THE RANDOM REVIEW 1982

THE
RANDOM
REVIEW
1982

Edited by
Gary Fisketjon
and Jonathan Galassi

BALLANTINE BOOKS · NEW YORK

The editors are grateful for permission to reprint the following:

"Jacklighting" by Ann Beattie. First published in *Antaeus*. Copyright © 1981 by Ann Beattie. Reprinted by permission of the author.
"The War of Vaslav Nijinsky" by Frank Bidart. First published in *The Paris Review*. Copyright © 1981 by Frank Bidart. Reprinted by permission of the author.
  The prose passages in "The War of Vaslav Nijinsky" are based on writings of Romola Nijinsky, Richard Buckle, Serge Lifar, and Maurice Sandoz. Quotations from Romola Nijinsky (*Nijinsky*, 1934) are reproduced by permission of Simon and Schuster.
"At the Ballard Locks" by Richard Blessing. First published in *The Seattle Review*. Copyright © 1981 by Richard Blessing. Reprinted by permission of the author.
"In the Sparrow Hills" by Emile Capouya. First published in *The Antioch Review*, Vol. 39, No. 2 (Spring 1981). Copyright © 1981 by The Antioch Review, Inc. Reprinted by permission of the editors.
"Cathedral" by Raymond Carver. First published in *The Atlantic*

For Donald Klopfer

Contents

Introduction
Acknowledgments

Introduction

The Random Review 1982, the first in an annual series, originated in our mutual conviction that there are many first-rate writers at work in America today, and that they too often remain secrets unto themselves and their kind. The reasons for this gap between individual achievement and public recognition are many and complex, but one of the more obvious difficulties has to do with the sheer number of books and periodicals published every year—a bewildering array of texts in which new or lesser-known authors can easily become lost, and which no reader, no matter how dedicated, could possibly sort out.

The Random Review is our attempt to select from over six hundred sources what we feel is the most stimulating new work, and to make that work readily available to the reader. Other anthologies have tried to collect the year's outstanding fiction or poetry or little-magazine writing, but until now no book has offered a critical survey of the best literary efforts—in short fiction, poetry, and the essay—from the full range of American periodicals.

In making our selection, we intended not to promote a particular sect of writers or, worse yet, writers with whom we have had personal or professional associations. Nor did we wish to join the agitated debate over the relative quality and merit of large as opposed to small magazines, and the other so-called issues that have divided the American literary community into discrete and even hostile camps, often with little attention paid to the work itself. We agreed at the outset not to favor the famous writer nor the establishment magazine; similarly, we have tried to resist the tendency to parade the prodigious "discovery" or to make a shrine of the small press. *The Random Review* is concise because it contains only work that we both admire wholeheartedly; when we have not been able to agree on a certain piece, we have left it out, relying on consensus to correct excessive personal enthusiasms. At the same time, we have dispensed with those democratic procedures that we feared might end in diffusion: nomination, lobbying, voting. Though we have made every effort to cover as many of America's magazines as possible, we cannot claim to have seen everything—no anthology is foolproof.

The community of writers in this country, as this book demonstrates, is a boisterous and unmanageable one, and luckily so. The variety of theme and technique here displayed is representative of the pluralism of our society, as is the diversity of sensibilities and points of view. If some of these writers have little to say to one another, we feel that each of them offers honest value to the reading public.

In short, we believe *The Random Review* gives ample evidence that literature in America is as healthy and adventurous as ever. We publish this book in the hope that these writers will, by force and virtue of their variously superior work, find the large group of discriminating and engaged readers that they deserve: a mutual admiration society of which no one could disapprove.

G.F. & J.G.
December 1981

Acknowledgments

We are grateful to the authors who have permitted us to reprint their work, to the many editors who have made their publications available to us, and to our colleagues at Random House and Ballantine Books who have made this venture possible, especially Marilyn Abraham, Jason Epstein, Peter Gethers, Keith Hollaman, Marc Jaffe, Robert Richman, Lelia Ruckenstein, and Jan Yamane. Special thanks go to Jay McInerney for his discrimination and enthusiasm.

THE
RANDOM
REVIEW
1982

Ann Beattie
Jacklighting

IT IS NICHOLAS'S BIRTHDAY: LAST YEAR HE WAS ALIVE, and we took him presents; a spiral notebook he pulled the pages out of, unable to write but liking the sound of paper tearing; magazines he flipped through, paying no attention to pictures, liking the blur of color. He had a radio, so we could not take a radio. More than the radio, he seemed to like the sound the metal drawer in his bedside table made, sliding open, clicking shut. He would open the drawer and look at the radio. He rarely took it out.

Nicholas's brother Spence has made jam. For days the cat has batted grapes around under the huge home-made kitchen table; dozens of bloody rags of cheesecloth have been thrown into the trash. There is grape jelly, raspberry jelly, strawberry, quince and lemon. Last month, a neighbor's pig escaped and ate Spence's newly planted fraise des bois plants, but overlooked the strawberry plants close to the house, heavy with berries. After that, Spence captured the pig and called his friend Andy, who came for it with his truck and took the pig to his farm in Warrenton. When Andy got home and looked in the back of the truck, he found three piglets curled against the pig.

In this part of Virginia, it is a hundred degrees in August. In June and July you can smell the ground, but in August it has been baked dry; instead of smelling the earth you smell flowers, hot breeze. There is a haze over the Blue Ridge Mountains that stays in the air like cigarette smoke. It is the same color as the eye shadow Spence's girlfriend, Pammy, wears. The rest of us are sunburned, with pink mosquito bites on our bodies, small scratches from gathering raspberries. Pammy has just arrived from

Washington. She is winter-pale. Since she is ten years
younger than the rest of us, a few scratches wouldn't make
her look as if she belonged, anyway. She is in medical
school at Georgetown, and her summer-school classes have
just ended. She arrived with leather sandals that squeak.
She is exhausted and sleeps half the day, upstairs, with
the fan blowing on her. All weekend the big fan has blown
on Spence, in the kitchen, boiling and bottling his jams
and jellies. The small fan blows on Pammy.

Wynn and I have come from New York. Every year we
borrow his mother's car and drive from Hoboken to Virginia. We used to take the trip to spend the week of Nicholas's birthday with him. Now we come to see Spence, who
lives alone in the house. He is making jam early, so we can
take jars back with us. He stays in the kitchen because he
is depressed and does not really want to talk to us. He
scolds the cat, curses when something goes wrong.

Wynn is in love. The girl he loves is twenty, or twenty-
one. Twenty-two. When he told me (top down on the car,
talking into the wind), I couldn't understand half of what
he was saying. There were enough facts to daze me; she
had a name, she was one of his students, she had canceled
her trip to Rome this summer. The day he told me about
her, he brought it up twice; first in the car, later in Spence's
kitchen. "That was *not* my mother calling the other night
to say she got the car tuned," Wynn said, smashing his
glass on the kitchen counter. I lifted his hand off the large
shard of glass, touching his fingers as gently as I'd touch a
cactus. When I steadied myself on the counter, a chip of
glass nicked my thumb. The pain shot through my body
and pulsed in my ribs. Wynn examined my hands; I examined his. A dust of fine glass coated our hands, gently
touching, late at night, looking out the window at the moon
shining on Spence's lemon tree with its one lemon, too
heavy to be growing on the slender branch. A jar of Lipton

iced tea was next to the tub the lemon tree grew out of—a joke, put there by Wynn, to encourage it to bear more fruit.

Wynn is standing in the field across from the house, pacing, head down, the bored little boy grown up.

"When wasn't he foolish?" Spence says, walking through the living room. "What kind of sense does it make to turn against him now for being a fool?"

"He calls it mid-life crisis, Spence, and he's going to be thirty-two in September."

"I know when his birthday is. You hint like this every year. Last year at the end of August you dropped it into conversation that the two of you were doing something or other to celebrate *his birthday*."

"We went to one of those places where a machine shoots baseballs at you. His birthday present was ten dollars' worth of balls pitched at him, I gave him a Red Sox baseball cap. He lost it the same day."

"How did he lose it?"

"We came out of a restaurant and a Doberman was tied by its leash to a stop sign, barking like mad—a very menacing dog. He tossed the cap, and it landed on the dog's head. It was funny until he wanted to get it back, and he couldn't go near it."

"He's one in a million. He deserves to have his birthday remembered. Call me later in the month and remind me."

Spence goes to the foot of the stairs. "Pammy," he calls.

"Come up and kill something for me," she says. The bed creaks. "Come kill a wasp on the bedpost. I hate to kill them. I hate the way they crunch."

He walks back to the living room and gets a newspaper and rolls it into a tight tube, slaps it against the palm of his hand.

Wynn, in the field, is swinging a broken branch, batting hickory nuts and squinting into the sun.

Nicholas lived for almost a year, brain-damaged, before he died. Even before the accident, he liked the way things felt. He always watched shadows. He was the man looking to the side in Cartier-Bresson's photograph, instead of putting his eye to the wall. He'd find pennies on the sidewalk when the rest of us walked down city streets obliviously, spot the chipped finger on a mannequin flawlessly dressed, sidestep the one piece of glass among shells scattered on the shore-line. It would really have taken something powerful to do him in. So that's what happened: a drunk in a van, speed-ing, head-on, Nicholas out for a midnight ride without his helmet. Earlier in the day he'd assembled a crazy nest of treasures in the helmet, when he was babysitting the neighbors' four-year-old daughter. Spence showed it to us— holding it forward as carefully as you'd hold a bomb, look-ing away the way you'd avoid looking at dead fish floating in a once nice aquarium, the way you'd look at an ugly scar, once the bandages had been removed, and want to lay the gauze back over it. While he was in the hospital, his fish tank overheated and all the black mollies died. The doctor unwound some of the bandages and the long brown curls had been shaved away, and there was a red scar down the side of his head that seemed as out of place as a line divid-ing a highway out west, a highway that nobody traveled anyway. It could have happened to any of us. We'd all rid-den on the Harley, bodies pressed into his back, hair whipped across our faces. How were we going to feel ourselves again, without Nicholas? In the hospital, it was clear that the thin intravenous tube was not dripping life back into him—that was as farfetched as the idea that the too-thin branch of the lemon tree could grow one more piece of fruit. In the helmet had been dried chrysanthemums, half of a robin's blue shell, a cat's-eye marble, yellow twine, a sprig of grapes, a piece of a broken ruler. I remember Wynn actually jump-ing back when he saw what was inside. I stared at the strangeness such ordinary things had taken on. Wynn had

been against his teaching me to ride his bike, but he had.
He taught me to trust myself and not to settle for seeing
things the same way. The lobster claw on a necklace he
made me was funny and beautiful. I never felt the same
way about lobsters or jewelry after that. "Psychologists
have figured out that infants start to laugh when they've
learned to be skeptical of danger," Nicholas had said.
Laughing on the back of his motorcycle. When he lowered
the necklace over my head, rearranging it, fingers on my
throat.

It is Nicholas's birthday, and so far no one has mentioned
it. Spence has made all the jam he can make from the fruit
and berries and has gone to the store and returned with
bags of flour to make bread. He brought the *Daily Progress*
to Pammy, and she is reading it, on the side porch where
there is no screening, drying her hair and stiffening when
bees fly away from the Rose of Sharon bushes. Her new
sandals are at the side of the chair. She has red toenails.
She rubs the small pimples on her chin the way men finger
their beards. I sit on the porch with her, catcher's mitt on
my lap, waiting for Wynn to get back from his walk so we
can take turns pitching to each other.

"Did he tell you I was a drug addict? Is that why you
hardly speak to me?" Pammy says. She is squinting at her
toes. "I'm older than I look," she says. "He says I'm twenty-
one, because I look so young. He doesn't know when to let
go of a joke, though. I don't like to be introduced to people
as some child prodigy."

"What were you addicted to?" I say.

"Speed," she says. "I had another life." She has brought
the bottle of polish with her, and begins brushing on a new
layer of red, the fingers of her other hand stuck between
her toes from underneath, separating them. "I don't get
the feeling you people had another life," she says. "After
all these years, I still feel funny when I'm around people

who've never lived the way I have. It's just snobbishness, I'm sure."

I cup the catcher's mitt over my knee. A bee has landed on the mitt. This is the most Pammy has talked. Now she interests me; I always like people who have gone through radical changes. It's snobbishness—it shows me that other people are confused, too.

"That was the summer of sixty-seven," she says. "I slept with a stockbroker for money. Sat through a lot of horror movies. That whole period's a blur. What I remember about it is being underground all the time, going places on the subway. I only had one real friend in the city. I can't remember where I was going." Pammy looks at the newspaper beside her chair. "Charlottesville, Virginia," she says. "My, my. Who would have thought twitchy little Pammy would end up here?"

Spence tosses the ball. I jump, mitt high above my head, and catch it. Spence throws again. Catch. Again. A hard pitch that lets me know the palm of my hand will be numb when I take off the catcher's mitt. Spence winds up. Pitches. As I'm leaning to get the ball, another ball sails by on my right. Spence has hidden a ball in his pocket all this time. Like his brother, he's always trying to make me smile.

"It's too hot to play ball," he says. "I can't spend the whole day trying to distract you because Wynn stalked off into the woods today."

"Come on," I say. "It was working."

"Why don't we all go to Virginia Beach next year instead of standing around down here smouldering? This isn't any tribute to my brother. How did this get started?"

"We came to be with you because we thought it would be hard. You didn't tell us about Pammy."

"Isn't that something? What that tells you is that you matter, and Wynn matters, and Nicholas mattered, but I don't even think to mention the person who's supposedly my lover."

"She said she had been an addict."

"She probably tried to tell you she wasn't twenty-one, too, didn't she?"

I sidestep a strawberry plant, notice one croquet post stuck in the field.

"It was a lie?" I say.

"No," he says. "I never know when to let my jokes die."

When Nicholas was alive, we'd celebrate his birthday with mint juleps and croquet games, stuffing ourselves with cake, going for midnight skinny-dips. Even if he were alive, I wonder if today would be anything like those birthdays of the past, or whether we'd have bogged down so hopelessly that even his childish enthusiasm would have had little effect. Wynn is sure that he's having a crisis and that it's not the real thing with his student because he also has a crush on Pammy. We are open about everything: he tells me about taking long walks and thinking about nothing but sex; Spence bakes the french bread too long, finds that he's lightly tapping a rock, sits on the kitchen counter, puts his hands over his face, and cries. Pammy says that she does not feel close to any of us—that Virginia was just a place to come to cool out. She isn't sure she wants to go on with medical school. I get depressed and think that if the birds could talk, they'd say that they didn't enjoy flying. The mountains have disappeared in the summer haze.

Late at night, alone on the porch, toasting Nicholas with a glass of wine, I remember that when I was younger, I assumed he'd be our guide: he saw us through acid trips, planned our vacations, he was always there to excite us and to give us advice. He started a game that went on for years. He had us close our eyes after we'd stared at something and made us envision it again. We had to describe it with our eyes closed. Wynn and Spence could talk about the things and make them more vivid than they were in life. They remembered well. When I closed my eyes, I squinted until the thing was lost to me. It kept going backwards into darkness.

Tonight, Nicholas's birthday, it is dark and late and I have been trying to pay him a sort of tribute by seeing something and closing my eyes and imagining it. Besides realizing that two glasses of wine can make me drunk, I have had this revelation: that you can look at something, close your eyes and see it again and still know nothing—like staring at the sky to figure out the distances between stars.

The drunk in the van that hit Nicholas thought that he had hit a deer.

Tonight, stars shine over the field with the intensity of flashlights. Every year, Spence calls the state police to report that on his property, people are jacklighting.

(Antaeus)

Frank Bidart
The War of Vaslav Nijinsky

Still gripped by the illusion of an horizon;
overcome with the finality of a broken tooth;
suspecting that habits are the only salvation,

—the Nineteenth Century's
guilt, *World War One,*

was danced

by Nijinsky on January 19, 1919.

. . .

. . . I am now reading *Ecce Homo*. Nietzsche
is *angry* with me—;

he hates "the Crucified One."

But he did not live through War—;
when the whole world painted its face

with blood.

Someone must expiate the blood.

. . .

No. Let what is past
be forgotten. Let even the blood

be forgotten—; there *can be no* "expiation."

Expiation is not necessary.

Suffering has made me what I am,—

I must not regret; or judge; or
struggle to escape it

in the indifference of (the ruthless
ecstasy of)
                CHANGE; "my endless RENEWAL";
                                        BECOMING.

—That is Nietzsche.

He wants to say *"Yes"* to life.

I am not Nietzsche. I am the bride of Christ.

            •   •   •

He was planning a new and original ballet. It was to be a
picture of sex life, with the scene laid in a *maison tolérée.*
The chief character was to be the owner—once a beautiful
cocotte, now aged and paralyzed as a result of her debauch-
ery; but, though her body is a wreck, her spirit is indomi-
table in the traffic of love. She deals with all the wares of
love, selling girls to boys, youth to age, woman to woman,
man to man.

    When he danced it, he succeeded in transmitting the
whole scale of sex life.

            •   •   •

    —Many times Diaghilev wanted me
to make love to him

as if he were
a woman—;

I did, I *refuse* to
regret it.
      At first, I felt humiliated for him,—

he saw this. He got angry
and said, "I enjoy it!"

Then, more calmly, he said,

"Vatza, we must not *regret* what we *feel*."

— I REGRETTED

        what I FELT . . . Not

making love, but that since the beginning
I wanted to *leave* him . . .
        That I stayed

out of "GRATITUDE,"—
        and *FEAR OF LIFE*,—
            and
            AMBITION . . .

That in my soul,
      I did *not* love him.

Now my wife wants to have
a second child. I am frightened;

the things a human being must learn,—
the things a child

must *learn* he FEELS,—

frighten me! I know people's faults

because in my soul,
                    I HAVE COMMITTED THEM.

The man who chops wood for us
was speaking, this morning, in the kitchen,

to my wife. As I passed in the hallway
I heard

whispering—; and LISTENED . . .

He said that as a child
in his village at Sils Maria

he worked for the writer, *Nietzsche*—;
he felt he must tell her

that just before the "famous man"
was taken away, INSANE,

he acted and looked

AS I DO NOW.

I can choose *"life"* for myself;—

but must I, again, again,
AGAIN,—
            for *any other* creature?

·   ·   ·

The Durcals arrived in St. Moritz, and were invited to tea.
Asked what he had been doing lately, Vaslav put on a worldly
air, leaned back on the sofa and said,
    "Well, I composed two ballets, I prepared a new program

for the next Paris season, and lately—I have played a part.
You see, I am an artist; I have no troupe now, so I miss the
stage. I thought it would be rather an interesting experiment to see how well I could act, and so for six weeks I
played the part of a lunatic; and the whole village, my
family, and even the physicians apparently believed it. I
have a male nurse to watch me, in the disguise of a *mas-
seur*."

Romola was overcome, torn between anger and relief.
She was confirmed in her supposition that her fears had
been groundless when the male nurse came, after ten days,
to assure her from his long experience that her husband
was completely sane.

         •   •   •

—Let me explain to you
what *"guilt"* is . . .

When I joke with my wife, and say,
"I think I will go back to Russia
and live as a peasant—"

she jokes back, and says,
"Do as you like! I will
divorce you, and marry

                a manufacturer . . ."

She looks at me, and I look at her.

What is terrible

is that I am serious—; and *she* is serious . . .

She is right, of course,—

                I do *not* have the right

to make her live differently, without servants,
rich friends, elegant clothes—
without her good and sane *habits;*

do not have the right even to trv
to *re-make* her . . .

But does *she* then have the right
to make *me* live like this, JUDGED, surrounded by
those who cannot understand or *feel* me,—

like a
manufacturer? . . .

She is angry, as I am angry.

We both are *right—;* and both angry . . .

Soon, she feels guilty, feels that she
has failed me—;

and I too

feel guilty . . .

The *GUILT* comes from *NOWHERE*.

Neither of us has done wrong!

But I am a good actor—and reassure her
that I love her; am indeed happy; and that
nothing will change . . .

I *want* to be a *good husband.*

Still, I am guilty.

. . . Why am I guilty?

My life is *FALSE*.

.   .   .

I know the psychology of lunatics;
if you don't contradict them, they like you.

But I am not insane.

My brother was insane. He died
in a lunatic asylum.

The reason I *know* I am *NOT* insane
is because, unlike my brother,

I *feel guilt.*

The insane do not feel guilt.

My brother was a dancer. He was older than I,
but still in the *corps* when I became
a soloist. He was ashamed, and jealous;

he went insane.

When the doctors questioned him, he showed
astonishing courage,—

                                he thought that everyone
in the company was paid

by the secret police, to gather
evidence against our family . . .

He displayed cunning, and stoic
fortitude, under the questions.

Even when he thought he faced death,
he lied
to protect my mother.

When he was taken away,
she cried, and cried . . .
                              She cried
visiting him,—

but that didn't make him feel GUILTY . . .

My wife thought because
I wore a large *cross* on my neck in the village,—

and told her certain dishes
served at our table were poisoned,—

I was insane.

But I *knew* that my actions
frightened her—; and I suffered.

Nietzsche was insane. He knew
we killed God.

              . . .This is the *end* of the story:

though He was dead, God was clever
and strong. God struck back,—

AND KILLED US.

If I *act* insane, people will call me
"mad clown," and forgive
                              even the truth—;

the insane feel anxiety and horror,

but are RELEASED
from GUILT . . .

I only want to know
things I've learned like this,—

these things I cannot *NOT* know.

　　　　• • •

His other ballet remained unfinished. It was his own life
put into a choreographic poem: a youth seeking truth
through life, first as a pupil, open to all artistic suggestions, to all the beauty that life and love can offer; then his
love for the woman, his mate, who successfully carries him
off.

　　He set it in the period of the High Renaissance. The
youth is a painter; his Master one of the greatest artists of
the period, part Genius and part Politician, just as Diaghilev seemed to him to be. This Master advances him,
and defends his daring work from the attacks of colleagues,
as long as he is a student; then he falls in love, and the
Master bitterly rejects not only him but his work.

　　　　• • •

　—Last night, once again, I nearly
abandoned my autobiographical ballet . . .

The plot has a good beginning
and middle,—
　　　　　THE PUZZLE

is the end . . .

The *nights* I spend—

reading and improving
Nietzsche, analysing and then abandoning

my life, working on the *Great Questions*

like WAR and GUILT and GOD
and MADNESS,—

I rise from my books, my endless, fascinating
researches, notations, projects,

dazzled.
—Is this happiness? . . .

I have invented a far more
accurate and specific notation for dance;

it has taken me two months
to write down the movement in my ten-minute

ballet, *L'Après-midi d'un Faune* . . .

There is a MORAL here

about how LONG you must live with
the consequences of a SHORT action,—

but I don't now feel
MORAL.
Soon I shall begin

Le Sacre du Printemps—; which
is longer . . .

I can understand the pleasures of War.

In War—
	where *killing* is a virtue: *camouflage*
a virtue: *revenge* a virtue:
pity a weakness—
			the world rediscovers

a *guiltless* PRE-HISTORY

"civilization" condemns . . .

In 1914, I was assured
the War would end in six weeks;

the Germans, in the summer, thought
they would enter Paris by the fall.

But the War
		was *NOT* an accident.

CUSTOM, and his Children,—

Glory. Honor. Privilege. Poverty.
Optimism. "The Balance of Power,"—

for four years

dug a large, long hole
(—a *TRENCH*—)
			in the earth of Europe;

when they approached the hole
to pin medals

on the puppets
they had thrown there,

they slipped in BLOOD,—

. . . AND FELL IN.

Poverty and *Privilege*
alone survived,

of all the customs of the past . . .

—Should the World
regret the War? Should I

REGRET MY LIFE?

. . . Let our epitaph be:

In Suffering, and Nightmare,
I woke at last

to my own nature.

* * *

One Sunday we decided to sleigh over to Maloja.

Kyra was glad and Vaslav was very joyful that morning.

It took us about three hours to get there; Kyra and I got very hungry during the long drive.

The road was extremely narrow during the winter, because it needed cleaning from the heavy snows, and in certain parts there was always a space to await the sleighs coming from the opposite direction.

Vaslav was as a rule a careful and excellent driver, but on this particular Sunday he did not wait, but simply *drove on into* the oncoming sleighs.

We were in danger of turning over; the horses got frightened.

The coachmen of the other sleighs cursed, but this did not make any difference.

Kyra screamed, and I begged Vaslav to be more careful, but the further we went the more fiercely he drove *against* the other sleighs.

I had to clutch on to Kyra and the sleigh to keep ourselves on.

I was furious, and said so to Vaslav.

He fixed me suddenly with a hard and metallic look which I had never seen before.

As we arrived at the Maloja Inn I ordered a meal.

We had to wait.

Vaslav asked for some bread and butter and macaroni.

"Ah, Tolstoy again," I thought, but did not say a word, and bit my lips.

Kyra was anxiously awaiting her steak, and as it was laid before her and she began to eat, Vaslav, with a quick gesture, snatched the plate away.

She began to cry from disappointment.

I exclaimed, "Now, Vaslav, please don't begin that Tolstoy nonsense again; you remember how weak you got by starving yourself on that vegetarian food. I can't stop you doing it, but I won't allow you to interfere with Kyra. The child must eat properly."

I went with Kyra to the other room to have our solitary lunch.

We drove home very quietly without a word.

•   •   •

—The second part of my ballet
Le Sacre du Printemps

is called "THE SACRIFICE."

A young girl, a virgin, is chosen
to die
so that the Spring will return,—

so that her Tribe (free
from *"pity," "introspection," "remorse"*)

out of her blood
can renew itself.

The fact that the earth's renewal
requires human blood

is unquestioned; a mystery.

She is chosen, from the whirling, stamping
circle of her peers, purely by chance—;

then, driven from the circle, surrounded
by the elders, by her peers, by animal
skulls impaled on pikes,

she dances,—

   at first, in paroxysms
of Grief, and Fear:—

      again and again, she leaps (—*NOT*

as a ballerina leaps, as if she
loved the air, as if
the air were her element—)

SHE LEAPS

BECAUSE SHE HATES THE GROUND.

But then, slowly, as others
join in, she finds that there is a self

WITHIN herself

that is *NOT* HERSELF

impelling her to accept,—and at last
to *LEAD*,—

      THE DANCE

that is her own sacrifice . . .

—In the end, exhausted, she falls
to the ground . . .

She dies; and her last breath
is the reawakened Earth's

orgasm,—
          a little upward run on the flutes
mimicking

      (—or perhaps MOCKING—)

the god's spilling
seed . . .

The Chosen Virgin
accepts her fate: without considering it,

she knows that her Tribe,—
the Earth itself,—
         are UNREMORSEFUL

that the price of continuance
is her BLOOD:—

she *accepts* their guilt,—

. . . THEIR GUILT

THAT THEY DO NOT KNOW EXISTS.

She has become, to use
our term, a *Saint.*

The dancer I chose for this role
detested it.

She would have preferred to do
a fandango, with a rose in her teeth . . .

The training she and I shared,—

training in the traditional
                              "academic" dance,—

emphasizes the illusion
                      of *Effortlessness,*
Ease, Smoothness, Equilibrium . . .

When I look into my life,
these are not the qualities
                              I find there.

Diaghilev, almost alone
in the Diaghilev Ballet, UNDERSTOOD;

though he is not now, after my marriage
and *"betrayal,"*

INTERESTED in my choreographic ambitions . . .

Nevertheless, to fill a theatre,
he can be persuaded

to *hire* me as a dancer . . .

Last night I dreamt

I was slowly climbing
a long flight of steps.

Then I saw Diaghilev
and my wife

arm in arm
climbing the steps behind me . . .

I began to hurry, so that
they would not see me.

Though I climbed
as fast as I could, the space

between us
NARROWED . . .

Soon, they were a few feet behind me,—
I could hear them laughing,

gossiping, discussing CONTRACTS
and LAWSUITS . . .

They understood each other perfectly.

I stopped.

        But they

DIDN'T STOP . . .

They climbed right past me,—
laughing, chatting,

NOT SEEING ME AT ALL . . .

—I should have been happy;

yet . . .
    wasn't.

I watched their backs,
as they happily

disappeared, climbing
up, out of my sight . . .

        •   •   •

Our days passed in continuous social activity.

Then one Thursday, the day when the governess and maid had their day off, I was making ready to take Kyra out for a walk when suddenly Vaslav came out of his room and looked at me very angrily.

"How dare you make such a noise? I can't work."

I looked up, surprised.

His face, his manner were strange; he had never spoken to me like this.

"I am sorry. I did not realize we were so loud."

Vaslav got hold of me then by my shoulders and shook me violently.

I clasped Kyra in my arms very close, then with one powerful movement Vaslav pushed me down the stairs.

I lost my balance, and fell with the child, who began to scream.

At the bottom, I got up, more astounded than terrified.

What was the matter with him?

He was still standing there menacingly.

I turned round, exclaiming, "You ought to be ashamed! You are behaving like a drunken *peasant.*"

A very changed Vaslav we found when we came home, docile and kind as ever.

I did not speak about the incident, either to him or to anybody else.

Then one day we went on an excursion and Vaslav again wore his cross over his sweater.

On our way home, he suddenly began to drive fiercely and the sleigh turned over.

Amazingly, no one was hurt.

I got really angry, and walked home with Kyra.

Of course, he was home ahead of us.

When I entered the house, the servant who worshipped Vaslav opened the door and said, "Madame, I think Monsieur Nijinsky is ill, or perhaps very drunk, for he acts so queerly. His voice is hoarse and his eyes all hazy. I am frightened."

I went to our bedroom.

Vaslav lay fully dressed on the bed, with the cross on, his eyes closed.

He seemed to be asleep.

I turned cautiously towards the door, and then noticed that heavy tears were streaming down his face.

"Vatza, how are you feeling? Are you angry with me?"

"It is nothing; let me sleep; I am tired."

• • •

Each night now I pray,
                    Let this cup

pass from me! . . .

But it is not a cup. It is my life.

I have *LEARNED*

> my *NATURE* . . .

I am insane,—
. . . or evil.

Today I walked out into the snow.

I said to myself:

> *THREE TIMES*
> *YOU TRIED TO HARM YOUR WIFE AND CHILD.*

I said:

> *LIE DOWN IN THE SNOW*
> *AND DIE. YOU ARE EVIL.*

I lay down in the snow . . .

I tried to go to sleep.
My HANDS

began to get cold, to FREEZE.

I was lying there a long, long time.
I did not feel cold any more . . .

Then, God said to me:

> *GO HOME*
> *AND TELL YOUR WIFE YOU ARE INSANE.*

I said:

Thank you, thank you, God!
I am not evil. I am insane.

I got up. I wanted to go home,—
and tell this news

to my wife.

Then, I said to God:

I am insane,—
my wife will suffer. I am guilty.

Forgive me for being insane.

God said:

GOD MADE YOU. GOD DOES NOT CARE
IF YOU ARE "GUILTY" OR NOT.

I said:

I CARE IF I AM GUILTY!

I CARE IF I AM GUILTY! . . .

God was silent.

Everything was SILENT.

I lay back down in the snow.

I wanted again to go to sleep, and die . . .

But my BODY did not want to die.
My BODY spoke to me:

There is no answer to your life.
You are insane; or evil.

There is only one thing that you can do:—

You must join YOUR GUILT

> *to the WORLD'S GUILT.*

I said to myself:

I must join MY GUILT

> *to the WORLD'S GUILT.*

I got up out of the snow.
. . . What did the words mean?

Then I realized what the words meant.

I said to myself:

You must join YOUR GUILT

> *to the WORLD'S GUILT.*

There is no answer to your life.
You are insane; or evil.

. . . Let this be the Body

through which the War has passed.

• • •

Nijinsky invited guests to a recital at the Suvretta House Hotel.

When the audience was seated, he picked up a chair,
sat down on it, and stared at them. Half an hour passed.
Then he took a few rolls of black and white velvet and
made a big cross the length of the room. He stood at the
head of it, his arms opened wide. He said: "Now, I will
dance you the War, which you did not prevent and for which
you are responsible." His dance reflected battle, horror,
catastrophe, apocalypse. An observer wrote: "At the end,
we were too much overwhelmed to applaud. We were looking at a corpse, and our silence was the silence that enfolds
the dead."

There was a collection for the Red Cross. Tea was served.
Nijinsky never again performed in public.

•   •   •

—The War is a *good* subject . . .

The audience, yesterday, liked
my dance.

The public does not understand *Art;*
it wants to be astonished.

I know how to astonish.

The War allowed me
to project,—
                    to EMBODY,—

an ultimate *"aspect"* of the *"self"* . . .

A member of the audience told me
I had always been able

"to smell a good subject."

God, on the other hand,—

                    who at times
has responded to my predilection

for *ACTIONS*

that are *METAPHYSICAL EXPERIMENTS,*—

perhaps felt threatened, or even
coerced—;

he perhaps felt that though he could
agree with me

that expiation *IS* necessary,—

he had to agree with
Nietzsche

that expiation is *NOT* possible . . .

In any case, he has chosen,—as
so often,—
                CAMOUFLAGE . . .

Now that the War has been over
two months, at times I almost
doubt if it existed—;

in truth,
       it never existed,—

. . . *BECAUSE IT HAS NEVER BEEN OVER.*

Twenty years ago, a boy of nine
was taken by his mother

to the Imperial School of Ballet,

to attempt to become a pupil;

the mother was poor, and
afraid of life; his father

had abandoned the family when the boy was four . . .

Even then, he had a good jump—;
he was admitted.

He had been taught by the priests
that because of Adam and Eve, all men were born
in *Original Sin,*—

              that all men were,
BY NATURE, guilty . . .

In his soul, he didn't believe it.

He was a good boy. His mother loved him.

He believed
in his essential innocence,—

he thought his nature
              GOOD . . .

He worked hard. He grew thinner,—
and started

      "dancing like God" . . .

Everyone talked about it.

But then,—
>   he LEARNED SOMETHING.

He learned that

>   *All life exists*

at the expense of other life . . .

When he began to succeed,
he saw that he was AMBITIOUS,—
>   JEALOUS
of the roles that others won . . .

—Then his brother
got sick . . .

THE ROCK
>   THAT GIVES SHADE TO ONE
>   CREATURE,—

FOR ANOTHER CREATURE

>   *JUST BLOCKS THE*
>   *SUN.*

. . . This is a problem of *BEING*.
>   I can imagine

no *SOLUTION* to this . . .

At sixteen, he met a Prince. He loved the Prince,—
but after a time

the Prince grew tired of him . . .

Then he met a Count—;
                                  whom he *didn't* love.

The Count gave him a piano . . .

He had heard of Diaghilev. Diaghilev
invited him
                    to the *Hotel Europe,*—

he went to seek his luck.

He found
his luck.

At once, he allowed Diaghilev
to make love to him.

Even then, he disliked Diaghilev
for his too self-assured voice . . .

He always had thought he was essentially
different from the people
                                  in books of HISTORY,—

with their lives of *betrayals; blindness;
greed;* and *miseries . . .*

He saw, one day, that this illusion,—
this FAITH,—

                          had, imperceptibly,

vanished—;

he was *NOT* different—;

he did not understand *WHY* he did
what he did, nor were his instincts

"GOOD" . . .

Then, I said to myself:

> "HISTORY *IS* HUMAN
> NATURE—;

TO SAY *I AM GUILTY*
IS TO ACCEPT
IMPLICATION
IN THE HUMAN RACE . . ."

—Now, for months and months,
I have found

ANOTHER MAN in me—;

HE is *NOT* me—; *I*

am afraid of him . . .

He hates my wife and child,—
and hates Diaghilev;

because he thinks GOODNESS and BEING
are incompatible,—

. . . *HE WANTS TO DESTROY THE WORLD*.

DESTROY it,—
or REDEEM it.

Are they the *same?* . . .

As a child, I was taught, by the priests,
to crave the Last Judgment:—

when the *Earth* will become a *Stage*,—

and WHAT IS RIGHT and WHAT IS WRONG

will at last show *clear,* and *distinct,*
and *separate,*—

and then,—

> *THE SLATE IS WIPED CLEAN* . . .

—Even now, I can see the World
wheeling on its axis . . . I

shout at it:—

> *CEASE. CHANGE,—*
> > *OR CEASE.*

The World says right back:—

*I must chop down the Tree of Life
to make coffins* . . .

Tomorrow, I will go to Zurich—
to live in an asylum.

MY SOUL IS SICK,—
> *NOT MY MIND.*

I *am* incurable . . . I did not
live long.

Death came
unexpectedly,—

> *for I wanted it to come.*

Romola. Diaghilev.

. . . I HAVE EATEN THE WORLD.

My life is the expiation for my life.

Nietzsche understood me.

When *he* was sick,—when his *SOUL*
was sick,—

> he wrote that he would have

much preferred to be a *Professor* at Basel

than *God—;*

> but that he did not dare to carry

his egotism
so far as to neglect the Creation of the World.

* * *

In 1923, Diaghilev came to see him. Vaslav by now got out
of bed in a strange fashion. First of all he went on all-fours;
then crawled around the room; and only then stood upright. In a general way, he seemed attracted by the floor, to
feel a need to be as low down as possible (his bed was
almost on a level with the floor) and to grab hold of something. As he walked he leaned forward and felt at his ease
only when lying down.

This was the first time Diaghilev had set eyes on him
since they had parted in wrath in Barcelona six years be-

fore. "Vatza, you are being lazy. Come, I need you. You must dance again for the Russian Ballet and for me."

Vaslav shook his head. "I cannot because I am mad."

• • •

Frightened to eat with a new set of teeth;
exhausted by the courage the insane have shown;
uncertain whether to REDEEM or to DESTROY THE
EARTH,

—the Nineteenth Century's
guilt, *World War One,*

was danced

by Nijinsky on January 19, 1919.

(The Paris Review)

Richard Blessing
At the Ballard Locks

Mid-summer.

We stand at the rail, stiff and dumb as
   pilings, linked
by the ropes of one another's arms. The salmon
   are running.

Fresh water madness is in them and they leap like sparks
from some windy chimney. It is only that they have come
   so far.

Or is it that they remind us of characters from that old
   movie,
lovers who age like apples on a sunny window sill,
   falling in
on themselves, dying at the end believing
   nothing dies?

It is only
that they remind us of ourselves, sprung jaw and raw tail,
   egg-white
for an eye, or torn, worthless fin.

Is there in nature or out
   of nature
or half in and out as here in this man-made channel
   locking fresh water
to the sea, these salmon ladders of poured cement,
   gawkers at every

porthole, no song but this one of self-
    mourning?

          They do not mourn.
They do not seem to mourn. See, there and there another
    one rises
out of the narrowed sea his shining body's length and
    higher.

They split the heart of the sun going down.

               Not feeding,
    someone says
along the rail. *They've come too far for that.*

                Still, they fling
their lives in violent, graceful gestures, four and five a
    minute,
falling with a smack flat as a butcher's palm.
                 I remember
on your birthday you were sad. *I won't be rich or famous,*
    you said.
And I don't have a baby. Now it's too late.

             Never too late,
the sea thrashes out and in. Look. How purely it is sex
    and death.
I pull you close. We have missed nothing. It is our only
    life.

               (The Seattle Review)

Emile Capouya
In the Sparrow Hills

THIS IS NOT A STORY. THE PEOPLE I MENTION HERE for purposes of corroboration are men of flesh and blood—or, as the Spaniards say, more tellingly, men of flesh and bone. Two of them are very much alive, and the third not long dead, all of them public figures in a small way, the only way in which literary men in our time are likely to be public figures if there is anything to them. I have no hesitation about mentioning their names. I haven't asked their permission, but the matter in regard to which I want them to back me with their testimony is a question of fact, quite impersonal. The one who is no longer alive can scarcely be my witness in any active sense, and yet he is for my purposes the most important of the three, since the business I have in mind falls directly within his professional specialty. I hope to be believed when I report what he said about it because I met him when I was very young, he was kind to me for something like thirty years, and I took the liberty of loving him. That is, I hope to be believed because it should be clear that I would not invoke his spirit falsely. Besides, we human beings live by trust. In this city, if you ask a passerby for directions the chances are very good that he will misdirect you. But I should judge that the chances of being purposely misdirected are just about zero. People are always in a hurry here. People are always confused. Only when they are abstracted does the look of confusion leave their faces—and then, when you awaken a stranger from his dream and put to him a puzzle in geography, about a place where he himself finds his way without reflection, by habit, it is only to be expected that his hurried answer will not always meet an ideal standard of accuracy.

I was thinking about all that the other evening in the restaurant. Then the waitress brought the bill, I looked at it, I handed her a credit card, and I went back to thinking about the propriety of mentioning Avrahm Yarmolinsky in order to have the support of his name for what I mean to say. I was thinking that the mere suspicion that I might be citing him for interested motives after his death would in a sense slander him by associating him with those interested motives. And I was thinking that since my motives were reducible to one, to establish a point of literary history on his testimony and that of two other gentlemen, I didn't see why anyone would want to impugn my credit. It's as if I were to announce that I had broken my leg in early March of 1965, as in fact I did do, and people who knew me at the time know that I did, though they cannot be expected to recollect the month and the year. Now, if I were to make that statement, why should it awaken doubts, and reflect badly on the integrity of my witnesses? The waitress came back and said, "Sorry, sir, your card has been declined."

She is a brusque, rawboned young woman. Not many weeks ago I was in the restaurant, and her hoarse voice sounded suddenly from the kitchen: "When I heard the Pope was dead I just freaked out. I mean I just freaked out." There was no mistaking the excitement in her tone, but since I couldn't see her face I had no way of judging the quality of her excitement. What sounded like a note of jubilation was almost certainly something else. It was hard to imagine that her life was so empty of excitement that she welcomed the Pope's death because it relieved the tedium. I call the place a restaurant, but it's more gin mill than restaurant, much more gin mill. It's just down the block and in that sense convenient, but it's noisy at night, lots of action, and waitressing is hard work. No doubt there's plenty of tedium in it, but plenty of excitement too. It wouldn't be that. But her words told me nothing by themselves—the beauty of that language is that it doesn't give anything away—and I could not see her face. I remember that I felt more friendly to her because she had been stirred, in some way, by the death of that old man.

She had slapped the card upon the table, as a card-player slaps down a card in triumph or disgust, and had turned away about her other business before I had understood what she had said. Declined? The term was oddly decorous. Had I gone beyond my limit? It was possible. When cash is short you use the card to take up the slack, and then card on card. But I was sure that I had paid the last installment. Or even if I hadn't, the credit company would not yet have had time to publish my card number with those of other delinquents in the closely printed booklet. Did the restaurant have a direct line to the company, and had they telephoned? How strange. The likeliest thing was that someone had made a mistake. And I began to feel offended that a regular customer should be treated so offhandedly when there was a good chance that he was not at fault. Then I noticed that the bill, too, was back on the table. I took out a ten and two singles, put them on top of the bill, and set about finishing my beer.

The waitress sailed by and picked up the money, awkward but swift. As she did, I saw something out of place, and a moment later I knew what it was. I had seen two tens and a single rise from the table with the bill. But if I was right about that, then I had made a mistake earlier when I thought I had taken a ten and two singles from my wallet. I counted the money I had left. It seemed about ten dollars short. But I am not reliable when it comes to things of that kind. I finished my beer, thinking that if I had overpaid the waitress, she'd soon be back.

She didn't come. The man behind the bar saw me tilt my chair and look round for her. He asked if he could help me. I told him my credit card had been refused, I didn't know why, but in any case I had given the waitress cash, a ten and two singles, I had thought, and then I had had the impression that it was a single and two tens. He said she'd be back. After a moment she appeared. "The check was $10.09. I gave the bartender a ten and nine cents and kept the two singles for my tip. Here, this is what I have in my pocket." She showed me a roll of singles. "I don't have a ten on me." I said, "Oh, I'm sorry. That's fine, then." And I felt relieved. I got up and went out into the street. But while walking I saw two tens and a single rise from the table, and I remembered that I seemed to be ten dollars short. But why would she have done a thing like that? I wasn't drunk. I had had a bottle of beer with my dinner. It would have been foolish of her to do a thing like that deliberately. At worst she had made a mistake, just as I certainly had done. To suspect her would be unjust. Besides, it was simply too painful to suspect people. We live by trust.

Now, I want to offer Avrahm Yarmolinsky's testimony on one small point—and certainly not least because I feel honored to be able to mention his name as that of a friend. Of course, he was a great scholar, and everyone respects such attainments. But, on the other hand, only a scholar in Yarmolinsky's field could really appreciate him on that ground. For me, respect for his learning was partly a form of superstition, relying on evidence of things unseen, the vulgar kind of faith that has the effect of making certain people popular because they are popular. What really moved me was his character.

For many years he was head of the Slavic Languages Division of the New York Public Library, and he worked at the Forty-second Street building. Whenever I enter that mausoleum I feel entombed. But though he spoke gently and was naturally self-effacing, as befitted a senior servitor of that great mortuary of books, he showed how much spirit and passion could find lodgment in such a place. His figure was slight, so that he looked like a grown-up boy, and he had a diffidence that seemed adolescent. His si-

lences seemed adolescent, but if they arose out of shyness I
never felt that they were self-regarding. In his presence
my own tormenting social awkwardness lost much of its
burden of self-regard. When I used to visit him and he
would come forward to shake my hand—carrying his own
hands in an odd way, knuckles to the fore—his Russian
head that was shaped like a slender keystone, with the
short, stiff hair brushed up *al Umberto,* would be slightly
tilted and would be regarding me like a block of cordial
granite. After our hands had met, his eyes would shift
gratefully elsewhere, and the ceremony of greeting, made
difficult by affection, would have been successfully accomplished.

He had very little small talk and no grand pronounce-
ments. I have never known a man who inquired how you
were with so clear an intention of listening to the answer.
It used to make me feel as if I were talking to my father,
and must be careful not to hurt him by giving too blunt an
account of my life and prospects. On the other hand I felt
obliged to tell him the truth, and I managed it by telling
him generalities: I found my job difficult because publishing houses were likely to be ignorant or venal—things of
that sort. I knew that if I were to give him instances or
details I should soon grow passionate and afflict him with
my professional *déboires.* That is what usually happened
when I talked about those things with my own father, for
he used to question me with an affectionate pertinacity
born of his illusion that his son was a romantic who needed
to be protected from the impulse to footless martyrdom.
But he himself was the romantic idealist, as his brothers
often told him, and not by way of praise. He had managed
to live decently, honorably, in a world now quite vanished.
I had earned my living in the new world by compounding
with the enemy on every important point. My father imagined that I was baring my breast to all God's dangers, like
the heroic Swiss who gathered the spears of six spearmen

into his bosom to make a breach in the enemy rank through which his comrades might pass. So when my father, affectionately reproachful, and with mild irony for what he supposed was my moonstruck vision of the world of commerce, would press me for the story of my latest discomfiture, I would lose all self-control, and tell him the circumstances of the prehistory of the incident, and then its history, and at last I would impart to him my moral reflections upon it—sometimes an hour's business. At the end of it he would be shaking his head sadly, and I would feel that I had abused him, for he is candid as a child and the news of the world's small evils appalls him forever. On one of those occasions he said to me, "What I cannot understand is that you haven't sat down with your boss and explained those things to him. He would surely see that it must be in everyone's interest to abandon such a policy—if policy it can be called, since it is so clearly retrograde." And after that demonstration of his hopeless good faith and naiveté I felt especially tender to him. He was a spar from the wreck of that old world, adrift in the new, unconscious that when the skies change, men's hearts change with the skies.

Avrahm Yarmolinsky was innocent in the same way, but he never pressed me. He may have been too diffident to examine his own sons and prescribe for them. In any case our relations did not authorize anything of the kind. It was I who asked most of the questions, and these were generally of the impersonal sort. I would ask him about Russian and Soviet literature—like most Americans I have almost no acquaintance with the literatures of the other Slavs. I remember him saying, with a pained smile, something like, "The literature of the recent Soviet period is really quite poor. Pasternak, Solzhenitsyn—those immensely gifted writers are not at all characteristic. They have skipped over generations, going back for their inspiration to the great Russian masters of the nineteenth century. A novelist like Sholokhov is a vigorous writer—one of few—but he has nothing like the imagination of the great nineteenth-century writers, nothing like their psychological penetration, let alone their moral impetus and philosophic power." All this hesitantly, with a pained smile from first to last.

Yet I had seen him an energumen. When I was in my early twenties, it must have been shortly after the war, I was his guest at a dinner party. Among the other guests was an affable man with a guitar—I gathered he was a neighbor—who sang very pleasantly, "The fox he run to his cosy den, there were his little ones, eight, nine, ten. . . ." And there was a young Czech woman, large-limbed and handsome, who took the guitar from him and sang something softly, her voice low and moving. There were two Poles, I think, and a Yugoslav. At times when no one sang, Yarmolinsky talked to his Slavic friends with startling volubility, turning from one to the other, and shifting from one tongue to another as if he were a mere mindless polyglot—but speaking in so emphatic a tone and with such evident high spirits that he seemed transformed by enthusiasm. It may be that while he wrote English very well, he did not really feel at home in the language, so that it was a relief to his spirit to talk with animated Slavs.

I never afterward saw him exhibit anything approaching abandon, but I had been pleased by that evidence of fire as a youngster is apt to be pleased, and liked him the more for it. It was the memory of having seen him exhilarated in that way that persuaded me to tell him, many years later, of a literary admiration of mine. I don't know why I am so disinclined to speak of such things ordinarily, but I am. Mostly, I am ashamed to speak of them. Among persons of a certain social class, as I have noticed, or at least in certain circles, enthusiasms of the kind are common coin. And I have worked in a trade—the book trade—in which grown men often say, "That's a manuscript that I'm really excited about." Perhaps it's because they say it often that my stomach turns. Perhaps it's because the expression, in a man's mouth, sounds faintly androgynous. But chiefly I think it is a kind of shrinking snobbery on my part that makes me take their professional excitement so seriously, since I know very well that they are not exposing their intimate feelings when they say things of the sort. Their emotion is aroused by the qualities that the manuscript in question offers under the aspect of a commodity. Everyone in the trade understands that very well. And in what sense would it be useful for people in a publishing house to be susceptible to the appeal of a manuscript that was destined to fall stone dead in the market? My snobbery isn't a response to the vulgarity of an enthusiasm domesticated for the purpose of selling books. It's that I shrink from avowing any literary enthusiasm at all, as if the subject were unfit for mention in mixed company. And the ebullient interest that the trade takes in books on which one can make a decent profit, for all its seeming innocence, its genuine innocence, glances too nearly at this foible of mine, simply because the object of the emotion is something that has been written. I am far from being immune to the values expressed in the practice of publishing houses; if you were, you couldn't work in one. No, I share them fully. But I feel it isn't decent to proclaim those values because in the nature of things they are at least distantly related to the ones that arise from genuine works of literature. That is an odd scruple that I myself cannot account for—seeing that I have spent many years in the trade— and that I am not at all proud of. If I were to be honest I should have to say that my violent delicacy on this question is cousin to my abhorrence of the waitress's patchouli. For she moves in a nimbus of the scent. She leaves it on the edge of a dish, on the lip of a glass, on the silver. Sometimes I am assailed by the smell hours later if I pass my hand near to my face. When that happens I can't understand how it is that I never remember how much I dislike the smell of the waitress until I have actually crossed the

threshold of that restaurant. And certainly I know that a
hoarse voice and patchouli do not amount to moral obliq-
uity. She is a young woman, doing the things that are
socially available for her to do. At most her pungent musk
represents a social error, and not even that, no doubt, among
her friends, who must include people who are estimable by
any reasonable standard and yet are in no way affronted
by the use of strong perfumes. I cannot bear it, but I hope I
am not such a fool as to make the practice my test for
decency, honor, self-respect.

The fact is that there is an ugly streak in my character,
a kind of repercussive violence that I am well aware of and
should be happy to be without. When I was young it sometimes took dangerous forms. The war had been over for a
couple of months when I sailed as A. B. on the *Waterbury
Victory,* New York to Antwerp, in midwinter. I was the
only A. B. on the ship who had a ticket—the others were
acting A. B.'s and by law could go no higher than ten feet
above the deck. The first day out, the mate had me go aloft
to the mainmast truck to chip and paint my way down the
mast. I eased into a bosun's chair, with a chipping hammer, a wire brush, and a pot of red lead secured to the
chair's bridle, and a marlinspike on a ropeyarn lanyard
over one shoulder and across my breast. It was blowing
half a gale, and I was swayed aloft by my gantline, whose
end had been taken to the winch. The bosun tended my
line, and he ran me up steadily, but he couldn't do anything
to keep the roll of the vessel from knocking me about. The
Waterbury Victory was a famous roller. Later on during
that passage, to see just how she rolled, I rigged a clinometer in the crew's mess, a hacksaw blade pivoted on a nail
in the bulkhead, and the degrees of its swing shown on an
arc drawn with a protractor. The certificate on the bridge
said that the ship was rated for forty degrees. The men took
the clinometer down at last because she would roll to forty-
four and hang there a long time before rolling as far the

other way. On this day she gave me a pounding. I reached the truck with bruised knees and skinned knuckles, in a temper that they would think to send a man aloft to do an anytime job when it was blowing fresh.

When I was nearly at the truck I balled up a fist and thrust it out to one side for the bosun to see. At once he slacked the line on the windlass drum and held me motionless. Then I made to marry the two parts of my gantline to hold me in place while he threw the line off the windlass. But I saw that the dangling paint pot would foul the long bight of line that I must overhaul with my free hand, in order to bring it up through the bridle and up and over my body to make the hitch that would support me aloft and allow me to descend at will, a few inches at a time. So I put out my fist again, looking down sidelong toward the winch and calling to the bosun to hold it. He nodded. It took me a few moments to shorten the tail on the pot and secure it to the other leg of the bridle. As I turned from doing that, the chair fell eight feet.

It would have fallen farther, but I had had a hand on one part of the gantline, and I had married it to the other almost before I knew that I was falling. Now with both hands holding the lines together, I looked below me. The bosun was gone, and one of the ordinaries, a green boy, was at the winch. Or rather six feet away and with his back to it. I shouted at him, and he began to haul me up with a snap that broke my grasp on the gantline and burned my hands. I shouted again and he stopped. It took a long time to make him understand that he must throw the turns off the winch. One's strength goes quickly aloft. I was weak by the time I started to haul up the long bight of the gantline with my right hand. There were many pauses, when I took the strain by pressing the line against the chair's bridle with my thigh, and it was a painful business getting a long loop through the bridle, and my legs and then the whole rig through the loop, till the hitch was formed at the bridle's throat. Then I sat for a while, getting over my scare and waiting for the strength to come back to my arms. I was safe now, and under my own steam, and the thing to do would be to stand on the seat of the bosun's chair, one hand for the ship and one hand for myself, and start to chip away at that six foot of topmast that I could no longer reach while sitting. But after a while it was clear that I hadn't the strength to wriggle my knees up above the level of the seat and pull myself to a standing position. By now, too, I had passed a frapping line around the mast to keep me from surging as the ship rolled, for her course kept us nearly in the trough of the sea; I was afraid to cast off that line and try to stand up. So I began to work where I was. My arms were so nearly numb that I had to shift the hammer from hand to hand.

Then the bosun called me from below. He motioned furiously, telling me to go higher. I shook my head. I attacked the mast again. A little after that I heard him shout from much closer. He had run up the ladder, which went as high as the crosstrees, and some twenty-five feet below me he was bellowing in the wind. He was tall and powerfully made, black Irish with raging blue eyes. The wind was so high that it stirred the thick black mustache bowed over the mouth that was venting fury at my bad seamanship. It seemed to me that I could see down his throat. I had been shivering in my thin clothes, mostly from weakness, but in an instant that was over. Seizing the heavy marlinspike that hung from my shoulder, I broke the lanyard with a jerk. "Boats, you left a green kid to tend my gantline. I'll settle with you when we're both on deck. Now stand from under or I'll drop this spike point-first." The bosun was a thorough seaman. His expression showed that he was appalled, not by the threat but by the breach of discipline—I must be raving mad. Almost at once he lowered his head and began to descend the ladder. He must have been a bold

man, too, because he never looked up to see what I might
be at.

I had painted my way down to the crosstrees when I was
called for my wheel watch. The paint locker was housed in
the mast tabernacle on deck, and I stowed my painting
gear there and drew kerosene from a drum with a spigot
on it to clean up a bit before going to the wheel. I was in a
fever, but I did not see the bosun. On the bridge the man at
the wheel told me the course and that she was carrying a
little left rudder as she sheered away from the seas. I saw
nothing in his expression, nor in the mate's. But I was in
no condition to notice, and from the bridge the mate, at
least, may have seen something amazing, a sailor aloft
holding out a marlinspike over the bosun's head. When my
watch was over, I saw the bosun in the mess, but we did
not speak. The next day during my watch I went to the
paint locker, and the bosun, his back to me, was mixing
paint. He sang,

How can it be, you fair young maiden,
No man has taken you to wife?
Are all the lads or blind or crazy?
Or do you love your single life?

I stopped a few feet from him. He stirred paint and sang.
After a while I moved forward again, and he turned and
handed me the paint pot, saying, "There you are." And
that was that. Except that I reflected for the first time that
I had offered to kill a man because he had been somewhat
overbearing. I thought, too, that my father, with his sol-
dierly sense of duty, would feel consternation if he were to
hear of it. But since then I have done other foolish things.

Now, I mean to make a small point of literary history,
not compose a work of art. If I were telling a story, I would
do it according to the rules. I would not ruminate on things

widely separated, and I would not be the subject of my own reflections. The work would be a narrative, it would have a shape, it would be faithful to itself. But I am engaged in something of a very different order, in which I am forced to speak of myself, and these wandering reflections are a way I have found that will permit me to talk about something that must seem surprising. These scattered memories as they arise have the effect of inspiriting me to go on to the historical matter I have it at heart to deliver. They remind me that I have a life, a self, as real as other men's—something I lose sight of whenever I am called to say what is counter to received opinion, or is simply unexpected, and if only for that reason somewhat disobliging. Then I doubt my right to speak. The sensation is of an attack of moral dizziness. But I should like to be able to persuade the reader, not that presently he will learn something to his advantage, as the writers of mystery stories used to say, but that he will learn something unexpected. Each new thing, it seems to me, changes the shape of the world. So I trust that all this military music, artless in the worst sense, will not prove a mere imposition when I have come to saying what it has been given to me to say.

I told Avrahm Yarmolinsky about a story of Chekhov that I had read while I was in college. It was in a volume that had the look of penury about it, bound in a cheap gray cloth filled with an unpleasant sizing, and the reedy lettering stamped in a blue that must always have looked faded and pinched. But that Chekhov collection had been assigned in a course I was taking, and I was glad to have come upon the last copy in the library. I was at college soon after the war. Many of the men in my class had been in the service for a long time; it was a great luxury for them to be in a college and reading books. They were eager to read, so that the books reserved for particular courses were hard to find. I carried off my dispirited-looking prize with satisfaction, and the two moods attended me as I read the stories. All of them appeared to me to have been composed expressly to be gathered into a volume bound in shoddy gray cloth with watery stamping. Nevertheless, to my astonishment, they were desolating and exalting.

One of those stories has been with me ever since. A gentleman walks out into the country—was it on the outskirts of St. Petersburg or of Moscow? The latter, perhaps, for I think I remember mention of the Sparrow Hills. Winter is near. The day is somber. Wandering absently, the gentleman is only half aware of the signs of the dying year about him, but his musings have taken their tone from the brown landscape and the wintry light. Then he comes upon a shepherd. Greeting him, he remarks on the cheerless look that the day has taken on. And after a moment the shepherd makes him this answer: "Your honor, the world is running down. A few years ago in these parts you would start a hare from his form at every step. If you paused among the poplars, the grouse would startle you with the sudden noise of his wings—sometimes two, three, four in succession bursting from the copse, each one taking you by surprise. The geese have been flying south all this month, but they are few, and most go by in silence. All my life long I was used to hear them before they could be seen, calling with a sound like the barking of dogs far off, and the flocks were so great that the long double line stretched to the limit of sight. The ducks are few now, too, in this season when they should be many. And each year in spring the woodcock would call in the clearings at twilight, then fly into the air and circle high up, and plummet down with their wild whistle—times I have heard them three at once, calling and whistling in different places. None came this past spring. The ewes scarcely bear. The grass is thin. The health is gone out of the world.

"Men are sickly in body and spirit. For how could the

increase fail and man's life be sound?"

And at these words the gentleman's heart contracts as if for a long time he has been suffering unaware and has just heard the name of his trouble. Or as if he has long been suppressing a painful intuition, and now his fellow has given it expression in terms that sweep away his resistance and leave him unmanned.

Something like that happened to me in New Orleans long ago, during the war. I was ashore, waiting for a ship, and so as not to be idle I had taken a job breaking freight for a trucking company. I worked at night, loading drums of lard, barrels of flour, cases and cartons of general merchandise for Shreveport or Lafayette or as far as Birmingham. It was interesting work. Sometimes the boss would give me directions, but mostly the strategy of loading was left to me, and I found it like ship stowage, though a good deal more simple since the tractor-trailer was not expected to roll and pitch with the seas. But still there was the job of getting the mass of goods out of the shed and into the trailer in the best order and with a minimum of double handling. It was tactically interesting, too. To break back a drum that weighed more than I did, slide the tongue of the hand-truck under it, draw it onto the hand-truck and start the load moving forward in the same instant in order to gain enough momentum on the narrow dock to be able to run it up the steel ramp into the body of the trailer—that took a little doing. And the heavy things had to be placed to best advantage, the case-goods and cartons had to be stacked in bulkheads so that they would not shift. The time went quickly between ten-thirty at night and four-thirty in the morning, and when I needed to straighten my back it was lawful to light a cigarette. Since it was summer, I would be going home in the first light. It was good work.

I was thinking of all that and feeling pleased as I knocked off one morning. I had just been paid. I had worked hard, but I had not been bored and I was not tired. I was looking forward to joining a ship in four days' time. I caught the streetcar. At the next stop a large blond man in white overalls boarded the car.

Though it was nearly empty, he took the seat beside me. He was in good spirits and he wanted to talk. He and his wife had come from Mississippi a few weeks ago so that he could take a job with a contractor who was building a government depot on the outskirts of the city. He said he did anything that had to do with framing—rough general carpentry for construction, as he summed it up. He added after a moment, "The money is good. And it's good work." That chimed in so well with my mood that when he asked me what I did I began to describe the pleasures of breaking freight. He said thoughtfully, "Every trade is interesting when you come to learn of it. Every trade." But I was anxious that he not think I was a warehouse laborer. I told him I was a seaman, and I began to talk of my art and mystery.

We had been sitting companionably in the rattling car, looking straight ahead but glancing at each other occasionally—it was a pleasure to look at his broad red open face, his fine mild eyes. But now he turned to me in surprise and commiseration. "Oh, you poor young man. Then you spend your life upon the sea. You have no woman to share your thoughts—" He broke off as if the idea were too immense for speech, or as if he felt that he had been indelicate in alluding to my friendless state. But after a while he said "There's pain in every life. Now, this job of mine is a godsend for the money it pays. The crew are all decent fellows. But I have to work nights, you see. If only I could work days, why, I'd be happy as a bird." I asked him if there was no chance of changing to the day shift. He shook his head. "Seems not. I've asked." I had put the question in sympathy, of course, and out of politeness, but also to give myself a breathing space. I had to take account of a new idea that threatened to change the aspect of the world. I can scarcely

recall now the sense of privilege I used to feel in bearing
the discipline of the vessel, the order of the watches, the
monotonous, workful, violent life. I liked living out in the
weather. Ships satisfied whatever aesthetic instinct I had.
I used to listen to the older seamen with the attentiveness
of a disciple, and in a short time I had grown skillful in my
calling. When I had been two years at sea, on board the
Jacob Thompson our Swede bosun asked to look at my
knife because he wanted to examine the pigtail of square
sennit I had put to the handle so that I could haul it out of
its deep sheath without a struggle. "That's delicate work.
How long you been going to sea?" I hesitated to tell him
how little salt water I had sailed over. "I know. You don't
want to say you're just a water-rat like me. I made my first
voyage as cabin boy when I was five years old. We come to
Bremerhaven and I try to walk home to Sweden." I felt
guilty at taking credit falsely, but I was delighted that the
bosun, who had shipped in sail, should mistake me for a
veteran. And since I was young, it was from the vantage
point of my office, as the Spaniards call it, that I saw all the
world. I took for my own the lines of my shipmate, Juan
Soto Galán, the ones that end his poem on Helen of Troy:

All talent is kin. What she cannot help,
The naked knife of her glance—
Leapt from the sheath to the hand, from the hand to the
    mark—
Is like the careless way I turn a splice,
Better than any rigger's loft ashore,
Or read the ship hull-down on the horizon
And tell my wondering mates her name and port.

I took those lines for my own, satisfied that the craft was
manly, but now that carpenter, a fellow man and a substantial one, had suggested to me that it was not fully

manlike, that it excluded something essential. The suggestion was painful and luminous. If after the war we had not sold most of our ships to the Greeks and the Norwegians, and registered what was left under flags of convenience, no doubt I should have been a seaman to this day. It's no easy thing to find good work, work that one is suited for. But when the carpenter spoke I understood that the life I had embraced was, in my own terms, no more than half a life.

That realization, unsettling as it was, concerned a relatively narrow train of conduct and custom. It knocked me off my pins for a time, but it was a long way short, in its unsettling effects, of the story in the Chekhov collection. That story, which I have compressed to the point of distorting everything but its import, though I could recite it at much greater length, and, I believe, very nearly in the words of the original—except that I will not introduce a work of art on a grander scale than is called for in an account whose proper business is with a modest item of literary history—that story, I have said, has been with me for many years. It made at once the same impression of painful enlightenment that the carpenter's words, his tone, the expression of his face, had made upon me, as if I had suddenly been enfranchised to suffer understandingly what I had hitherto borne unaware. But it was very much more powerful and lasting, a kind of astonishment of discovery possibly equal to the change occasioned by the shepherd's words in the soul of that wanderer in the Sparrow Hills. In both cases the prophet's ignorance as well as his knowledge vouched for his saying. But what the shepherd said struck me as more impersonal in its application and not to be eluded. Chekhov, out of the *trop plein* of his energies and passions, and out of the pessimism of a dying man— for he was dying of tuberculosis—had composed that threnody for his world. And that world was indeed ready for death. In a quarter-century it was dead. It is a universal assumption that the world we inherited from that time is a dead world. Naturally we ignore the fact. Life has always been hard, no doubt. But to live in a dead world calls for a ceaseless tautening of the imagination that has made us a race of hysterics. However, that is by the by.

I told Avrahm Yarmolinsky how I had come upon the Chekhov story in my college course years back. I made no reflections upon it. I was meaning to ask him if he knew of the collection in which I had found it, or any other that contained it, since I wanted to read it again. But at one point in my detailing of the incident I began to falter. Something in his manner had made me lose the clue of my thought. The current of sympathetic attention that flows from the listener to sustain the speaker had been suddenly interrupted. Yarmolinsky's grave face was stony. I felt that before I was aware of what it meant. But then experience told me what was about to happen, and I began at once to feel ashamed, like a man caught out. The first instance of it that I can recall consciously had happened some years before, when I was working for Jack Steinberg in the one-horse publishing firm that he later made into a notable house. He was about to entrust some copy-editing to me, and he asked me if I knew what to do with commas and periods when they occurred in the neighborhood of quotation marks. I answered bouncily with a homemade formula. Jack was a passionate man who habitually spoke gently. He was easy to work for—indeed, endlessly indulgent. And I used to feel rather reassured than not by the glint of iron under his affable habit. This time his expression changed abruptly. He said, "Here's *The Chicago Manual of Style*. Take it home, go through the whole thing, so you'll know that it covers everything. And the index is complete. Don't go near that manuscript till you have some idea of what the questions are and where you can find the answers." But I had known myself to be inexcusably at fault before he spoke, simply from the rigidity of his face. And only a few months ago in conversation with a friend, I said casually that I didn't think much of a science of clinical psychology that had changed the definitions of psychosis and neurosis twice in my lifetime. My friend is a physician, profound and droll, with a manic comicality of invention; in discussion a playful tiger. Now all drollery ceased together. His face set, he told me that those definitions had not changed, and he quoted the textbook formulae. What I had meant to say was that their meanings had changed, since they were being applied to clusters of symptoms that were in practice regarded in quite another way than they had been when the definitions were first adopted. One indication was the discovery—less than twenty years old—that neurosis is not the monopoly of the middle class, and psychosis not the specialty of coarse natures lower in the social scale. But I could say none of that, for my friend's face was implacable. I think of Marlow in *Lord Jim,* consulting the French naval officer about the moral bearings of Jim's case, and being much heartened by his ready understanding of the natural fear that had overcome the young man. And so Marlow finds the courage to ask, then, if he is not disposed to take a lenient view of Jim's conduct. And the Frenchman scrambles to his feet, as if eager to keep his garments from contamination by the possibility of leniency, and announces the judgment of his entire nation upon the matter: There is still the question of honor. And as for what may come when honor is forfeit, he can offer no opinion because he knows nothing about that. Implacable. Though I think he is in the right.

Yarmolinsky said quietly, mournfully, "There is no such story of Chekhov. Almost every scrap attributable to Chekhov that is of literary significance has been collected. That story is not in the corpus."

I understood that the judgment could not be appealed.

Yarmolinsky had edited Chekhov, written about him. And I am unreliable about literary sources, my acquirements in such matters being a late growth. But that I should mistake the authorship of a story that corresponded to my buried premonitions of the meaning of my own life, that I should be wrong about the gray binding and faded blue lettering that I had borne for years like a weight upon the heart—had I ever been inside that library, did I attend that college?—these things seemed astounding. Learned men have erred. But then, it could not be Turgenev. I had read *A Sportsman's Notebook* over and over. And it was not Tolstoy or Gogol. And of the small number of Russian and Soviet writers with whom I was familiar, it was inconceivable to me that the author of that sketch might be anyone but Chekhov.

I N THE WEEK THAT HAS GONE BY SINCE MY CREDIT CARD was rejected in the restaurant, I have received the monthly statement of account. From that statement it is clear that if the company had allowed me to charge my restaurant bill of $10.09, there would still have been a balance in my favor of over thirteen dollars. I won't use that card again. I don't like to pay interest to capricious people. I've read that one of the credit card companies, I forget which, has issued fifty million cards. A number of that magnitude guarantees many chances for error, but it also makes discourtesy routine, and suspicion business as usual. How often I've tendered a card for some small purchase, and the clerk has reached under the counter to get the closely printed booklet, and run down the columns of figures to see if the man standing before him is to be regarded as a citizen or a pariah. I used sometimes to pretend ignorance. I would ask, "Are those the good ones or the bad ones?" Usually the clerk would seem a bit taken aback, even embarrassed. "The bad ones." "And have you found any yet?" I never spoke to a clerk who had. But some said that at other counters, elsewhere in the store, or at a branch in another borough, a bad one had turned up. I dropped the game after a while. Those were the terms on which the clerk earned his living. I had thought to educate him about his relations with his fellows, but that was presumptuous. If I had accomplished anything, it was to add a drop of bitterness to his cup.

But it's like trying to give your check for a purchase in a department store. In this city you must produce your driver's license or no soap. Once I had my passport with me, and I was curious to see if the spread eagle and the Great Seal of the United States of America, and the endorsement of the secretary of state, and my photograph—bearded, however—and my signature would turn the trick. No. I had to produce my driver's license. "Patience," my father says when I confront him with things of the kind. But I had a French friend once who used to exclaim on such occasions, *"Quelle époque!"* More pointed and more heartfelt. For our nerves are raw from the climate of affronts and suspicion that we have accustomed ourselves to endure. I go to some lengths myself not to add to the miasma rising from the marsh. Many years ago, a man named Hardesty, from Wilmington, Delaware, borrowed ten dollars from me in a Southern port. He didn't mention that he was shipping out next day. He had been cadet master of our class at the school in St. Petersburg, Florida, where we were to be dubbed (wonders of the war!) ensign, second lieutenant, or third mate if we passed the courses. On our very first evening at the school, while we were in formation in the street outside our barracks, Hardesty had awarded me ten demerits—thirteen meant expulsion. He said, textually, "That will cost you ten demerits." We had been laughing at a mild joke an officer had made; my laughter had gone on a hemidemisemiquaver too long. I said, "That will cost you more than that." And I stepped out of the rank to strike him. But the officer, a lieutenant named Sargent—a very decent man—said quietly, "Stop, mister." The honorific mister was an earnest of my prospective translation to third mate. "Go back to your formation."

In my three months at the school I never collected the last three demerits, so I was duly graduated as an officer in the merchant marine. Hardesty was too. (I believe he had no demerits whatsoever. How would he have come by any?) Four months after that, both of us happened to be in New Orleans, waiting to ship out. I came upon him in Bourbon Street. I think we had not spoken since the night he had awarded me ten demerits. He said, "I'm flat broke. Lend me ten till Saturday." Since I detested the man I could not refuse him the money. And he was gone next day. Recently I told the story to a friend of mine. I told him that by accident I had just learned that there were people of that name still living in Wilmington, that I was going to go there some day and get back my ten dollars with interest. My friend said, "Don't talk like that. Don't even think like that." Now, I am opposed to capital punishment. I can scarcely imagine a nastier custom than allowing public functionaries to assume our responsibility for condemning and murdering a human being. But I have nothing against private vengeance—though I would think it reasonable that my fellow citizens try to restrain me if they believe that I intend an act of violence.

But what was I to make of the announcement, on the part of a scholar in the field of Russian letters—specifically an editor and biographer of Chekhov—that the volume I had read as a class assignment, containing the story I have mentioned, was not by Chekhov at all? Of course, Yarmolinsky did not say precisely that. He simply denied that the story I had told him in summary had been written by Chekhov. Well, I made nothing of it. If the theory of the heliocentric organization of the solar system were overthrown tomorrow, I should be very much interested in the new ingenuities that science was substituting for the familiar ones. But of course one expects some such overthrow. And science does not demand of us a slack-jawed faith in its proposals, just a provisional acceptance of the presumed state of the art, so that investigation may proceed. The Chekhov story is another matter. It happened to me. It is part of my life. I made nothing of Yarmolinsky's denial. And there is a further oddity in all this. Why hadn't Yarmolinsky told me the true authorship of the story? He knew Russian literature as the dog knows the coverts, as at one time, a pilot of the Hudson River, I knew the courses, buoys, lights, and landmarks from Ambrose Light to Albany. It is not credible that in my desultory reading I had happened upon a wonderful Russian author unknown to him. That seemed scarcely more likely than that some writer entirely foreign to Russia would set his sketch of the end of the world in the Sparrow Hills, and report it as a colloquy between a muzhik and a gentleman. I could make nothing of Yarmolinsky's denial.

T HE POET M. L. ROSENTHAL IS STEEPED IN Chekhov. Not, I imagine, because he takes him for Aeschylus or Shakespeare, but because there are strains in that music that touch his heart. I understand that very well. When I was young, it was Auden, not Yeats, who touched me most. Yeats was the bigger man, Auden the more clubbable—not that his throwaway manner is without a kind of diffident nobility:

England to me is my own tongue,
And what I did when I was young . . .

In any case, Rosenthal is my friend, and some years after Yarmolinsky had set me that puzzle, he happened to speak of Chekhov's "Ward Six." There's no doubt about that one, at least. And then he mentioned the film that the Russians had made of Chekhov's "The Lady with the Dog." I had seen that. For a few moments two middle-aged men thought of Chekhov, his plays, his stories—and the plague that those stories have unleashed upon us because their atmosphere of things unresolved, of less than heroic pain, can be evoked readily enough by writers who have no genius. And one thing leads to another: I told him my Chekhov story. He said he had never read it. He was surprised. How could one miss a story like that? He would look for it.

But he never did unearth it. He said later that it sounded like something that Chekhov might have written, but apparently he hadn't. At least he himself could find no trace of it among the editions of Chekhov that he had looked through. He wondered if it might not be another writer.

Yes, but who? The problem is rendered more acute by the scantiness of my information about Russian authors. If I know of no more than a dozen, how can I possibly make a mistake? Reviewing them while counting on my fingers, it is clear that none of them except Chekhov could possibly be the author. Well, Gorky and Isaac Babel are remote possibilities. But Gorky did not take that view of life. To introduce the shepherd's monologue somewhere in a story—that would be possible for him. But to make it the high point of a sketch designed to express an intuition of cosmic failure is simply not Gorky. And Babel writes in saber strokes. The impractical-seeming parries that guard cheek and flank, the florid moulinets that are nevertheless the shortest route to an opening, the sudden attack with the point—these make a wild skirling music, an exuberant *Totentanz*. He would never let a peasant speak connectedly, collectedly, so long a speech, one that gave no occasion for explosive satisfaction in bitterness. Now, I am not even remotely a scholar, but in these matters I have a certain flair. I told my friend—the one who said I must not dream of spilling Hardesty's blood—that in these matters I had absolute pitch. He said, "In these matters no one has absolute pitch." Of course. But absolute pitch is relative; some people are tone-deaf. I have relative absolute pitch, and I will not abate my claim any further, because I have a duty to the truth. And it's a small enough talent that I claim. It would seem that I haven't a shred of imagination. And I can't even read Babel or Gorky or Chekhov in their own language. But the Chekhov story cannot have been written by either of the others. It might have been written by Turgenev, but I have read no other stories or sketches of his except those that figure in *A Sportsman's Notebook*, and it is not among them. How can I be mistaken when I have too little information to make any confusion of the kind remotely plausible?

Certainly ignorance can lead one into error sometimes, and sometimes into sin. But this is not that sort of occasion. I know because I have been led into both, and I can recognize them. Once, for example, when I was on the *Jean-Baptiste LeMoyne,* south of the Florida Keys, I made a serious mistake at the wheel. We had been steering southeast, and the mate told me to come right easy, meet her, and steady her on one-eight-nine. We were making a long plunge into the Caribbean. I carried out the order and reported, "Steady on one-eight-nine, sir." He said, "Keep her so." He left the wheelhouse and went up the vertical ladder to the flying bridge. I heard him stride across the deck above my head. I assumed he meant to take an azimuth of the sun. Then he called down through the speaking tube, "What is your heading now?" I had looked up involuntarily when I first heard his voice, and I looked at the gyro compass again. "One-eight-nine, sir." He asked me the same question two more times in the next two minutes. The compass did not go a single click right or left—the sea was calm—and each time I answered confidently, "One-eight-nine." Then he ran across the deck above my head, tumbled down the ladder, and came into the wheelhouse on the run. He stared at the compass. He said, "Your heading is one-nine-four." I looked. That's what the compass said, and I had been certain that it had not moved. I had been reading one-nine-four as one-eight-nine, steering five degrees off course. He said, "You deliberately tried to fool me." My shame at having wandered from the course kept me from understanding the accusation. He said, "You tried to make a fool of me." When I could speak, I said, "I'd be a fool to try that. I made a mistake. You were taking an azimuth, weren't you? You had the gyro repeater right under your nose." That wasn't polite, but I was terribly rattled. He said, "You tried to make a fool of me. I won't forget that." To be unskillful was bad enough. To be taken for a cheat and a liar was nearly unbearable. There was nothing more I could say. I thought bitterly that I was the best sailor in the watch. It did not even occur to me that he may have thought so too, and could not account for my being off course during long minutes, cheerfully answering one-eight-nine the while, unless I had meant to mislead him. We were to load oil in Aruba for Valparaiso, but from Aruba we carried the oil back to Perth Amboy, so that the voyage was over in three more weeks. That was lucky. When I signed off the vessel, I said to him, "Mister mate, I misread the steering compass. There's no excuse for that. But I wasn't trying to fool you." He said, "I know what you were trying to do." And that was that. It has troubled me for thirty years, and not because it was the worst mistake I ever made. I've done worse things, all right. It's that the man thought I had lied about something I would never lie about. Since then lovers have said I lied about things one doesn't lie about, and the accusation has hurt less. Men and women are not to understand one another. But that ship's officer and I were members of the same craft. There was nothing to misunderstand. I have never forgiven him.

Here is an odd thing. That man could not be persuaded, years ago, because he had been disappointed in his expectations. A good helmsman stays on course, and if in heavy weather the ship's head is nearly ungovernable, he meets her on each swing to keep her as much as possible from ranging, and tries to average his course—as a young man I heard with a curious elation that "govern" was related to the Greek word for "rudder." And many years later I am obdurate about that man because he felt that I had broken the bond of faith that sustains us all. He was a good seaman, and he should have known my heart by his own. At one time a woman who had a tenderness for me nevertheless found that every action, every gesture of mine, was an offense. I asked her, "Why did you choose me, then?" Her answer undid me: "Everyone lives in a dream of love." The most painful lines in *Don Quixote* turn on the grim joke of our illusions. The don is at last persuaded that what he had taken for a castle and for noble courtesy were hired lodging and professional hospitality. He says, "This is an inn, then?" "And a right good one," the innkeeper returns with perfect satisfaction. The don says, "I have been sadly deluded all this while." The Spanish is more virile and more hopeless—*"Engañado he vivido hasta aquí."*

It must be for reasons like these that I feel an unlikely twinge of resentment at Avrahm Yarmolinsky for having denied my testimony, and at my friend Mack Rosenthal. It is as if they sought to dispel a kindly illusion. No doubt they could not consider what the result might be if they succeeded, since they were themselves testifying to their best knowledge. They were testifying to what they knew, and we owe one another just that.

Now, Rosenthal is a remarkable poet, and the measure of it is that he is, statistically speaking, insane; an essential part of his trade is to conciliate his generation, but he takes no interest in the job. Hamlet says of Osric, "He did comply with his dug before he sucked it." Yes, but Osric has got on, hasn't he, and at the end of the play he is hale and hearty, and in a position to commend his services to

Fortinbras. Rosenthal has no such gift. Like every real poet he has had to invent a new language, but his language is unacceptable to the nation we have become. It is not hieratic, remote, like the language of Stevens. It is not a fit vehicle for sly, poisoned confession, like the language of so and so. He doesn't know how to talk tough, like the tribe of the terrified tough. The most noted of his fellow poets are a generation of Malvolios who have had greatness thrust upon 'em. He has no talent for that. A painful case.

He has courage that he would do well to keep out of his verse, courage of readiness and courage of compunction. I was lunching with him one day at his college. Holding our trays before us, we were in line to pay the man at the cash register. There was a foreigner ahead of us in line. He was confused, and the man at the register was insolent. I turned away, mentally, from the business. I'm a modern American. My motto is, Don't look at me—I just work here. I paid, and waited for my friend to join me. He said in a low tone to the man at the register, "I heard what passed between you and that man. He's a foreign visitor, a guest of the university, a guest of the country." The man at the register said something negligently exculpatory. Mack said, "That won't do. I'm going to see to it that you won't be impolite to a stranger again." I felt embarrassed for my friend. He seems to think he lives here, not on Mars or on television.

Another time we had lunch at the White Horse. As we entered we saw a big fellow sitting on a stool with his back to the bar, his elbows braced on it. He was heavy-bodied, with a sunburned face, and his nose looked as if someone had broken it for him not too long ago. He was drunk. He seemed to find us amusing. I excused myself to make a phone call and went past the end of the bar to the public phone. While I was dialing the number I heard Mack's voice. I glanced over that way, and things didn't look right. When the phone had rung five times I hung up. I steamed over to Mack and said, fatuously, "Do you know this man?" He said, "No, I don't. But he seems to think that he knows me." "I know you," the man said, and he laughed. I turned to him, but Rosenthal took my arm and said, "Let's go into the other room." We did, and we ordered our lunch and the house's infamous half-and-half. Suddenly Mack said, "My God, it's Delmore Schwartz. I didn't recognize him. He's gained a lot of weight, and he looks as if he's been in a fight. I have to apologize to him." With great difficulty I kept him from doing that; in Schwartz's condition it would have been a mistake. "That's terrible," Mack said. "I never recognized him. I'll have to find someone who knows where he's living now, and write to him." I had always thought of Delmore Schwartz as the man who had at the outset the essential gift that most of the poets who were his exact contemporaries never chose to demonstrate, the ability to make a great line. He made only a half-dozen of them, but they are perfectly diagnostic for poetry. One would be enough—"The scrimmage of appetite everywhere." That line is Dantesque. So I was thinking that on my meeting that extraordinary man I had tried to edge him into a brawl.

But what I had begun to say is that Rosenthal is magnanimous and not sentimental, and he can't seem to keep the first quality out of his poems, nor inject into them a saving dose of the other. In sum, he lacks a decent respect to the opinion of mankind. On his head be it.

As might be imagined, those traits make him an inconvenient friend. I get back at him as best I can. He admired, rightly, Horace Gregory's version of Catullus's *"Nil nimium studeo, Caesar"*: "I shall not raise my hand to please you, Caesar, Nor do I care if you are black or white."

I brooded on that, and the next day telephoned him to say that I had made a better version: "I couldn't care less about pleasing you, Caesar. You can be white or black—it don't make me no never-mind."

There was a pause. Mack asked, "And did you introduce the ungrammatical expression in order to conform to the original?" I said loftily that I had employed an American idiom to render in a contemporary mode the unbuttoned impertinence of the original. "I see," he said. "Would you repeat the lines for me? I'd like to write them down." So that one missed fire. I doubt that it will stop me, though. I have observed that experience does not teach, though it may canker.

But what it comes down to is that, with less reason to do so than Avrahm Yarmolinsky, since he has not like Yarmolinsky devoted a good part of his life to a scholarly investigation of Chekhov, and with equal lack of concern for the possible consequences to me, Rosenthal has concluded that I am mistaken, and in an unimportant way, about the authorship of the Chekhov story. That, from a close friend, strikes me as cavalier. On the basis of an investigation that could not, in the nature of the case, be systematic, let alone exhaustive, he has decided that I am not to be believed on this point—indifferent to him, capital to me.

Now, the trouble with being alone in the world, in the sense that no one agrees with you and the world's experience does not ratify your instinctive feelings, is that you go crazy. I do not mean in a statistical sense. Since no one agrees, you repeat, you exaggerate, you shout. And at last you shout not from outraged conviction but from terror, from distrust of your feelings, since they are coin that does not pass current and you cannot rid yourself of them. At that point you understand that you are crazy. And a man is a social animal. How can you believe that you are in the right when everyone knows that you're crazy?

When I was second mate on the *Ulla Madsen* I invented a method of finding longitude at noon. It came to me suddenly on a day when I was taking the usual noon sights to establish the latitude—just as once, when I was a child riding on the subway and seeing the lights of the tunnel slide by, it came to me that motion in space was the graph of time, and time elapsed the measure of motion. For hundreds of years men had been measuring the angular distance of the sun above the noon horizon, applying a correction for the date, and setting down the result as their latitude. Longitude was a very different matter. To arrive at it one worked cumbersome problems in spherical trigonometry, or, more recently, with one's sight entered volumes of tables and in about ten minutes could hope to come up with a "line of position" that gave an estimated longitude that was close enough for the purposes of a vessel that could not run into danger any faster than fourteen knots. But a dozen or so entries on a form are required, and petty calculations, and there is plenty of chance for error. It came to me that at one moment of the day—noon—one could find longitude almost as one finds latitude, almost by inspection.

Every deepwater ship carries two timepieces, the ship's clock that is set approximately to local time, and the chronometer that is set as precisely as may be to Greenwich time, with its rate of error written down in the log every day after comparison with radio signals. You start to take sights a few moments before noon by the ship's clock, and note the time of each sight with a watch set to local time. The sun is climbing to its greatest altitude, and the successive sights show a larger and larger angle with the horizon. At last the sextant shows a smaller reading—and you know that the sight taken just before that one represents high noon. From it you get your latitude, as usual. Then, by comparing the ship's clock, showing local time, with the chronometer, set to Greenwich time, correcting only for the moments elapsed since that penultimate sight, you have your longitude. The sun passed over Greenwich before it passed over your head, and the difference in time between those two transits is the measure of your distance from the prime meridian at Greenwich—which is longitude. The only calculation required is to change time to degrees and minutes of arc, at the rate of fifteen degrees to the hour, for that is the speed of the sun's apparent motion through the sky.

At first I wondered why the books did not mention it. I must be wrong. Or perhaps it was because the method is usable only at noon, when the sun is on your meridian. But that did not seem a sufficient reason, since the navigator's "day's work" required him to shoot the sun at noon in any case.

Well, I never had a skipper who let me use that discovery. There had to be something wrong with it, though it sounded right. I used the method secretly because it was quick. And since it is inherently more accurate than the method of looking up tables and making entries and manipulations on a form, every day I had to nudge my noon position on the chart and ease it over toward the old man's. But that is an old sea-custom anyway.

Many are the persons I have told of my discovery. Always they looked sympathetic and skeptical. The more they knew of the subject the more careful they were to look sympathetic—*on ne badine pas avec l'amour*—but they were skeptical. I bore it all. Then, last summer, I picked up a yachting magazine on a newsstand, for I love boats and shall never have one now. In it there was an advertisement for an electronic pocket calculator that would solve various problems in navigation and piloting. My eye went down the list of problems disapprovingly: I detest those machines. All at once my heart jumped. You know how it is when you miss your footing on the stair. The first you know of it is that your hand has seized the rail—your body knew the danger before you did, and your heart has jumped. One of the items read, "Longitude by Meridian Altitude." The technical term means one thing only. My method, my rejected method is now so much a matter of course that it is programmed on a pocket calculator. And for thirty years I had thought myself mad.

So when my friend Mack Rosenthal adopts with me the tone of a man visiting a sickroom, and says it sounds as if it might be Chekhov, but it appears after all that it isn't, he cannot possibly know that his tactful tone is an exacerbation. He is driving me to the verge of recklessness, something to which my unfortunate temperament lends itself in any case. So, too, is my other friend who is nameless here because he does not properly figure in the foreground of the account I have to render—the one who tells me, "In these matters no one has absolute pitch." After these excitements of my reason and my blood, and given a certain instability which is after all my business alone, though it is probably patent to that small portion of the world that knows of my existence, I think it will be understandable if I do something characteristic and out of character. Then who will be mad and who will be sane?

T HE THIRD PERSON WHOM I MUST INTRODUCE HERE FOR the sake of his testimony is Mr. Monroe Engel, who is well enough known as a scholar and man of letters, I trust. He is quite as well known as is agreeable with honesty, and no grander notoriety would serve my particular purposes. I met him three years ago, when both of us served on a literary jury. We had two prizes to award. One of these went, as of right, to the foremost American novelist—now in his dotage but who served the Republic well while he still had all his marbles. The question was, what younger deserving writer should be granted the second award? It had been decided by a kind of unofficial consensus to bestow it upon one who deals in the necrology of our dead world, taking his cue from a hint in T. S. Eliot regarding rusted iron, stonecrop, merds. And that made me think of another and most gifted writer who was still blindly

evoking memories of life, the possibility of tragedy. Then I
did something unseemly, for I know how to sway a committee: a child's heartbroken insistence, or the calm lucidity
of the paranoiac, or a new proposal put forward with manly
firmness when everyone is looking at his watch and thinking of his luncheon engagement—these are features of my
armamentarium. I think none of my fellow committee
members understood the willfulness of my filibuster in
favor of vanished hope, except a young woman—herself a
notable writer—the youngest member of the committee.
She understood because she is hostage to death by reason
of her youth, with her teeth set against vain sentiment.
But she was outvoted.

After the formal session there were a few minutes of
conversation, and Monroe Engel spoke to me. He was cordial, as if I were a man and a brother rather than a person
secretly convinced that his literary passions had more than
a tinge of defensiveness. And we are a social animal; Mr.
Engel's manner made me feel readmitted to human con-
verse. Our discussion before the vote had provoked the
mention of Chekhov, and Mr. Engel told me now that he
was editing a collection of the stories. I told him of my
Chekhov story. I asked if he was acquainted with it. In
putting the question I tried to disguise my eagerness to be
delivered of the burden it has come to represent to me.
He said he hadn't come across it, but that he would be reviewing the entire corpus, and he would let me know if he
found it.

People say those things, but life intervenes, and you do
not hear from them. So I was touched to get a postcard
from Monroe Engel some time afterward. I have it before
me now—the only physical document in the case:

January 8
I've not been able to find the Chekhov story you described.
Perhaps it will turn up in the one volume of stories (the stories of

1894) that has not yet been issued. If not, you have a collector's memory.

Sorry not to be more helpful.

Sincerely,
Monroe Engel

A collector's memory. That is an interesting coinage. Under other circumstances I suppose I should think it pleasantly witty, signifying the substance of things hoped for that cannot possibly exist. I am in any case very grateful to Monroe Engel for his courtesy, and I hope he will not think it an ill return that I hale him before the public on my business without asking leave. For my need is great. I am too old to imagine that the volume containing the stories of 1894 (my father was at that time a child of five) will sustain my claim. Besides, more than two years have passed. Mr. Engel has no doubt finished his review of the Chekhov corpus some time ago. I am sure that he would have let me know if he had come upon the story.

Now, that puts me in a very difficult position, though I might appear to have sought it. I may resent—not on trivial grounds, but on grounds that are scarcely avowable nonetheless—Avrahm Yarmolinsky's ukase in the matter, and the pronouncement in the same sense of my friend M. L. Rosenthal. The fact remains that I appealed to their special knowledge, and they answered me according to their understanding of the case, as they were bound to do. Marshalling their testimony in this account has been painful to me, but I have gone through with it doggedly. Monroe Engel's report I cannot resent at all, though he has delivered the latest blow to my hopes. The problem is severe, and it is not simply a matter of my having been hopelessly wrong about a literary ascription that has had special meaning for me. I have been wrong in worse cases and survived. I mentioned how Mack came to the defense of a foreigner—unknown to the man himself, simply on principle, because that man was the stranger within our gates. Well, I have had very different relations with foreigners in my time. I shall not dilate upon an incident in a Latin-American port where, one night, drunk and about to be arrested (for cause), I snatched the policeman's saber from its sheath, foined at him with the point to gain a moment's start on him and his companion, ran along the wharves in the darkness, came on a providential *lancha* with oars in her whose painter I cast adrift, pulled away towards the anchor lights of the shipping in the roadstead, made my own vessel at last, having run into the stage at the foot of her lowered accommodation ladder, discovered the accursed sword still beside me on the thwart—the pommel gouging my hip and the point jammed under the stretcher against which my feet were braced—hurled it away from me into the water and from the stage spurned off the *lancha* to drop down-current, all with no thought of the policeman who was answerable for that saber nor the waterman whose livelihood was that boat. That happened far away, in a far-off time, and I had the excuse of being drunk and frightened. But not long ago I was crossing Seventh Avenue from the west, and the traffic light changed before I had reached the sidewalk. Immediately I heard the baleful blast of a highway horn at my back, and the car passed so close that I had to jump for the curb. The driver shook a fist at me as he sailed around the corner into Bleecker Street. I began to run, and I pressed on until I caught up with the car at Sixth Avenue where it had stopped for the light. It was liver-colored. When I pulled the door open the driver shrank away as far as he could without letting go of the steering wheel. He was a dark man. At that moment he looked as if he had been hit with a single-jack. I thrust my head and shoulders inside the car and said murderously, "The pedestrian has the right of way in this city." "You cross with red light." Cars that had come up behind us sounded their horns. I felt disgust and savage pleasure at his fear. "In your country, no doubt, a man in a car can run over any man on foot. Don't ever try that again here." I slammed the door, exulting in the noise. The liver-colored car moved away and the next car sounded its horn indignantly at me as it went by. I could scarcely see. For a few minutes I found it hard to walk because I was shaking, and as that began to leave me my satisfaction too ebbed away. The business took on an ugly look. I was ashamed.

No one, I trust, will imagine that I have described here the worst actions of my life. I have done worse things. And the swan's breast stems the turbid flood and takes no stain, but the things of man are otherwise disposed. Every act of prepotence or cowardice has left a sediment in my spirit that darkens for me the stream of life. But somewhere I keep a measure, as they say a meter stick is preserved at Paris to try the truth of all the others. Even in this city that offers no horizon I find out a level and a perpendicular. In the end I know how much things come to, which way is up. To suppose that I would be ashamed to acknowledge that I have been dim-wittedly ascribing to Chekhov a story of which he is innocent, would be to deny me all sense of proportion, as if I could not tell the difference between footlessness and faithlessness. It's true I can't say how it comes about that I should be so mistaken, but I long ago resigned the childish passion for knowing the inessential—if I want to be fully informed I can always read the *New York Times*. It is something else that troubles me. For even as I loathe with all my soul the waitress's musky aura, her hoarse voice, the matter-of-fact brutality that informs her brisk, awkward movements, so I hate the artist's mountebank suppleness of self-exposure, his gift for uniforms and posturing, for being all things to all men, for taking on willingly the tincture of the stream of his times. I know there is in it a certain temporal majesty, marked with grime, as there is grimy majesty in empire or in the vulgar power of Concorde. But it troubles me exceedingly to confess what at this point the reader may already suspect. It was not what I intended at the outset, I could swear to that. But do I know what I intended? And to take responsibility is one thing; to feel myself complicit is another. Nevertheless it appears, against all likelihood, that in a certain season, when day was drawing off, the brown air taking the creatures of earth from their labors, all alone I girded myself for the journey and its pain, and composed—magisterially—the myth of our times. It was a signal and thankless effort, but the mere mention of it has persuaded men of judgment to consider for a moment its admission to the canon. It seems certain now—in my own despite—that I am the author of the Chekhov story. What genius I had then.

(The Antioch Review)

Raymond Carver
Cathedral

THIS BLIND MAN, AN OLD FRIEND OF MY WIFE'S, HE WAS on his way to spend the night. His wife had died. So he was visiting the dead wife's relatives in Connecticut. He called my wife from his in-laws'. Arrangements were made. He would come by train, a five-hour trip, and my wife would meet him at the station. She hadn't seen him since she worked for him one summer in Seattle ten years ago. But she and the blind man had kept in touch. They made tapes and mailed them back and forth. I wasn't enthusiastic about his visit. He was no one I knew. And his being blind bothered me. My idea of blindness came from the movies. In movies, the blind moved slowly and never laughed. Sometimes they were led by seeing-eye dogs. A blind man in my house was not something I looked forward to.

That summer in Seattle she had needed a job. She didn't have any money. The man she was going to marry at the end of the summer was in officer's training school. He didn't have any money, either. But she was in love with the guy, and he was in love with her, etc. She'd seen something in the paper: Help Wanted—Reading for Blind Man, and a telephone number. She phoned and went over, was hired on the spot. She'd worked with this blind man all summer. She read stuff to him, case studies, reports, that sort of thing. She helped him organize his little office in the county social service department. They'd become good friends, my wife and the blind man. How do I know these things? She told me. And she told me something else. On her last day in the office, the blind man asked if he could touch her face. She agreed to this. She told me he ran his fingers over every part of her face, her nose—even her neck! She never forgot it. She even tried to write a poem about it. She was always writing a poem. She wrote a poem or two every year, usually after something really important had happened to her.

When we first started going out together, she showed me the poem. In the poem she recalled his fingers and the way they had moved around her face. In the poem she talked about what she had felt at the time, about what went through her mind as he touched her nose and lips. I can recall I didn't think much of the poem. Of course I didn't tell her that. Maybe I just don't understand poetry. I admit it's not the first thing I reach for when I pick up something to read.

Anyway, this man who'd first enjoyed her favors, the officer-to-be, he'd been her childhood sweetheart. So okay. I'm saying that at the end of the summer she let the blind man run his hands over her face, said goodbye to him, married her childhood etc., who was now a commissioned officer, and she moved away from Seattle. But they'd kept in touch, she and the blind man. She made the first contact after a year or so. She called him up one night from an Air Force base in Alabama. She wanted to talk. They talked. He asked her to send him a tape and tell him about her life. She did this. She sent the tape. On the tape she told the blind man about her husband and about their life together in the military. She told the blind man she loved her husband but she didn't like it where they lived and she didn't like it that he was a part of the military-industrial complex. She told the blind man she'd written a poem and he was in it. She told him that she was writing a poem about what it was like to be an Air Force officer's wife in the Deep South. The poem wasn't finished yet. She was still writing it. The blind man made a tape. He sent her the tape. She made a tape. This went on for years. My wife's officer was posted to one base and then another. She sent tapes from Moody AFB, McGuire, McConnell, and finally

Travis, near Sacramento, where one night she got to feeling lonely and cut off from people she kept losing in that moving-around life. She balked, couldn't go it another step. She went in and swallowed all the pills and capsules in the medicine cabinet and washed them down with a bottle of gin. Then she got into a hot bath and passed out.

But instead of dying she got sick. She threw up. Her officer—Why should he have a name? He was the childhood sweetheart, and what more does he want?—came home from a training mission, found her, and called the ambulance. In time, she put it on the tape and sent the tape to the blind man. Over the years she put all kinds of stuff on tapes and sent the tapes off lickety-split. Next to writing a poem every year, I think it was her chief means of recreation. On one tape she told the blind man she'd decided to live away from her officer for a time. On another tape she told him about her divorce. She and I began going out, and of course she told her blind man about this. She told him everything, or so it seemed to me. Once she asked me if I'd like to hear the latest tape from the blind man. This was a year ago. I was on the tape, she said. So I said okay, I'd listen to it. I got us drinks and we settled down in the living room. We made ready to listen. First she inserted the tape into the player and adjusted a couple of dials. Then she pushed a lever. The tape squeaked and someone began to talk in this loud voice. She lowered the volume. After a few minutes of harmless chitchat, I heard my own name rasped out by this stranger, this man I didn't even know! And then this: "From all you've said about him, I can only conclude—" But we were interrupted, a knock at the door, something, and we didn't get back to the tape. Maybe it was just as well. I'd heard enough, anyway.

Now this same blind stranger was coming to sleep in my house.

"Maybe I could take him bowling," I said to my wife. She

was at the draining board doing scalloped potatoes. She put down the knife she was using on the onion and turned around.

"If you love me," she said, "you can do this for me. If you don't love me, okay. But if you had a friend, any friend, and the friend came to visit, I'd make him feel comfortable." She wiped her hands with the dish towel.

"I don't have any blind friends," I said.

"You don't have *any* friends," she said. "Period. Besides," she said, "goddammit, his wife's just died! Don't you understand that? The man's lost his wife!"

I didn't answer. She'd told me a little about the blind man's wife. The wife's name was Beulah. Beulah! That's a name for a colored woman.

"Was his wife a Negro?" I asked.

"Are you crazy?" my wife said. "Have you just flipped or something?" She picked up the onion. I saw it hit the floor, then roll under the stove. "What's wrong with you?" she said. "Are you drunk?"

"I'm just asking," I said.

Right then my wife filled me in with more detail than I cared to know. I made a drink and sat at the kitchen table to listen. Pieces of the story began to fall into place.

Beulah had gone to work for the blind man the summer after my wife had stopped working for him. Pretty soon Beulah and the blind man had themselves a church wedding. It was a little wedding—Who'd be anxious to attend such a wedding in the first place?—just the two of them, and the minister and the minister's wife. But it was a church wedding just the same. What Beulah had wanted, he'd said. But even then Beulah must have been carrying cancer in her lymph glands. After they had been inseparable for eight years—my wife's word, "inseparable"—Beulah's health went into a rapid decline. She died in a Seattle hospital room, the blind man sitting beside the bed and holding on to her hand. They'd married, lived and worked together, slept together—had sex, sure—and then the blind man buried her. All this without his having ever seen what the goddamned woman looked like. It was beyond my understanding. Hearing this, I felt sorry for the blind man for a minute. And then I found myself thinking what a pitiful life this woman must have led. Imagine a woman who could never see herself reflected in the eyes of her loved one. A woman who could go on day after day and never receive the smallest compliment from her beloved. A woman whose husband would never read the expression on her face, be it misery or something better. Someone who could wear makeup or not—what difference to him? She could, if she wanted, wear green eye shadow around one eye, a straight pin in her nostril, yellow slacks and burgundy pumps, no matter. And then to slip off into death, the blind man's hand on her hand, his blind eyes streaming tears— I'm imagining now—her last thought maybe this: that her beloved never knew what she looked like, and she on an express to the grave. Robert was left with a small insurance policy and half of a twenty-peso Mexican coin. The other half of the coin went into the box with her. Pathetic.

S O WHEN THE TIME ROLLED AROUND, MY WIFE WENT to the rail station. With nothing to do but wait—and sure, I blamed him for that—I was having a drink and watching TV when I heard the car pull into the drive. I got up from the sofa with my drink and went to the window to have a look.

I saw my wife laughing as she parked the car. I saw her get out of the car and shut the door. She was still wearing a smile. Just amazing. She went around to the other side of the car to where the blind man was already starting to get out. This blind man, feature this, he was wearing a full beard! A beard on a blind man! Too much, I say. The blind man reached into the back seat and dragged out a suitcase.

My wife took his arm, shut the car door, and, talking all the way, moved him down the drive and then up the steps to the front porch. I turned off the TV. I finished my drink, rinsed the glass, dried my hands. Then I went to the door.

My wife said, "I want you to meet Robert. Robert, this is my husband. I've told you all about him." She closed the porch screen. She was beaming. She had this blind man by his coat sleeve.

The blind man let go of his suitcase and up came his hand.

I took it. He squeezed hard, held my hand, and then he let it go.

"I feel like we've already met," he boomed.

"Likewise," I said. I didn't know what else to say. Then I said, "Welcome. I've heard a lot about you." We began to move then, a little group, from the porch into the living room, my wife guiding him by the arm. He carried his suitcase in his other hand. My wife said things like, "To your left here, Robert. That's right. Now watch it, there's a chair. That's it. Sit down right here. This is the sofa. We just bought this sofa two weeks ago."

I started to say something about the old sofa. I'd liked that old sofa. But I didn't say anything. Then I wanted to say something else, small talk, about the scenic Hudson River. How going *to* New York, sit on the right-hand side of the train, and coming *from* New York, the left-hand side.

"Did you have a good train ride?" I said. "Which side of the train did you sit on, by the way?"

"What a question, which side!" my wife said. "What's it matter which side?" she said.

"I just asked," I said.

"Right side," the blind man said. "For the sun. Until this morning," the blind man said, "I hadn't been on a train in nearly forty years. Not since I was a kid. With my folks. That's been a long time. I'd nearly forgotten that sensation. I have winter in my beard now," he said. "So I've been told, anyway. Do I look distinguished, my dear?" he said to my wife.

"You look distinguished, Robert," she said. "Robert," she said. "Robert, it's just so good to see you." My wife finally took her eyes off the blind man and looked at me.

I had the distinct feeling she didn't like what she saw. I shrugged.

I'd never met or personally known anyone who was blind. This blind man was late forties, a heavyset, balding man with stooped shoulders, as if he carried a great weight there. He wore brown slacks, brown cordovan shoes, a light-brown shirt, a tie, a sports coat. Spiffy. He also had this full beard. But he didn't carry a cane and he didn't wear dark glasses. I'd always thought dark glasses were a must for the blind. Fact was, I wished he had a pair. At first glance, his eyes looked like anyone else's eyes. But if you looked close there was something different about them. Too much white in the iris, for one thing, and the pupils seemed to move around in the sockets without his knowing it or being able to control it. Creepy. As I stared at his face, I saw the left pupil turn in toward his nose, while the other made a futile effort to keep in one place. But it was only an effort, for that eye was on the roam without his knowing it or wanting it to be.

I said, "Let me get you a drink. What's your pleasure? We have a little of everything. It's one of our pastimes."

"Bub, I'm a scotch man myself," he said fast enough, in this big voice.

"Right," I said. Bub! "Sure you are. I knew it."

He let his fingers touch his suitcase, which was sitting alongside the sofa. He was taking his bearings. I didn't blame him for that.

"I'll move that up to your room," my wife said.

"No, that's fine," he said loudly. "It can go up when I go up."

"A little water with the scotch?" I said.

"Very little," he said.

"I knew it," I said.

He said, "Just a tad. The Irish actor, Barry Fitzgerald? I'm like that fellow. When I drink water, Fitzgerald said, I drink water. When I drink whiskey, I drink whiskey." My wife laughed. The blind man brought his hand up under his beard. He lifted his beard slowly and let it drop.

I DID THE DRINKS, THREE BIG GLASSES OF SCOTCH WITH a splash of water in each. Then we made ourselves comfortable and talked about Robert's travels. First the long flight from the West Coast to Connecticut, we covered that. Then from Connecticut up here by train. We had another drink concerning that leg of the trip.

I remembered having read somewhere that the blind didn't smoke because, speculation had it, they couldn't see the smoke they exhaled. I thought I knew that much and that much only about blind people. But this blind man smoked his cigarette down to the nubbin and then lit another one. This blind man filled his ashtray and my wife emptied it.

When we sat down to the table for dinner we had another drink. My wife heaped Robert's plate with cube steak, scalloped potatoes, green beans. I buttered him up two slices of bread. I said, "Here's bread and butter for you." I swallowed some of my drink. "Now let us pray," I said, and the blind man lowered his head. My wife looked at me, her mouth agape. "Pray the phone won't ring and the food doesn't get cold," I said.

We dug in. We ate everything there was to eat on the table. We ate like there was no tomorrow. We didn't talk. We ate. We scarfed. We grazed that table. We were into serious eating. The blind man had right away located his foods, he knew just where everything was on his plate. I watched with admiration as he used his knife and fork on the meat. He'd cut two pieces of meat, fork the meat into his mouth, and then go all out for the scalloped potatoes, the beans next, and then he'd tear off a hunk of buttered bread and eat that. He'd follow this up with a big drink of milk. It didn't seem to bother him to use his fingers once in a while, either. He used his bread to scoop beans.

We finished everything, including half of a strawberry pie. For a few moments we sat as if stunned. Sweat beaded on our faces. Finally, we got up from the table and left the dirty plates. We didn't look back. We took ourselves into the living room and sank into our places again. Robert and my wife sat on the sofa. I took the big chair. We had us two or three more drinks while they talked about the major things that had transpired for them in the past ten years. For the most part, I just listened. Now and then I joined in. I didn't want him to think I'd left the room, and I didn't want her to think I was feeling left out. They talked of things that had happened to them—to them!—these past ten years. I waited in vain to hear my name on my wife's sweet lips: "And then my dear husband came into my life"— something like that. But I heard nothing of the sort. More talk of Robert. Robert had done a little of everything, it seemed, a regular blind jack-of-all-trades. But most recently he and his wife had had an Amway distributorship, from which, I gathered, they'd earned their living, such as it was. The blind man was also a ham radio operator. He talked in his loud voice about conversations he'd had with fellow operators in Guam, the Philippines, Alaska, even Tahiti. He said he'd have a lot of friends there if he ever wanted to go visit those places. From time to time he'd turn his blind face toward me, put his hand under his beard, ask me something. How long had I been at my present position? (Three years.) Did I like my work? (I didn't.) Was I going to stay with it? (What were the options?)

Finally, when I thought he was beginning to run down, I got up and turned on the TV.

My wife looked at me with irritation. She was heading toward a boil. Then she looked at the blind man and said, "Robert, do you have a TV?"

The blind man said, "My dear, I have two TVs. I have a color set and a black-and-white thing, an old relic. It's funny, but if I turn the TV on, and I'm always turning it on, I turn the color set on. Always. It's funny."

I didn't know what to say to that. I had absolutely nothing to say about that. No opinion. So I watched the news program and tried to listen to what the announcer was saying.

"This is a color TV," the blind man said. "Don't ask me how, but I can tell."

"We traded up a while ago," I said.

The blind man had another taste of his drink. He lifted his beard, sniffed it, and let it fall. He leaned forward on the sofa. He positioned his ashtray on the coffee table, then put the lighter to his cigarette. He leaned back on the sofa and crossed his legs at the ankles.

My wife covered her mouth, and then she yawned. She stretched. She said, "I think I'll go upstairs and put on my robe. I think I'll change into something else. Robert, you make yourself comfortable," she said.

"I'm comfortable," the blind man said.

"I want you to feel comfortable in this house," she said.

"I am comfortable," the blind man said.

After she'd left the room, he and I listened to the weather report and then to the sports roundup. My wife had been gone so long I didn't know if she was going to come back. I thought she might have gone to bed. I wished she'd come back downstairs. I didn't want to be left alone with a blind man. I asked him if he wanted another drink, and he said sure. Then I asked if he wanted to smoke dope with me. I said I'd just rolled a number. I hadn't, but I planned to do so in about two shakes.

"I'll try some with you," he said.

"Damn right," I said. "That's the stuff."

I got our drinks and sat down on the sofa with him. Then I rolled us two fat numbers. I lit one and passed it. I brought it to his fingers. He took it and inhaled.

"Hold it as long as you can," I said. I could tell he didn't know the first thing.

My wife came back downstairs wearing her robe and pink slippers. "What do I smell?" she said.

"We thought we'd have us some cannabis," I said.

My wife gave me a purely savage look. Then she looked at him and said, "Robert, I didn't know you smoked."

He said, "I do now, my dear. First time for everything," he said. "But I don't feel anything yet."

"This stuff is pretty mellow," I said. "This stuff is mild. It's dope you can reason with. It doesn't mess you up."

"Not much it doesn't, bub," he said, and laughed.

My wife sat on the sofa between the blind man and me. I passed her the number. She took it and inhaled and then passed it back to me. "Which way is this going?" she said. Then she said, "I shouldn't be smoking this. I can hardly keep my eyes open as it is. That dinner did me in. I shouldn't have eaten so much."

"It was the strawberry pie," the blind man said. "That's what did it," he said, and he laughed his big laugh. Then he shook his head.

"There's more strawberry pie," I said.

"Do you want some more, Robert?" my wife asked.

"Maybe in a little while," he said.

We gave our attention to the TV. My wife yawned again. She said, "Your bed is made up when you feel like going to bed, Robert. I know you must have had a long day. When you're ready to go to bed, say so." She pulled his arm. "Robert?"

He came to and said, "I've had a real nice time. This beats tapes, doesn't it?"

I said, "Coming at you," and I put the number between

his fingers. He inhaled, held the smoke, and then let it go. It was like he'd been doing it since he was nine years old.

"Thanks, bub," he said. "But I think this is all for me. I think I'm beginning to feel it," he said. He held the burning roach out for my wife.

"Same here," she said. "Ditto. Me too." She took the roach and passed it to me. "I may just sit here for a while between you two guys with my eyes closed. But don't let me bother you, okay? Either one of you. If it bothers you, say so. Otherwise, I may just sit here with my eyes closed until you're ready to go to bed," she said. "Your bed's made up, Robert, when you're ready. It's right next to our room at the top of the stairs. We'll show you up when you're ready. You wake me up now, you guys, if I fall asleep." She said that and then she closed her eyes and went to sleep.

The news program ended. I got up and turned the channel. I sat back down on the sofa. I wished my wife hadn't pooped out. Her head lay across the back of the sofa, her mouth open. She'd turned so that her robe had slipped away from her legs, exposing a juicy thigh. I reached to draw her robe over the thigh, and it was then I glanced at the blind man. What the hell! I flipped the robe open again.

"You say when you want some strawberry pie," I said.

"I will," he said.

I said, "Are you tired? Do you want me to take you up to your bed? Are you ready to hit the hay?"

"Not yet," he said. "No, I'll stay up with you, bub. If that's all right. I'll stay up until you're ready to turn in. We haven't had a chance to talk. Know what I mean? I feel like me and her monopolized the evening." He lifted his beard and he let it fall. He picked up his cigarettes and his lighter.

"That's all right." I said. Then I said, "I'm glad for the company." And I guess I was. Every night I smoked dope and stayed up as long as I could before I fell asleep. My wife and I hardly ever went to bed at the same time. When I did go to sleep, I had these dreams. Sometimes I'd wake up from one of them, the heart going crazy.

S OMETHING ABOUT THE CHURCH AND THE MIDDLE ages, narrated by an Englishman, was on the TV. Not your run-of-the-mill TV fare. I wanted to watch something else. I turned to the other channels. But there was nothing on them, either. So I turned back to the first channel and apologized.

"Bub, it's all right," he said. "It's fine with me. Whatever you want to watch is okay. I'm always learning something. Learning never ends. It won't hurt me to learn something tonight. I got ears," he said.

We didn't say anything for a time. He was leaning forward with his head turned at me, while his right ear was aimed in the direction of the set. Very disconcerting. Now and then his eyelids drooped and then they snapped open again. Now and then he put his fingers into his beard and tugged, as if thinking about something he was hearing on the television.

On the screen a group of men wearing cowls was being set upon and tormented by men dressed in skeleton costumes and men dressed as devils. The men dressed as devils wore devil masks, horns, and long tails. This pageant was part of a procession. The Englishman said it all took place in Málaga, Spain, once a year. I tried to explain to the blind man what was happening.

"Skeletons," he said. "I know about skeletons," he said, and he nodded.

The TV showed Chartres Cathedral. Then there was a long slow look at Sainte Chapelle. Finally the picture switched to Notre Dame, with its flying buttresses, its spires

reaching toward clouds. The camera pulled away to show
the whole of the cathedral rising above the skyline.

There were times when the Englishman who was telling
the thing would shut up, would simply let the camera move
around over the cathedrals. Or else the camera would tour
the countryside, men in fields walking behind oxen. I waited
as long as I could. Then I felt I had to say something. I said,
"They're showing the outside of this cathedral now. Gar-
goyles. Little statues carved to look like monsters. Now I
guess they're in Italy. Yeah, they're in Italy. There's fresco
paintings on the walls of this one church."

"What's fresco painting, bub?" he asked, and he sipped
from his drink.

I reached for my glass. But it was empty. I tried to remember what I could remember about frescoes. "You're
asking me what are frescoes?" I said. "That's a good question. I don't know."

The camera moved to a cathedral outside Lisbon, Portugal. The differences in the Portuguese cathedral compared
with the French and Italian were not that great. But they
were there. Mostly the interior stuff. Then something occurred to me and I said, "Something has occurred to me.
Do you have an idea what a cathedral is? What they look
like, that is? Do you follow me? If somebody says *cathedral*
to you, do you have any notion what they're talking about?
Do you know the difference between that and a Baptist
church, say? Or that and a mosque, or synagogue?"

He let the smoke issue from his mouth. "I know they
took hundreds of workers fifty or a hundred years to build,"
he said. "I just heard the man say that, of course. I know
generations of the same families worked on a cathedral. I
heard him say that, too. The men who began their life's
work on them, they never lived to see the completion of
their work. In that wise, bub, they're no different from the
rest of us, right?" He laughed. Then his eyelids drooped

again. His head nodded. He seemed to be snoozing. Maybe he was imagining himself in Portugal. The TV was showing another cathedral now. This one was in Germany. The Englishman's voice droned on. "Cathedrals," the blind man said. He sat up and rolled his head back and forth. "If you want the truth, bub, that's about all I know. What I just said. What I heard him say. But maybe you could describe one to me? I wish you'd do it. I'd like that. If you want to know, I really don't have a good idea."

I stared hard at the shot of the cathedral on the TV. It held a minute. Then it was gone, and the view was of the inside with rows of benches and high windows. How could I even begin to describe it? But say my life depended on it. Say my life was being threatened by an insane Turkish bey.

They took the camera outside again. I stared some more at the cathedral before the picture flipped off into the countryside. There was no use. I turned to the blind man and said, "To begin with, they're very tall. Very, very tall." I was looking around the room for clues. I tried again. "They reach way up. Up and up. Toward the sky. They soar. They're like poetry, that's what they're like. They're so big, some of them, they have to have these supports. To help hold them up, so to speak. These supports are called buttresses. They remind me of viaducts for some reason. But maybe you don't know viaducts, either? Sometimes the cathedrals have devils and such carved into the front. Sometimes great lords and ladies. Don't ask me why this is," I said. He was nodding. The whole upper part of his body seemed to be moving back and forth. "I'm not doing so good, am I?" I said.

He stopped nodding and leaned forward on the edge of the sofa. As he listened to me, he was running his fingers through his beard. I wasn't getting through to him though, I could see that. But he waited for me to go on just the same. He nodded, as if trying to encourage me. I tried to think what else I could say. "They're really big. They're massive. They're built of stone. Marble, too, sometimes. In those old days, when they built cathedrals, men aspired to be close to God. In those days God was an important part of everyone's life. This was reflected in their cathedral-building. I'm sorry," I said, "but it looks like that's the best I can do for you. I'm just no good at it."

"That's all right, bub," he said. "Hey, listen. I hope you don't mind my asking you. Can I ask you something? Let me ask you a simple question, yes or no. I'm just curious and there's no offense. You're my host. But let me ask if you are in any way religious? You don't mind my asking?"

I shook my head. He couldn't see that, though. A wink is the same as a nod to a blind man. "I guess I'm agnostic or something. No, the fact is, I don't believe in it. Anything. Sometimes it's hard. You know what I'm saying?"

"Sure, I do," he said.

"Right," I said.

The Englishman was still holding forth. My wife sighed in her sleep. She drew a long breath and continued with her sleep.

"You'll have to forgive me," I said. "But I can't tell you what a cathedral looks like. It just isn't in me to do it. I can't do any more than I've done." The blind man sat very still, his head down, as he listened to me. "The truth is, cathedrals don't mean anything special to me. Nothing. Cathedrals. They're something to look at on late-night TV. That's all they are."

It was then he cleared his throat. He brought something up. He took a handkerchief from his back pocket. In a minute he said, "I get it, bub. It's okay. It happens. Don't worry about it," he said. "Hey, listen to me. Will you do me a favor? I got an idea. Why don't you find us some heavy paper? And a pen. We'll do something. An experiment.

Sure, you can do it. You can. We'll draw one together. Get us a pen and some heavy paper. Go on, bub, get the stuff," he said.

S O I WENT UPSTAIRS. MY LEGS FELT LIKE THEY didn't have any strength in them. They felt like they did sometimes after I'd run a couple of miles. In my wife's room I looked around. I found some ballpoints in a little basket on her table. And then I tried to think where to look for the kind of paper he was talking about.

Downstairs, in the kitchen, I found a shopping bag with onion skins in the bottom of the bag. I emptied the bag and shook it. I brought it into the living room and sat down with it near his legs. I moved some things, smoothed the wrinkles from the bag, spread it out on the coffee table. The blind man got down from the sofa and sat next to me on the carpet.

He ran his fingers over the paper. He went up and down the sides of the paper and the edges, top and bottom. He fingered the corners. "All right," he said. "All right. Let's do her."

He found my hand, the hand with the pen. He closed his hand over my hand. "Go ahead, bub, draw," he said. "Draw. You'll see. I'll follow along with you. It'll be all right. Just begin now, like I'm telling you. You'll see. Draw," he said.

So I began. First I drew a box that resembled a house. It could have been the house I lived in. Then I put a roof on the house. At either end of the roof I drew spires. Crazy.

"Swell," he said. "Terrific. You're doing fine," he said. "Never thought anything like this could happen in your lifetime, did you? Well, it's a strange life, bub, we all know that. Go on now. Keep it up."

I put in windows with arches. I drew flying buttresses. I hung great doors. I couldn't stop. The TV station went off the air. I put down the pen and closed and opened my fingers. The blind man felt around over the paper. He moved the tips of his fingers slowly over the paper, over what I'd drawn, and he nodded. "Doing fine," he said.

I took up the pen, and he found my hand once more. I kept at it. I'm no artist. But I kept drawing just the same.

My wife opened her eyes and gazed at us. She sat up on the sofa, her robe hanging open. She said, "What are you doing? What in the world are you doing?"

I didn't answer her. The blind man said, "We're drawing a cathedral, dear. Me and him are working on something important. Press hard now," he said to me. "That's right. That's good," he said. "Sure. You got it, bub. I can tell. You didn't think you could. But you can, can't you? You're cooking with Crisco now. You'll see. Know what I'm saying? We're going to have us something here in a minute. How's the old arm?" he said. "Put some people in there now. What's a church without people, bub?"

"What's going on?" my wife said. "Robert, what are you doing? What's going on?"

"It's all right," he said to her. "Close your eyes now, bub," he said.

I did that. I closed them just like he said.

"Are they closed?" he said. "Don't fudge."

"They're closed," I said.

"Keep them that way," he said. He said, "Don't stop now." So we kept on with it. His fingers rode my fingers as my hand went over the rough paper. It was like nothing else in my life up to now.

In a minute he said, "I think that's enough. I think you got the idea," he said. "Take a look. What do you think?"

But I had my eyes closed. I thought I'd keep them closed a little longer. I thought it was something I ought not to forget.

"Well?" he said. "Are you looking?"

My eyes were still closed. I was in my house and I knew that. But I didn't feel inside anything.

"It's really something," I said.

(The Atlantic Monthly)

Terrence Des Pres
Into the Mire: The Case of Bertolt Brecht

I F WE HOLD WITH THE SORT OF INNOCENCE STILL
lingering in American literary criticism, then what
Hannah Arendt called "the case of Bertolt Brecht" would
seem to be closed. Nobody denies his genius. There is general
agreement that he is one of our century's best poets
and that his plays are the most significant contribution to
serious drama since Ibsen. That ought to be the end of it,
but just here the difficulties start. As Eric Bentley wrote
to James Laughlin after Brecht had caused endless trouble
over small details of publication: "Both you and I have a
right to be out of patience with Brecht. But he is still important
as an artist." Bentley's sentiments were voiced
countless times during Brecht's life, often in terms much
stronger, and this double attitude toward him—that he
was a genius of doubtful humanity—has echoed in his wake
ever since. I think Brecht's "case" comes out in his favor,
but the crossover between life and art, or the way extraliterary
matters play a part in literary judgment, has become
a permanent element in our response to Brecht's
work. Situations wherein the artist's life reflects importantly
upon his art are on the increase, and Brecht would
hardly have become the center of such stiff-necked debate
were it not for the fact that what we make of him extends
what we make of the art/life problem generally.

In the latest collection of *Paris Review* interviews, Francine
du Plessix Gray warns that one of the most "alarming"
developments since the Second World War has been "our
ravenous appetite for the Artist's Personality." True enough;
the fastest way to literary fame nowadays is not to write a

book of fine poems but to interview a batch of poets. Given the work, we want the life as well. Insofar as what we are after is dirty linen, then "alarming" is not too strong a word for the tendency Gray describes. But she is wrong in at least one respect; our need to measure life and art in terms of each other corresponds to an important shift in literary awareness, and it is not a recent development. What is new—and here Gray's reference to the Second World War affords insight—is the degree to which politics gives special import to the relation between the artist and his work. Prior to the sort of political intrusion which now infects everything, we had worked out a remarkably flexible method for handling art/life problems, a method now in doubt because of poets like Brecht.

Both Byron and Rimbaud, for example, share affinities with Brecht and might even be thought to prefigure him. Both, as a contemporary said of Byron, were mad, bad, and dangerous to know. They were antisocial, sexually wild, destructive to themselves, and hurtful to their friends. In other words, splendid examples of the *poète maudit*. They were, as I said, more than a little like Brecht, yet we do not hold their personal behavior very much against them. And when we pass judgment on artists of their kind we look to the importance of their art and allow it to redeem, or at least mitigate, the way they lived. To create great poetry takes great talent which, in turn, deserves special privilege. Or so we have supposed, subscribing to the cult of Art and Genius that has been the core of our Romantic inheritance. For at least two centuries, revolt and self-indulgence have seemed natural to artistic integrity, and if on occasion this sort of license causes local wreckage, we have assumed that the human cost is small compared to the largeness of spirit set free.

But artists themselves have so often abused this benefit—think, for example, of Mailer or Capote today—that we might expect only fools to keep faith. On the contrary, the cult of genius has survived not only internal betrayal; it holds its own against a countermovement which might have but did not demolish the myth of the artist's superior humanity. Ironically—since he so honored genius and loved art—Freud did much to put both in question. Quite apart from the connection between art and neurosis, Freud simply let loose the suspicion that a flawed soul can do fine work and still be flawed; or finally that creativity is as much a muddle as a mystery. Taken all the way, Freud's emphasis on the dark drives of the unconscious turns the venerable myth of the "daemon" into the disquieting idea that some force truly demonic directs the artist at his task.

Few of us are hard-line Freudians, but the "suspicion" of which I speak is now so widespread that no biographer, even with the best of intentions, would attempt a poet's portrait without first digging for unpleasant facts, some evidence of that necessary wound which allows art's mighty bow to bend full-strength. The aim of this process is to push past decorum in order to capture, as Coleridge said of the poet, "the whole man active." As it turns out, some of these poets are rather deplorable people. Robert Frost, for example, was pretty much the "old-stone savage armed" he described as his double in one of his poems; and Lawrance Thompson's big biography of Frost stands as a sort of landmark in the arena of serious debunking. More recently, Harold Bloom has carried the whole business to extremes by telling us that great poets are, well, monsters. At some fearsome psychic depth, poetic patricide is what makes the burning fountain burn.

We might thus suppose that our Romantic notions of the artist's high estate have undergone steep discount. But no, the wounded archangel is an archangel still. We know that art is essential, and if the golden egg comes flecked in dross the goose is still no ordinary bird. In general, then, we say for example that Dickens was an awful fellow, that the domestic damage he caused was unfortunate, but that thereby he did write those fabulous books. We are even beginning to believe that the monomania of a Tolstoy or a Wagner or a Picasso was necessary; work on such grand scale required egos that mistook themselves for God. And Byron, Rimbaud? Their story endings anticipate Brecht's but the society of their times *was* degenerate, and not to rebel would have been capitulation. So now we have it both ways. If art justifies the way artists live, their reckless lives add credence to their art.

As a method for handling cases in which the artist's life puts his art into question, this has been a clever if slippery solution. It has been applied to Brecht, but never to general satisfaction. And it can also backfire. Martin Esslin, for example, has been one of Brecht's toughest defenders; his 1959 study is still probably the best short introduction to the man and his work. In *Mediations,* Esslin's 1980 collection of essays, he again comes to Brecht's defense. He praises the recent translation of Brecht's poetry, *Poems 1913–1956,* which is indeed excellent. Esslin's main business, however, is to save Brecht from academic cultists, who want to canonize Brecht's every word, and more importantly, to take Brecht out of the hands of his Soviet apologists, who attempt to deify him and use his fame for political advantage. In particular Esslin attacks the image of Brecht as the genial genius of East Berlin, the Marxist sage untroubled and at home in the world Stalin built. Esslin's strategy is direct; he quotes pointedly from Brecht's later prose (mostly unavailable in English) and demonstrates that Brecht was consistently critical of the Soviet system. To rid Brecht of any Stalinist taint is Esslin's aim, but by establishing moral distance between Brecht and Soviet reality, Esslin inadvertently throws the current method of handling art/life problems into reverse. For if Brecht knew the system was perverse, doesn't work inspired by Marxist ideals become suspect? Or, if his art is acceptable beyond dispute, can it redeem a man who remained silent during

times truly terrible when, in fact, his artistic privilege
gave him the chance to speak out?

Esslin is on Brecht's side and we understand his point
despite the questions he raises. But the problem persists
and has reached a high point in James K. Lyon's *Bertolt
Brecht in America,* published in 1980, a book which in
itself, and in the ciritical response it has provoked, has
magnified Brecht's "case" wholesale. Lyon too favors Brecht,
but his account of Brecht's American exile contains so much
unfavorable material that late in the narrative Lyon breaks
in with a special plea for Brecht's essential decency. And
Lyon too relies on the current method of justifying the life
and the art in terms of each other. He repeatedly excuses
Brecht's offensive social behavior and his heedless treat-
ment of colleagues by pointing to the way—admittedly
amazing—those whom Brecht wronged so often tended to
put up with him and give him the benefit of the doubt. The
assumption is that only genius could merit pardon so
sweeping. For example, Brecht confounded his faithful
supporters again and again, Eric Bentley and H. R. Hays
especially. Bentley admits to being badly used, but he never
wavered in his assistance and readily calls Brecht "the
most fascinating man I have ever met." Lyon says of H. R.
Hays that "like so many collaborators who admired or were
fascinated with Brecht, he continued to promote the writer's works and reputation until the end of Brecht's American exile." And when, as Lyon records, Brecht offended
Joseph Losey so keenly that Losey quit his job as director
of *Galileo,* Charles Laughton got on the phone to Losey
and said, "Please come back." "I will," Losey replied, "if
Brecht apologizes to me." Shortly thereafter, Laughton
phoned again with this message: "Brecht says please come
back, and he also says you should know Brecht never apologizes." Losey went back.

Responses of this kind suggest deep regard for Brecht's
genius, and Lyon goes so far in praise of this uncommonly

demanding spirit—hypercritical, adversative, uncompromising—as to assert that Brecht had to behave as he did: "Brecht believed that goodness or friendliness, not evil or anger, was man's normal state, and that indignation over injustice tended to wear off in time. Therefore he resolved to remain critical by exerting himself to keep his anger alive, i.e., to be the 'evil' one by playing the role of the adversary." No doubt there is justice in Lyon's reasoning, and ordinarily these would be acceptable arguments. Why, then, does our standard method of disposing of the art/life problem falter in Brecht's case?

The answer takes us into territory still largely unexplored—the unacknowledged but increasingly urgent relation between art and politics. In poetry of Brecht's kind, literary issues are questions of conscience and decency as well. Any aesthetic enterprise which claims to be more than art for art's sake must ground its claim outside itself. It must acknowledge, as most lyrical poetry for example does not, its relation to social reality. Both tragedy and satire are instances of art ministering to the social health of the community. Didactic art, on the other hand, points either to the authority of the past or the promise of the future in order to justify its appeal. It either expresses the ethic of established institutions or, as in Brecht's case, it clarifies the moral vision inherent in an ideology which, not yet actualized, has no concrete backing beyond the poet's embodiment in his own life of what, through his art, he would have others be and do. Which is to say that when art becomes overtly political, we have some right to suppose that how the artist conducts his public life will certify or jeopardize his work's authority; and we may also suppose that excellence, while it excuses much, cannot condone its own betrayal.

When in 1979 the English translation of Brecht's *Diaries 1920–1922* appeared, response was predictable. Here was a portrait of the artist as a young man, done in the artist's own hand; and what we see is mainly an artist brazenly self-centered, a man in his early twenties whose chief gift to others was havoc. Among initial reviews, I recall none which took these diaries as an occasion for further questioning, namely, how could an ego so seemingly insolent go on to produce a body of art whose definitive mark is its moral intelligence, or have come in the later journals and especially in the later poetry to speak in a voice undeniably compassionate and wise. Here again James Lyon's account of Brecht's years in the United States offers unexpected insight. Lyon hit upon the opportunity for using Brecht's own theory that art reveals most when it presents familiar action in an unfamiliar context. Lyon gives us the portrait of an artist out of his element. And what happens in Brecht's plays happens in Lyon's book: two versions of reality are made to appear, to contend and provoke us to thought.

Exile wasn't the problem. Brecht rather liked the idea of being forced out by Hitler. What got him down was being on the dole, being a famous playwright suddenly unknown and unvalued, being at the peak of his creative powers without the means to exercise them, and being, finally, trapped in Hollywood, then the crassest corner of America. These were circumstances that Brecht never mastered; his predicament brought out the worst as well as the best in him, and his American experience may thus be used as solid *ad hominem* evidence against him. This is unfortunate and misleading, because those who thrive on gossip or whose idea of biography never gets past personal anecdote will miss the one time in Brecht's life when he was caught off his guard and allowed his soul to show.

From the time of his arrival in California in July 1941, until October 31, 1947, his last day in New York, Brecht's personal style created a flood of negative response. He was, according to one of his associates, "enormously energetic, enormously stubborn, enormously sarcastic, enormously difficult." His arrogance was as unbearable as the smell of his unbathed body. His lack of social grace was as glaring as his two-day's growth of beard, his omnipresent cheap cigar, or the fact, as one of his friends put it, that Brecht "ate very little, drank very little, and fornicated a great deal." In this latter respect, most of us know dozens of poets and writers who can match Brecht's performance—except, of course, for the drinking. This level of detail, nevertheless, is the matter that reviewers of Lyon's book have fastened upon, starting with Auden's remark that of the few people who might deserve the death sentence, Brecht was one and that he, Auden, could imagine doing it himself. The other *de rigueur* item in this Brechtian file comes from the occasion on which, in 1935, he came briefly to New York to oversee direction of *The Mother* and found that the American style of acting was as appalling to him as the reinterpretations that were mangling his original text. At rehearsal he finally exploded with the words that now stand as the slogan of Brecht's behavior in America: *Das ist Scheisse! Das ist Dreck!* That critics have simply presumed that stuff of this sort takes us into Brecht's final character suggests not only our attachment to trivia, but the more serious error of mixing personal tics with conduct meriting real criticism—thereby making of Brecht not a complex case to be understood, but a mess to be endured or dismissed as we wish.

In the wake of such confusion we need to recall the serious case against Brecht, which was put forth most forcefully by Hannah Arendt in 1966 and is now included in her *Men in Dark Times*. Her argument—the only one that counts—comes down to this: while poets may go further than ordinary mortals ("more is permitted"), they may yet go so far ("sin so gravely") that they damage their authority and their art to a terminal degree. To her credit, Arendt views the vagaries of Brecht's private life as beneath the dignity of his "case" or of her own evaluation. She observes instead that the root of his art is compassion and that in his life he was utterly devoid of self-pity. Her main concern is therefore with acts and decisions which, for the poet with a political identity, may be said to constitute his "sins." And here Arendt approaches solid ground. Whereas Brecht was heroic in his stand against Hitler, and whereas his commitment to Marxist ideals was admirable and genuine, his failure to speak out against Stalin was an abomination pure and simple. And in Arendt's view, Brecht's failure came to its culmination when he returned from exile to spend his last years in East Berlin as director of the Berliner Ensemble.

Always the moralist, Arendt was also exceptionally sensitive to literature, and it is on literary grounds that she would make her final indictment. She argues that after Brecht's return to the Soviet sector of Germany this great poet ceased to write great poetry or anything else worth respecting. When he betrayed his muse, his muse abandoned him. And unlike Ezra Pound—that other "case"— Brecht was not a madman but a shrewd, extremely intelligent man who always knew what he was doing. That, really, is his crime in Arendt's judgment: he knew. Here is the sum of the serious case against Brecht:

... it is precisely [his] extraordinary intelligence, breaking like lightning through the rumble of Marxist platitudes, that has made it so difficult for good men to forgive Brecht his sins, or to reconcile themselves to the fact that he could sin *and* write good poetry. But, finally, when he went back to East Germany, essentially for artistic reasons, because its government would give him a theater—that is, for that "art for art's sake" he had vehemently denounced for nearly thirty years—his punishment caught up with him. Now reality overwhelmed him to the point where he could no longer be its voice; he had succeeded in being in the thick of it—and had proved that this is no good place for a poet to be.

The mark of a good argument is that it opens up, rather than closes down, the range of issues involved; and since Martin Heidegger was one of Arendt's heroes, we might go on to ask if for philosophers, too, "being in the thick of things" is no good place to be. Arendt, in other words, has touched upon one of the paramount problems defining the life of art and thought in our century. The predicament is not new—when he had his chance to be a second Socrates, Aristotle went Brecht's way. But in our time the pace of events, the magnitude of catastrophes, the increasing pressure of political forces make escape, or even a bit of entirely private breathing space, less and less possible.

In the nineteenth century, simply fulfilling the role of the *poète maudit* was sufficient; and once their revolt had been guaranteed through their art, poets could—like their apolitical counterparts today—debauch, so to speak, with dignity. Today that's not enough. If an artist takes up an adversary stance his position is a sham unless accompanied by some index of conviction which also touches upon the way life is lived. This is true not only because social criticism spills over into conflict openly political, but more deeply because the integrity of art is nothing if not rooted in our common struggle for spiritual autonomy in a world where governments of every stamp are determined to smash human rights, silence dissent, and by using language for propaganda and "big" lies, pervert that potency of words on which poetry and moral discernment depend. Arendt's sense of how difficult the role of the poet has become does much to explain her hardness toward Brecht.

But to what extent was she right? Brecht surely got himself into the thick of terrible things, but a similar position has been endured by other of our great modern poets, Mandelstam, Akhmatova, and Milosz among them. It does not follow that political turmoil ruins art. Brecht's brilliant early poetry was written in opposition to the Nazi rise, and after Hitler came to power and Brecht went into exile he produced some of his finest poems and plays. For the vehemence of his poetry against war (his "Legend of the Dead Soldier" in particular) he earned the hatred of Hitler's brown-shirts long before 1933, and in that fatal year he wrote his "Hitler Chorales," a group of satires to be sung to the melodies of famous Lutheran hymns, the first of which begins, "Now thank we all our God / For sending Hitler to us," and which ends:

> He'll paint the filth and rot
> Until it's spick and span
> So thank we all our God
> For sending us this man.

Brecht's irony, ferocious and jubilant, suggests the vigorous will with which he launched his attacks. He was, in all ways, a man on the offensive. What gives any body of poetry its character is the specific tension arising from the poet's private relation to the world. And in Brecht's case there is no doubt what this relation was. Keeping in mind that "the house-painter" was his term of derision for Hitler, here from a poem entitled "Bad Time For Poetry" is Brecht's position:

> Inside me contend
> Delight at the apple tree in blossom
> And horror at the house-painter's speeches.
> But only the second
> Drives me to my desk.

That was written in 1939; the previous year Brecht wrote the following stanza from "To Those Born Later," one of his most telling poems:

> All roads led into the mire in my time.
> My tongue betrayed me to the butchers.

There was little I could do. But those in power
Sat safer without me: that was my hope.
So passed my time
Which had been given to me on earth.

That is Brecht's view of his calling, and let us be sure we
have heard him aright. Armed with nothing but his art,
he declares a one-man war on the State. At first this seems
ridiculous, a sort of unilateral suicide pact. But when we
go on to consider the extent to which, in many countries,
writers are arrested, shot, or forced into exile, the relation
between the solitary artist and the State takes on the aspect of real war. And even though there is something hard
to credit—arrogant, delusional, even monomaniacal—about
such a lopsided stand, Brecht is not alone. Solzhenitsyn is
the most visible current example, but there are dozens like
him—poets who sense that one of the profoundest battles
of our time is between the individual and his own government, poets like Joseph Brodsky (Russian), Reza Baraheni
(Iranian), or Kim Chi Ha (Korean), all of whom have suffered political persecution for their art.

But if that is Brecht's true position, and yet he never
attacked Stalin with anything like the ferocity he leveled
at Hitler, isn't Arendt right? He arrived in East Berlin on
October 22, 1948, and he lived there seven and a half years
before he died in 1956 at the age of fifty-eight. That is a
short time for any artist—especially amid political unrest
on all sides—to begin a new life, to set up a theatre company and see to its success. When he first returned he was
refused entry to the American sector of Berlin, but he
would have gone to the Eastern zone anyway. He was a
Marxist and this would be Marxism on German soil, *his*
nation's chance to rebuild itself from the rubble according
to socialist principles. That is a cardinal point to keep in
mind when weighing Brecht's return. Germany was not
yet two nations and Brecht had enormous hope for a unified

Germany. With a national theatre in mind, and knowing the urgency of gathering the cream of German talent before it dispersed across Europe, Brecht urged Piscator to join him: "It is a good moment, one should not put it off much longer, everything is still in a state of flux and the direction things take will be determined by the forces at hand." Brecht desperately wanted to gather sufficient "forces at hand."

We now know for certain that Brecht was never bribed to live in East Berlin by the promise of his own theatre. His most recent German biographer, Klaus Völker, is emphatic on this point. There was no "official invitation." In *Brecht: A Biography,* Völker states "it would be truer to say that [Brecht] forced his way in." The theatre was Brecht's idea, and it met first with indifference and then with much difficulty before it opened officially, more than two years after Brecht's departure from America, and the Berliner Ensemble would not have its own building until March of 1954. The amount of time and energy that went into this struggle must have been very great; and even so, only six productions were staged before, in 1951, a new round of Soviet purges and the vicious atmosphere of the Cold War destroyed, once and for all, Brecht's hope for a national theatre which would contribute to the creation of a new Germany. It was at this point that Brecht observed: "Time will show if pessimism is to be rated negatively."

During these crucial last years, then, Brecht was intensely busy. He was politically active, speaking, going to rallies, traveling in a semiofficial capacity. He was creating his own theatre and keeping Soviet censorship at bay. He was building up a first-rate acting company. He was adapting plays to fit his own ideas of dramatic art. He had begun to write new plays. He was doing what he most loved and what he had missed most while in America—directing without interference, solely in accord with his own deepest principles. And he was also writing poetry. His last poems

are spare and swift and might appear slight on first reading, but many are excellent, the "Buckow Elegies" in particular. And what chiefly characterizes his poetry during
these last years is the increasing frequency and bitterness
of poems bearing anti-Soviet sentiment, such as "Still At
It," the theme of which—everything has changed and
nothing has changed—was strong in Brecht's work at this
time:

> The plates are slammed down so hard
> The soup slops over.
> In shrill tones
> Resounds the order: Now eat!
>
> The Prussian eagle
> Jabbing food down
> The gullets of its young.

Some of his late poems are sarcastic in the fiery early style,
as is the case, for instance, in "The Solution"; after the
East German regime had crushed the workers' uprising of
June 17, 1953, Brecht writes that perhaps the best course
of government would be to "dissolve the people / And elect
another." More of the late poems, however, are muted and
subtle, as if these were the last, half-uttered words of a
man talking only to himself, a man, say, whose entire life
had taught him that "As always the lovely and sensitive /
Are no longer," and who steps into the ragged shade of an
abandoned greenhouse to see "the remains of the rare
flowers."

If most of Arendt's indictment is not borne out by the
facts, that is not completely her fault; in time of upheaval,
facts are hard to come by. But on one point—and here the
mystery of Brecht deepens—Arendt was right. Brecht always knew. In Russia, personal friends had been shot or

had died in concentration camps. In his late prose (I quote from one of Esslin's essays) Brecht contemplates the Soviet situation and observes that the whole vast system "still works very badly and not very organically and needs so much effort and use of violence that the freedoms of individuals are very limited." There is, he goes on, "compulsion everywhere and no real rule of the people." As for the goals to be realized, the violence and coercion "prove that all the basic elements of the *great order* are far from realized as yet, are far from being developed at the moment."

The repetition of those last phrases beginning "are far" gives Brecht's view a strange, almost mesmerized quality, as if he were evoking despair and hope in exactly equal measure. Without illusion, expecting nothing, he simply won't let go, won't foreclose on a dream gone forfeit. And this, I would now suggest, is precisely the element of character most strikingly revealed by Brecht in exile. As Lyon points out, Brecht waited so long to make his escape from Hitler's advancing armies that he very nearly did not make it. He sailed, in fact, on the last ship that could get him to America. Pondering this, Lyon remarks: "Few optimists have had fewer illusions than Brecht and remained optimists. He refused to quit Europe until the situation was hopeless." But wasn't this Brecht's style in all things?

The first two years in America were spent in Hollywood, where "to sell" was the cardinal verb in the new language Brecht confronted. Were this anyone but Brecht, the spectacle of a genius doggedly trying to turn out inane "film stories" would be pathetic. But not in Brecht's case. He eventually wrote more than fifty of these "stories," but with the partial exception of *Hangmen Also Die*, nothing he worked on succeeded. What was wanted was a "Metro-Goldwyn-Mayer Gospel for the Little Man," as Brecht referred to the prevailing formula, with its mandatory love interest and its taboo against any hint of class antagonism. But like Bartleby the scrivener, Brecht preferred not to.

The more he saw what success meant, "the more steadfastly he resolved to write film stories for Hollywood on his own terms or not at all." That, of course, ensured his defeat, and for a man as lucid as Brecht, knowing what he was doing must have made him all the more irascible. But just here the Brechtian element comes plainly into view: he would have his art handled "on his own terms or not at all." Nothing could sway him in matters bearing directly upon his own work. And in this respect Brecht is perhaps the supreme example of what Lyon calls "obdurate genius."

Lyon's careful tracking offers much evidence that Brecht was "obsessed" with Broadway. Since his youth, America had exerted the deep pull of myth on Brecht's genius, and now he wanted American recognition for his work, which of course meant acceptance in New York. But here again the intractable Brechtian element asserted itself. When, for example, Le Gallienne, whom Lyon calls "the guiding spirit of the American Repertory Theater and one of the best-known American actresses of the day," asked to play the lead in *Mother Courage,* Brecht replied in English: "Over my dead body." He had seen her perform, and her Stanislavski style was anathema to Brecht. *The Caucasian Chalk Circle* got so far as a signed contract, but Brecht withdrew when he could not persuade Auden to rework the translation. And when his old friend Erwin Piscator, who was already established, told Brecht he wanted to do *The Good Woman of Setzuan,* Lyon observes that a "New York production might have taken place without delay." Except that Brecht wanted Piscator to do a different play, and then haggled over the situation until all foundered.

The production history of *Galileo,* which did not reach Broadway until Brecht was back in Europe, is a summa of Brechtian resistance. At various points he turned down Orson Welles and Mike Todd, both eager to produce the play, either of whom would have ensured a hit. Perhaps

Brecht's saddest run-in was with Harold Clurman, then a director who not only respected Brecht but whose political sense and willingness to work with experimental forms made him the perfect person to launch *Galileo* in New York. Clurman asked for the job and was turned down because Brecht saw him as a member of the Stanislavski camp. Clurman persisted, suggesting that Brecht misunderstood him. He assured Brecht that he would be happy to "learn" the proper Brechtian principles of drama, but again no. Brecht thus spurned a talented and sympathetic man whose connections would have helped guarantee a warm reception for *Galileo*.

Brecht's behavior, in the examples just cited, almost amounts to a third case against him. Are we to interpret such action as egomania, as madness, as perverse delight in complication? Brecht's "obdurate genius" certainly caused trouble on all sides, but it was also the source of his greatness, the distinguishing characteristic of this artist's power. As Lyon points out, "The word 'compromise' was not in the vocabulary of a dramatist determined to change the existing theatrical world." And again politics is the heart of the matter, for by changing the theatrical world Brecht intended to release a powerful cultural force which would work to change *the* world. That Brecht did aim to change the world follows from his commitment to Marxism. The key, however, is that for a poet whose genius was profoundly rooted in the demotic authority of spoken German—language of the street, market, bar, and gutter, culturally grounded in Luther's lingual usurpation of the Bible—when Brecht spoke of changing the world he meant (at least first) Germany.

Unlike many of his fellow exiles during the war, Brecht was dead set against "Americanization," and he was not bothered by his status as a German exile. This, in fact, was the proof of his German as opposed to Nazi spirit, just as today, for example, the Russian poet Joseph Brodsky takes his exile as proof that against the Soviet perversion he is the true repository of Russian soul. There is much evidence, especially in his poetry, to suggest that Brecht identified his genius with the fate of his country, and beyond doubt his calling as a poet was at the service of Germany's downtrodden masses. In a way not presently apparent in America, poets of other nations—Poland and Hungary are strong examples—have traditionally identified themselves and their art with their country. We did have Whitman, and more recently Williams; but thinking of Eliot and Pound, or the suspect glamour of our expatriates, we might more readily see our poets and writers in pursuit, as a famous critic put it, of "a world elsewhere."

Brecht's fierce care for the destiny of his nation might therefore seem of little consequence, but, on the contrary, it was of absolute importance, and it accounts for much that has been questionable in his public conduct. The American acting style, for example, was dreck because it wasn't Brechtian, i.e., German, in Brecht's interpretation. And the most significant outcome of his relation to German identity was that Hitler loomed infinitely larger, more real and menacing, than Stalin. Toward Hitler there was hatred violently personal; toward Stalin, on the other hand, Brecht was perplexed, critical, horrified, but also detached. If Brecht identified as strongly with the German people as I think he did, then of course Hitler was more threatening than Stalin, despite Brecht's knowledge of the Soviet catastrophe.

One of the most instructive chapters in *Bertolt Brecht in America* describes the ugly conflict between Brecht and Thomas Mann. Mann called Brecht "very gifted, unfortunately." Brecht referred to Mann as "that short story writer." Hostility was mutual, and at least on Brecht's side it amounted to outright hate. Some of this arose from the usual antipathy of genius for its double. But Brecht could not abide the bourgeois basis of Mann's art, and he had been critical of Mann long before they arrived in America. When the two giants finally came face to face in California, an explosion was inevitable, and the form it took was, again, very revealing. The issue this time was whom to blame for the war, and the degree to which Germany in general should be punished.

Mann held that the Nazi movement was homegrown, the outcome of something demonic in the German soul. He went so far (if we can believe Brecht's journal) as to say that he "would not find it unjust if the allies punished Germany for ten to twenty years." This, of course, infuriated Brecht. He demanded a sharp distinction between the Nazi regime, which kept the country in tow through terror, and the German people at large, most of whom had suffered inhuman hardship since the defeat of the previous war. Brecht did not absolve the citizens of this culprit nation from their share of guilt, but he insisted that the Nazi regime had represented, and had been supported by, a very small portion of German citizens, mainly the industrialists and leaders of big business. Here Brecht's reliance on Marxist analysis failed him, for although firms like Krupp and I. G. Farben did indeed profit grandly, *this* government was not an extension of capitalist designs. Like the rest of us, Brecht could not account for the Nazi mentality. The point of the Mann-Brecht conflict, however, is the emphatic clarity with which Brecht revealed his need to save Germany from political division and from still more spiritual despair. The terrible irony is that by identifying his fate with the fate of his country, what happened to Germany happened to Brecht: both ended divided, at the center of endless controversy and international strife.

Quite apart from political questions, however, Brecht's artistic contribution has come to seem decisive; his influence has so thoroughly penetrated the vanguard of theatrical and cinematic techniques that he seems "modern" in a sense more commanding than his "modernist" contemporaries. This turn of events, while true in itself, blinds us to the special relation between art and life in Brecht's case and obscures his calling as a poet. His preference for forms like ballads, street songs, doggerel, jingles, and church hymns, especially within the context of an art that is overwhelmingly didactic, surely raises doubts about Brecht's apparent modernity. And, in fact, to understand him we must see Brecht as a poet of the traditional, premodern type—in other words, the poet as repository of tribal wisdom, as voice and conscience of the community as a whole, the magician whose capacity to praise and curse extends even to keeping kings and tyrants in line, but whose powers will also be called up, like the "rat-rhymers" of medieval times, to stand before the village granary and through poetic incantation drive out the rats.

This was Brecht's job as a poet—to drive out the rats, starting with his own barn. Esslin and others have argued that Brecht's Marxism was the intellectual consequence of his basic poetic disposition, a point which is fairly obvious from Brecht's journals and which can also be seen from his early poetry. In its ideal form, Marxism gave Brecht's explosive genius the discipline and clearness of aim he needed. It also gave him something even more valuable. For Brecht, Marxism was a form of mediation between himself as an alienated individual from the middle class, and the bedrock commonality of the German populace. If this sounds odd, let us recall that Romanticism was the point in the development of our cultural heritage when, for the first time, a literary movement and political awareness began to merge, as may be seen in Shelley and Blake, in Hölderlin, in Hugo, and in a host of others. And as the nineteenth century advanced, the poles of the modern predicament were increasingly defined in terms of two extremes: on the one hand social estrangement as fate, on the other the Marxist dream of harmonious community as historical promise.

That was the gap that poets like Byron and Rimbaud faced but could not close. And the hope of closing it has always been Marxism's secret appeal for intellectuals and artists who feel in the world but not of it. Certainly this was how Marxism helped Brecht resolve his major problem—how to allow the single individual and the communion of suffering humanity to meet, or how to warrant the collective validity of personal vision. Such was the function of Marxism in Brecht's case. Thereby the poet gave over his gift to the community he served, and thereby his commitment to a modern ideology took on the ancient, mythical identity of the soothsayer amid a people sorely afflicted.

Looked upon in this way, Brecht's "case" begins to be greatly more positive and offers an occasion for rethinking an array of presumed conclusions. Usually an ideology dominates the individual, but in Brecht's example the enormous power of this headstrong man dominated the ideology. His art never suffered reduction, or diminishment of invention, or any of the closing-down effects, including the sacrifice of private integrity, which critics (mainly in America) charge against any poet who is so bold as to confront in his art what all of us, every day, confront in our lives. Brecht's genius was equal to the theories available at his historical moment, and this accounts likewise for the fact that with no illusions about the Soviet defeat of Marxist ideals, Brecht would not permit his own vision of the Marxist dream to die. Defeat, yes; capitulation, no. There is thus a strong element of tragedy in Brecht's case, and there is evidence, as in the following poem, that he knew exactly where he stood:

At the time when their fall was certain—
On the ramparts the lament for the dead had begun—

The Trojans adjusted small pieces, small pieces
In the triple wooden gates, small pieces.
And began to take courage, to hope.

The Trojans too, then.

That is one of Brecht's late poems. His sense of failure
and betrayal is bitterly present, and that amazing last line,
by turning history back upon itself, captures in an instant
the tragic dialectic between struggle and defeat. More deeply
than Arendt intended, this poet *knew*. And knowing, he
gathered his strength to survive and carry on. This, I take
it, is the final character of Brecht's "obdurate genius." He
was dead at fifty-eight, but had he lived as long as, say,
Thomas Mann, who died at eighty, I cannot believe that
Brecht's oppositional nature, or his Marxist idealism, or
his care for his country would have allowed him to remain
silent when, two months after his death, the uprising began in Hungary which the Soviets would so brutally smash,
or that he would not have spoken out loudly indeed when,
in 1961, the Berlin Wall went up.

If the "case" against Brecht persists, it feeds on the predicament that any artist with the courage to face political
issues must endure. Art is perfect as life can never be. In
terms of our ideals and convictions, all of us may be measured and found wanting. The political poet is thus caught
in a double bind. No institution or society—think of the
Church, think of America—lives up to the beliefs which
inform it. And no poet can live up to those finest moments
of vision which make the poetry itself invaluable. Political
events, furthermore, can discredit in a day the hard-held
convictions of a lifetime. When, therefore, we measure
Brecht's life and art against each other or against our own
standards, we can reject him for his faults or accept him
with honor for his astonishing tenacity. And we might

remember too, as Brecht wrote in "To Those Born Later," that commitment entails cost; that anger, even against injustice, makes the voice hoarse.

(The Yale Review)

Jim Gauer
The Other Takes the Morning Off

Can it be that in spite of everything this morning
People are out walking around like
Walking people, people who walk
Past each other and people who smile to themselves
Like smiling people, or smiles that walk around?
What a simple day for a smile
To walk around, in spite of everything, for the sidewalk to
    be
There where it is, for the cars to be parked
Just where we parked them, and the grocer to stand
On the spot that he does stand, in his perfect apron,
    pushing
That exact broom, the first broom
Of morning, his impossible broom that says
I'm awake! and he is awake, and so am I.
Can it be that the trees this morning are
As tall as trees are, with just
That many blossoms, and branches that reach
As far as they do reach, and no further?
Is it conceivable that the paper this morning was this
    morning's paper?
Somehow the news that I read there was just
The news that was, in those words, and no other.
I see a woman waving. She is the woman who waves.
I see a small crowd gather. That is the gathering crowd.
I see myself in reflection. I see myself in reflection. I walk
From where I was to where I am without falling
Into semblances, and when I tell you I walk
You believe me, you are smiling and I am talking

And you are the one who smiles.
And I tell you, beyond all that I've told you, that these
Are only examples, but these are
The examples that are.
In spite of everything, in spite of the long sigh
Of occupied buildings, in spite of the way
Buildings are sighing like sighing buildings, when I
    awoke
This morning, I was awake
And smiling, smiling just those
Ribbons into the children's hair.

(The Kenyon Review)

Linda Gregg
Death Looks Down

Death looks down on the salmon.
A male and a female in two pools, one above
the other. The female turns back along the path
of water to the male, does not touch him,
and returns to the place she had been.

I know what death will do. Their bodies already
are sour and ragged. Blood has risen
to the surface under the scales. One side
of his jaw is unhinged. Death will pick them up.
Put them under his coat against his skin
and belt them in there. Will walk away
up the path through the bay trees.
Through the dry grass of California to where
the mountain begins. Where a few deer
almost the color of the hills will look up
until he is under the trees again and the road ends
and there is a gate. He will climb over that
with his treasure. It will be dark by then.

But for now he does nothing. He does not disturb
the silence at all. Nor the occasional sound
of leaves, of ferns touching, of grass or stream.
For now he looks down at the salmon large and whole
motionless days and nights in the cold water.
Lying still, always facing the constant motion.

(Columbia)

Stephanie C. Gunn
Bunny Says It's the Death Watch

MY YOUNGER BROTHER PETE IS AS TALL AS A horse. He calls everybody Fred. No matter what his name is, or who he is, or what he does. He calls even our father Fred. Father doesn't know. Mother does and thinks it's funny. She'd been looking for a name for him ever since he moved away into a new house painted white, in the beach town next to ours. He moved into a new sky-blue sailboat that leaks when it heels to starboard, and a new wife, exactly half his age, who sleeps in mascara, who ties her pig and pony tails up in red wrapping bows. Mother's been looking all over for a name for Father ever since he moved away into that new house with the new silver slide in the front yard. The slide squeaks when his two new children go down it. Their midget shorts and skirts ride up their infantile bare legs. Their elastic-loose underpants ride up their white bottoms that become pink bottoms when they squeak down the slide.

His two new children land on Father's new grass that has some of Father's new woodchips lying in it. Amongst the woodchips there is a fleet of Father's old iron toy soldiers that were once made, by little hands, to do great battle. Now the toy soldiers lie forgotten except when a foot of one of Father's new children finds one and, only for a second, feels it before running on, before sinking it into the grass, sinking some toy soldiers that no longer have painted faces, and others that have lost their heads, and still others that have lost their shoes that had their feet in them.

Mother has been looking everywhere for a name for Father ever since he moved to that woodchip driveway lined with old skinny pine trees that, in the summer sun, bleed their sticky sap all down their barks. Mother has been looking. But it was Pete who found it. Pete found: Fred.

The sun melts the trees, melts their insides out. The sun sets the crickets to doing whatever they do with their legs to make that ZZZZZ, that ZZZZZ that means that they're hot and have to tell each other, or else one of Father's happy, hand-clapping children, or else both of Father's happy children clapping. The crickets ZZZZZ and give away where they are, and then they are chased and cornered and caught and suffocated in two hands or all four little hands. They ZZZZZ and they become members of the cricket corpse collection in the garage in Father's sail box.

Don't tell Father.

Father ties ropes with rings onto the pines lining the woodchip driveway and snaps the clues of wet spinnakers onto these rings. The sails dry in the wind, in the sticky needles and cones. They swell bright red and bright blue and bright yellow, they are as big as airplanes. You have to put your aerial down coming up the drive. You have to turn off the radio and get out of the car and put the aerial down. Father considers the sails to be the flags of his estate, his own country. He flies them at all times except in small craft warning winds. He flies them and, in foul weather gear and rubber boots, stands under them and hoses their bellies saltless. The new woodchips get all salty.

Father tells his small children of mahogany eyes and lips like raspberries that the trees come by colored parachutes. That's how they were born. They were dropped out of the sky in twins in a long row down the driveway. The trees like to have spinnakers tied to them, he says. The tugging sails comfort them, remind them of a past. He actually TELLS his children this. He fuels their little minds, pliant, with myths and magic before they grow up, before they're fed to the wolves. That's how he puts it. The world,

the wolves, what's the difference? He teaches them fun so
they'll always have had at least THAT with him. When
they are in their adolescence and he is an old man they
will remember his stories. Trees by parachute. What about
babies? Them by parachute, too? I ask Father who shrugs
and smiles and knows that by the time they'll be interested
in that kind of thing, they will likely hear all about it from
some place else. He says, They're only six and four. I know,
I say. And the one who's four looks up at me and says, Six
and four, that's ten—right? That's how many fingers—
right? And how many toes? I ask her. And she sits down on
Father's new woodchips, takes off her summer sandals,
and counts.

Mother has not talked to Fred in many years. She does
not want to. She SAYS that she doesn't want to. She forbids
him to call our house. But sometimes he calls. If there is
an emergency, say, if the wind comes cruel, if the spinnakers rip, if the trees work at flying, if the new woodchips
rise and swirl, making a bonfire out of themselves, Father
calls our house.

If, when he calls, Mother answers, he hangs up. Then
Mother finds one of us on the patio watching through German submarine binoculars. We watch the strong off-shore
breeze and all that goes with it to the horizon: a lady in a
tire, boys in a stalled motor boat emptying cans of beer
into themselves, and an all-colored beach ball. One of us
watches the all-colored beach ball being grieved over by a
child on the end of a jetty with her fists in her eyes, or does
she grieve the loss of the lady in the tire? Not the boys in
the boat with the beer? Mother finds one of us and says,
"You-know-who just called. Why don't you call him back.
I'll go into my room."

They lived together for twenty-nine years. She can tell
the difference between him and a person who, having the
wrong number, hangs up without a word.

After Mother delivers this message of hers, she disap-

pears into her end of the house. On the half-hour you can
hear her yell from behind her door, "Is it safe to come out
yet?"

Today, it is summertime and we are in Dennisport. Waves
are shush-shushing outside the house, up onto the beach,
up onto the foot of the seawall. Pete and I are in the kitchen
in bare feet. The radio is on behind the basket of seedless
sea-green grapes and plums as purple as fresh bad bruises.
Reggae is all over the kitchen. Last night's popcorn dish is
in the sink soaking. There is the toaster going up and
down, and a pair of wooden toast tweezers are stuck onto
it by magnets. Pete is using a knife to unlodge an English
muffin from the toaster's inner combings.

"What do you think these are for, Pete-baby?" I point to
the toast tweezers. "The decor? Your imagination? Your
bicycle?"

"Yep," Pete says. He is not yet fully awake. Sleep is caked
on his eyelashes like oatmeal, and he has sliced the muffin
in the toaster into quarters and still can't get it out.

Frankie, our oldest brother, walks into the kitchen holding between his index finger and his thumb, as far away
from himself as he can, a pair of white boxer underpants.
They are as big as a pillow case.

"Did you put these in my room?" Frankie's voice is much
louder than the reggae. There is disturbance in his eyes.

Mother steps in through the back door screen in her
bathing suit that looks like a sundress. It is blue with
bunches of seedless sea-green grapes on it. She has been
lying outdoors in the sun and there is a piece of aluminum
foil folded over her nose. There is sun-prevention lipstick
on her chin and cheeks and lips. Frankie is staring at Pete
in his inside-out red elephant pajamas. Frankie is staring
at me wrapped in an over-sized crimson towel, my hair
dripping like a faucet. Frankie is staring at Mother in her
bathing suit that goes down to her knees.

"Well?" he asks.

There is a draft of air coming in from the back door. It is surprisingly cool for a sunny day like today, not a cloud in the sky. Frankie fixes his eyes on Pete who, leaning over his blue and white breakfast plate, jams a whole buttered blueberry muffin into his mouth. Pete is tapping his foot that is hard and thick from walking on our rock road and Fred's new woodchips, he is tapping his foot to AM reggae.

"Well?" Frankie asks again. "Did you?"

Pete swallows before he says, "Nope."

"Who put them in my room, then?" Frankie's black eyebrows are down over his eyes. "Whose are they?"

Mother stops pouring cranberry juice into a glass crowded with ice. She looks over at Frankie from under her visor hat. There is the moment of everyone thinking. You can see that Mother is thinking. I am thinking. Even Pete is thinking. Pete is looking at the underpants in their reflection in the toaster. Whose ARE they? As big as a pillow case. Whose else.

"Throw them in the garbage!" Mother says through her sun-prevention lipstick. "I mean it. In the garbage right now!"

"Gee, I'm sorry, Mum," Pete says licking blueberry off his thumbs. "They must have gotten into my backpack or something. I wonder how THAT happened." Pete goes off into himself wondering.

"In the garbage!" Mother says in a loud voice, a very loud voice, not like Mother at all.

"You mean, just because you're divorced, you're not going to do Fred's laundry any more?" I ask her, but just then, Frankie lurches to the back door and in a strong underhand, throws them outside. Through the kitchen window Mother and Pete and I see their white blob flash across the patio and hook themselves onto the arm of a three-and-a-half-legged deck chair.

"They look very nice there, Frankie. Very nice. Don't they improve breakfast," I say.

"Frankie! What are you doing? What are they doing there?" Mother wants to know. She is quite serious but then she is about to laugh. Now she is laughing, not a lot, not from the stomach, but she is laughing, which is something.

"I threw them there!" Frankie replies, making kisses at her in the air. His navy blue eyes are smiling. A hero, he is thinking. Then, right off his mouth, right out of his eyes, his smile fades. He bends his head down to look at the floor. A morning couple of black locks falls over his face like gloved fingers. He leaves them there.

"Well, where else?"

"In the compost heap?" I ask.

"They cannot stay THERE!" Mother says and she walks away into her room.

And they don't, of course. They don't stay there at all.

Pete stuffs them into his backpack on his way to the end of the road to meet Fred. They are going sailing together. They are going to try to figure out a way to fix the leak under the railing by the starboard side-stay. Eventually, around noon, Pete will probably beach the boat and scrape barnacles off of the bottom. He will take a little paint off, too. He will make the bottom of the boat as smooth as the bottoms of Father's new little ones. That's how Father puts it. That's how Father puts what he wants done.

Wearing cutoffs, Pete is walking up the hill in our road. Fred will be along any minute in his red-interior convertible. Its front seat is very low, and when Fred drives it he has to sit forward to see over the dashboard. Mother has seen Father in this car. He looks like a child in it, she has said. She does not see him often. They live in neighboring towns and it is not surprising that they should stand together in the same check-out line at the grocery stores, or the same teller line at the bank. It is not surprising that they should sit in seats that share the same arm in a movie theater. But of course they never do.

But that doesn't mean to say that they don't spy on each other. Mother drives by Father's white house on her way to play tennis or on her way to visit her sister, Bunny. This is how she knows that one of Father's children is a foot taller than the other. That wearing orange life preservers going down the slide is one of their favorite things to do. What she does not know is that they yell, Man Overboard! as they go down, that they are pretending to be part of a 747 emergency landing. She does not know that they love airplanes, and the sky. That they love the thought of trees arriving by parachute. That their eyes are ever up in the air watching for more births. If their eyes were down the driveway, they would see Mother slowing in her car, they would see her watching them slide.

And Fred, the same goes for Fred. He, pretending impatience, will drive up the hill in our road and wait at its top. He will honk his horn. He will sit there and die to know what is going on in our house, his old one. He will spy on the baby carrots in the garden, the seawall crumbling under the tides, and of course, Mother, always Mother. He will want to see her.

Freckles on Pete's shoulders and their sharp blades have run into each other. He is at the top of the hill when he hears an upstairs window fly open. He turns his head to look back at our house.

"Don't get stuck wheelbarrowing!" Frankie yells at him through the screen of his bedroom window. Frankie laughs to himself all the way over to a set of golf clubs in the corner. He picks out a putter, drops two Titalists onto the wooden floor, and aims for a bed leg. He begins an imitation of the very low excited voice of a sport's announcer. And now here we are on the eighteenth green. Fred is attempting a nine-foot putt. If he sinks this one he will total out at ten under, certainly a winning score here at the Fred Open. If he sinks it.

Pete sits in the deep, clean beach sand that has found its way to the road's end, or was there before the road was. He puts on his beaten running shoes, and waits. His shoes have holes in their toes, and their laces are broken and not long enough to go all their way around. He takes apart an oak leaf at its veins. He aims a rock at a dog's water dish across the street. Aims a couple of more rocks there. The dog's not around. He gets one right in the bowl, a tiny spurt of water jumps out of it and lies in the sand, a dead crooked snake. The sun is out and hot, the snake is disappearing. Fred's not around either. Pete throws one more rock as far as he can into the woods on the other side of the road, far beyond the dog dish. He doesn't hear where it ends up. So he just lies down in tree shadow, his head on his backpack, and dozes off. The pine trees melt all around him. Crickets start their ZZZZZ sound and just when he's getting used to them, just when he doesn't hear them any more, they stop. Their stopping, as sudden as their starting, nearly wakes up Pete.

An hour later, Mother wants to drive to the store. She says, "Do you think it's safe?" She waits half an hour more and just as she is walking out the back door, the phone rings. It might be her tennis partner or her sister, Bunny, and she answers it. "Hello?" she asks. There is dial tone.

"It was you-know-who," she says to me. I am at the kitchen sink cleaning out the gold fish bowl. Two gold fish and one red and white one are squirming for space in a drinking glass that is too small for the three of them to be in. The red and white one lies on the bottom of the glass and fights with itself to keep belly-down. Not a good sign, I think as I rinse the fake coral piece that the fish adore swimming in and out of. But the red and white one must be at least a year old. I try to count the months but I cannot remember the time I first saw the fish. Why not throw ALL of them into seawater at a low tide, I think. What a good idea. At low tide so that they can get used to sea motion before the tide gets deep and carries them away.

The gold ones are bumping into each other soundlessly. They wave their see-through fins at each other and their mouths are startled, their mouths are saying O. Their eyes are skidding their way along the inside of the glass. The fish are gulping air out of the water, feed out of the water, water out of itself. Through the glass you can see the threads of their bowels as dark as pencil lines. You can see the threads come right out of the fish and swim behind them like spouses. The threads are all over the bottom of the bowl. At full speed boiling water runs into the bowl and up to the bowl's lip and over. I let it run by itself. Through the glass the fish watch their bowl come clean.

Just as a hand of Mother's is on the back door pushing to get out, the phone rings. THIS time it might be her tennis partner or her sister, Bunny. She answers it.

"No, I'm sorry, he's not. WHAT?"

I hear her slam down the phone.

"Lord, what I go through!"

I wipe my hands on the hem of my oversized crimson towel and peek around the corner at Mother, who sits in the rocker beside the phone, rocking. Rocking, rocking, with her hands in a white-knuckled grip of the chair's arms.

"What is it?"

"That man, that man," she is saying.

"Fred?"

"Do you know what that was? Do you?" she asks me.

"No. WHO?" She does not answer. "Who was it, Mother?"

"I said, Hello, and this little voice asked to speak to Pete." Mother breathes in, then out. The piece of aluminum foil falls off her nose into her lap. With the care of a blind woman learning a jigsaw piece so that she can fit it, Mother fingers the foil. "I said that Pete wasn't here, then

SHE said, the little voice said, Oh, well, just tell him to call up Daddy."

"Oh, dear," I say.

"I just can't get over that man sometimes." Mother's head is shaking slowly from side to side, she is slowly rocking herself back and forth.

"I know."

"You can tell that Father of yours not to do that ever again. He just can't do that to me." Mother is not crying. She will not either. Her cheeks are as soft and worried as pillows after night, her eyes are true blue, her hair is a bright white, and has been since the day Frankie was born. Tomorrow she will make jokes about talking on the phone to one of Father's new little ones. But it is not tomorrow yet.

At the end of the road, right beside the sleeping Pete, Mother honks her horn. Pete sits up abruptly.

"Oh, hi, Mum!"

"Hi, darling. You having fun? Fred just called. Probably looking for his underwear. And you'll never guess who ELSE I talked to. He must be desperate for them. BYE!" Mother says and off she drives. She has one eye out for Fred in his red-interior convertible. Off she drives and Pete hears her voice, when she stops the car a block away, yelling back at him.

"Pete, please don't sleep in the road!"

Nearly evening, the bowl is clean, the fish are back in it and they are swimming through their fake coral reef. Outside the house clouds have been rolling in. Wind has picked up. The seas have begun to turn. Thunder from the sky shakes the silver candlesticks on the warped dining room table. They move closer together, scared children. The cooking pots on nails on the kitchen wall shake, their tops hung over them clatter. The fish in the water in the bowl quiver. Hanging tea cups in a closed kitchen cabinet tink each other in delicate toasts. Thunder loosens the magnets holding the wooden toast tweezers and they, the tweezers, fall off the toaster and lie in burnt crumbs in the toaster tray.

Deck chairs from the front of the house slide past side windows to the back of the house. They screech on the patio like copulating cats. Some lift off and bang against the side of the house in flight. They are trying to get into the house through the walls. One deck chair gets stuck in a bush thats arms are open wide as if it's been waiting for this moment all its life, to hold something, anything, the deck chair. The three-and-a-half-legged deck chair flies off onto the driveway. Mother is going to run it over when she drives home from shopping.

Ocean waves are up all over the picture windows. Waves and rain both come hard. There is a window upstairs that is open too much or too little. It has caught the wind, and is a fog horn.

Through the storm I rush outside to the clothesline. In the darkness white pajama legs are slapping at each other. As I near them they slap at me. Like coats of plaster, wet towels stick to me. The hooks of Mother's bras are sharp at my face but I make them stop. I take the linen into my arms into the house. I drape them over the arms and across the shoulders of the living room chairs and couches, and they are people who have been in a boating accident. They drip and make the rug black.

Lightning comes in fast from the outside. I run with pots from the kitchen to places I know in the house, to places where the rain is leaking. I make Frankie run, too.

Staring out the picture windows, I wait three lightning flashes before I say, "Hey, Frankie. There's a boat out there."

Frankie and I look out at the sailboat shooting under and then up over the ocean's blackness and whiteness and waves.

"I can't believe ANYBODY'd be crazy enough to be out in this weather," Frankie says.

I grab the German submarine binoculars from the sill of the picture windows.

"Frankie, that boat looks sky-blue to me."

"I don't believe it," Frankie says flatly and goes up the stairs.

All the pots are off their nails in the kitchen. There are many more leaks than pots. I begin with pot tops but soon there are none left of them either. I put the fish bowl on the floor in the upstairs bathroom under the slowest leak. When the drops fall into the bowl, the fish open their mouths, then shut them quickly and open them again. They do not bump into each other, or that fake coral piece. They are not THAT confused. But they do dart this way and that. Is it eating time? Is it time to clean the bowl? Didn't we do that this morning?

The wind blows, blows the house down. The house creaks, an old ship keeling over. There is the wind moving through the blankets on the beds. I go up the stairs four at a time and shut the window that is making the fog horn noise. Now there is the sound of the pots overflowing, the splashing of the water on the rugs. I can hear from upstairs the splashing downstairs. I run down and call for Frankie to help. But there is thunder and he cannot hear. Or else he does hear but he does not come.

I hear the roll of golf balls on the floor above. I hear one in five hit a bed leg. I hear one escape the course altogether and run down the hall to where the stairs come down. But the ball doesn't. It stays at the top.

Every light goes out.

"Power's off!" Frankie yells. "Hey, the power's off!" He is beside me in a second.

Mother blows in through the back door with groceries in wet paper bags and her sister, Bunny.

"There's a boat out there," I tell Mother and Bunny.

"In this storm?" Mother says wiping the side of her face with the back of her hand.

"Yah," I say. "And I think," I catch Mother's blue eyes in mine. "I think it's Fred."

Mother goes to the picture windows. Her breath fogs the glass as she speaks, "Who else would it be?"

In her boy's haircut, Bunny stands beside Mother. Glaring through the German submarine binoculars she says, "Sure, it's him. Fred and all the little bastards in their foul weather coats and orange life preservers."

"How can you see in the dark?" Mother asks.

"Oh, I can FEEL it when he's around. I wonder if he'll hit a jetty or run aground and sink," Bunny says.

I think of the white bottoms that become pink bottoms when they squeak down the new silver slide. In their orange life preservers. In their pretend emergency landings. If the sky-blue sailboat sinks today, Father's new little ones will know exactly how to behave.

"I suppose Pete's out there with him," Mother says staring out into the electric air, out to where her son sails.

"I mean, one would like to think of their Father as a sensible man?" This is a question I ask Mother. She turns from me to light the fireplace fire and, for a while, we all sit in front of it.

Upstairs, by the light of one candle, I dump water from the full pots into the sink. As suddenly as a cat, Frankie stands beside me. "You might as well know the facts," he says. He is combing his black hair back. He is wearing a golf glove, three T shirts one on top of the other, ankle socks that don't match or have heels, and a pair of pink golf pants.

"Why do you think Fred orders us around all the time, has us do all the work? So SHE won't have to do it. He wants her to be ready for him in bed." The roof is low, a hat over our heads. The rain spits and splatters on it. Frankie's eyes are shyly at the mirror as if he were seeing in it himself as a child. Frankie parts his hair cleanly on the left. "He wants her to be ready for him. Not tired like Mum. That's one of the reasons Dad left, you know. He told me. Mum was too out to lunch in bed at night. I'm too tired, she would say. That's why he had to look elsewhere. And now he has us doing the wheelbarrowing. Oh, yah, Dad's pretty cagey. He has us doing HER work. But I'm not going to do it any more. No, sir. Not me. Oh, no wonder my golf's lousy!" Frankie flips his comb into the sink. "I can't even go over there without him telling me to wheelbarrow a ton of woodchips from the back of the house and spread them evenly all over the dumb driveway, and SHE's always standing there watching, stamping her foot saying, Not over THERE, over HERE!"

"Stop arguing!" Mother yells up the stairs at us.

"We're not!" Frankie yells back in a very excited voice. He stomps into his room and comes out with a driver in his hand. He extends the club down the stairwell to see its silver shaft glimmer in the downstairs fire light.

"Frankie! Are you playing golf in this weather?" Mother's voice is laughing until it is cut off by a bonehard clap of thunder. Frankie runs back into his room.

"Frankie?" I stand in his doorway. The chimney that runs up the center of the house is heating the upstairs now, it is heating Frankie and me. I can hear Frankie tapping balls. I can hear them rolling. He is putting in the dark. "Hey, Frankie? I wouldn't take it so hard. Listen, I do the wheelbarrowing, too, when I'm—"

"Oh, shut up!" Frankie says.

With my hands feeling the way of the hall, I take myself back into the bathroom. The fish bowl has overflowed and the red and white one is on the floor. I pick it up by the tail and lay it on my palm. Its eyes are dry. I flip it back into the bowl. And it is not dead. It is slithering through the water. Be thankful for the little things in life, I think. The little things that happen one after the next. Cupping my hands over the bowl's lip, I pour half of its water out, and sit it under the slow leak that had quickened. The red and white one trembles around the gold ones and the fake coral piece. It is asking them if they saw it through the glass, on the outside of the bowl, on the wooden bathroom floor.

Now it is evening. We are all in front of the fire. Even Pete is here. He has emptied his plate of swordfish and is warming his toes as wrinkled as sponges. He is calling each toe Fred. This Fred went to market, this Fred stayed home.

It is Frankie's night to do the dishes and he is going at it crash bang in the candlelit kitchen. He is yelling about the popcorn pot. It was from LAST night and last night was Pete's night to do the dishes, so why doesn't HE do it? Pete is poking at the fire with a stick. Now he is setting up a game of checkers beside him on the floor. He positions the checkers as big as bracelets on the black and red checkered rug that is the size of a card table. Pete is setting up the game and waiting for his partner, Frankie The Dishwasher, to be through.

While Mother and Bunny are in the kitchen drying and putting away, Pete is telling me that Fred had not taken the spinnakers down before their sail, before the storm, and when the sailors returned they found the spinnakers ruined. Fred had gone into his sail box in the garage to count how many he had left. Pulling out three, they had filled up the garage, and then they had deflated onto the floor. With their little hands on their cheeks, Father's new little ones had watched their carefully piled cricket corpses fly into the air like bird seed. They had watched as each cricket corpse became, upon landing, ash. Father had yelled, Now, WHAT'S THIS? The sails outside are soaked and stretched beyond any light of hope, and these sails inside are full of bugs! Father's new little ones had mourned ever so silently the loss of their cricket corpse collection. And when Father had seen the sorrow in their mahogany eyes, he had patted them on their heads and ruffled up their hair. He had said, Oh, don't worry, girls. Now we can leave the sails up over the driveway forever. Now we no longer have to worry about the winds that blow bigger than the small craft warning winds.

"Now," added Pete to me, "we don't have to put the aerial down when we drive up the drive. We can leave the radio on, and the aerial where it is, and we can slice the spinnakers into streamers."

"Did you tell this to Fred?" I ask him.

"No. He'll find out," Pete replies.

"Who will find what out?" Bunny asks.

She and Mother come to sit beside the fire and Peter stops his talking about Fred. He removes some of the giant checkers off the rug-board and works at setting up an impossible checker situation. Crawling on hands and knees from the black side to the red, he plays at both.

"Who will find what out?" Bunny asks again.

"Pete was just telling me that Frankie will find out that doing the popcorn pot is good for his golf swing," I say. There is laughter from all except Frankie, who does not hear our talk. Or else he is pretending not to. Now, in the fire light, we are all quiet, and out of this quiet Mother begins to speak.

"Well, alright," she says. Now Mother has had a bit of scotch. To warm herself up. Not too much. A bit. She sits on the floor with her legs stretched out in front of her and while she talks, she works at touching her toes. "So, your Father's not home, aye?" Bunny has taken her turn with the stick and is brightening up the fire. She is throwing on another log and then brushing her hands together. Under her plucked eyebrows, she has dark eyes. They are being hypnotized by the fire, by Mother's voice, the rain on the roof, the rain on the rug. Mother has a soft sweater on, her eyes are sapphire. She is touching the tips of her fingers to her ankles and saying, "So, your Father's not even in the country." She is turning to me. "I'm pregnant with you. I don't know whether to have you or not. Frankie doesn't walk. He doesn't talk. He won't eat. I take him to a psychiatric clinic at Yale. Bunny comes with me. I don't know WHAT I would have done without Bunny." Pete has got two red kings into a corner with a black one. Not one can make a move. He has his hand under his chin and is frowning thoughtfully.

"The Yale doctor talked to me for four full hours. I told him everything. I thought I might as well. Things I've never told anyone. Things I never told your Father. Well, at the end of our session, the doctor didn't even want to see Frankie. He watched him for a minute, and then he said to me, There's nothing wrong with that child. That boy is fine. YOU need someone to talk to. Someone, your husband. That's what he said. That's all he said."

When the clock bongs twelve times, the storm lessens outside. Bunny looks out the picture windows and then drives her car over the three-and-a-half-legged deck chair and up the hill in our road and down the other side. Rain stops coming into our house. Frankie is finished with the washing of the popcorn pot. Thunder and lightning have gone far enough, have stopped. Have now gone away. There is no wind in the blankets on the beds. Only Pete is in his bed, and Mother is in hers. They are sleeping warm and dry, dreaming dreams. The air outside is cool like fall time. The sea is smoothing itself like a lady does her skirt. A little at a time. The waves have thrown up onto the shore seaweed the size of human bodies, horse-shoe crabs that have lost their tails, and conks. We will see these things on the beach tomorrow. Logs, that turned into a million radiant fingernails, are now turning black. The fire dies. The light on Frankie's and my faces stops.

Frankie has heard every word Mother has said about him. Him at the age of three. Him at the psychiatric clinic.

Frankie is the last to go up to bed. Before I go to sleep, I move the fish bowl from the bathroom floor onto a dresser in the hall. Bunny is driving through our town and into the next. She is driving by Father's new white house. There are the drowned spinnakers hanging from the pines. In the proper beds Father's two new little ones, and Father's new wife half his age, sleep on their backs and on their fronts like the toy soldiers that lie under the grass beside the slide.

There is one light on in Father's new house.

Beside it, Fred is wide awake.

(Fiction)

Robert Hass
Listening and Making

I TOLD A FRIEND I WAS GOING TO TRY TO WRITE something about prosody and he said, "Oh great." The two-beat phrase is a very American form of terminal irony. A guy in a bar in Charlottesville turned to me once and said, loudly but confidentially, "Ahmo find me a woman and fuck her twenty ways till Sunday." That's also a characteristic rhythm: ahmo FIND ME a WOman / and FUCK her TWENty WAYS till SUNday. Three beats and then a more emphatic four. A woman down the bar doubled the two-beat put-down. She said, "Good luck, asshole." Rhythms and rhythmic play make texture in our lives but they are hard to talk about and besides people don't like them to be talked about. Another friend wrote to me about an essay of mine in which I commented at some point on a "metrical inversion" in a line from a poem by Robert Lowell. He said he liked the piece well enough, but that one phrase—that finical tic of the educated mind—had filled him with rage. I think I understand why.

For a long time anthropological theory treated shamanism and spirit possession as separate phenomena. Shamanism was seen as a priestly tradition, a repertoire of techniques for acquiring vision. Spirit possession was a peripheral phenomenon, occurring mostly among women on some borderline between hysteria and Pentecostal religion. Or so it seemed until an English anthropologist, Ian Lewis, began to study the continuities between them. At which point it became clear that shamanism was usually a fully developed, male-dominated, politically central evolution of spirit possession, and that, in the harshly repressed lives of women in most primitive societies, new songs, chants, visions and psychic experiences keep welling up into cults which have their force because they are outside the entrenched means to vision. Because rhythm has direct access to the unconscious, because it can hypnotize us, enter our bodies and make us move, it is a power. And power is political.

That is why rhythm is always revolutionary ground. It is always the place where the organic rises to abolish the mechanical and where energy announces the abolition of tradition. New rhythms are new perceptions. In the nineteenth century, blank verse, the ode and ballad forms overthrew the heroic couplet. In the twentieth, vers libre overthrew the metrical dexterities of the Victorians. The latest of these revolutions occurred in the 1950s. It is variously dated from Charles Olson's essay "Projective Verse," from Allen Ginsberg's *Howl* and Jack Kerouac's spontaneous poetics or from Robert Lowell's conversion to William Carlos Williams in *Life Studies*. In the second generation of poets since 1950, the same slogans have been advanced and there is, in the magazines, an orthodoxy of relaxed free verse. Statements about rhythm emphasize its natural character. The rhythm of poetry is sometimes said to be based on the rhythm of work, but no one wonders then why we work rhythmically. The heartbeat—pa-thunk, pa-thunk, pa-thunk—is pointed to as a basis for rhythm, but if you think about it for a minute, it seems obvious that it is a little monotonous to account for much. Prosody is not much taught or talked about, since it was a form of institutional terrorism in the previous, metrical orthodoxy. And during this time, I think, there has been an observable falling off in the inventive force of poetry. A likely outcome would be an equally mindless metrical revival. And I think that would be too bad. The range of possibilities for the poem—from chant to prose—have been extended enormously in English in the past seventy years. Very few living poets—Robert Duncan comes to mind—work with that full range. What I want to try to do in this essay is talk about the part rhythm plays in the work of the imagination and suggest a way of thinking about the prosody of free verse. It is listening that I am interested in—in writers and readers—and the kind of making that can come from live, attentive listening.

Here is a poem by Gary Snyder, "August on Sourdough, A Visit from Dick Brewer":

You hitched a thousand miles
            north from San Francisco
Hiked up the mountainside   a mile in the air
The little cabin—one room—
               walled in glass
Meadows and snowfields,   hundreds of peaks.
We lay in our sleeping bags
             talking half the night;
Wind in the guy-cables   summer mountain rain.
Next morning I went with you
          as far as the cliffs,
Loaned you my poncho—   the rain across the shale—
You down the snowfield
           flapping in the wind
Waving a last goodbye   half-hidden in the clouds
To go on hitching
          clear to New York:
Me back to my mountain   and far, far, west.

This poem is beautifully made, casual, tender, alive with space. It is worth remembering, since I want to argue that rhythm is at least partly a psychological matter, that twenty-five years ago the editors of most American literary magazines would have found it thin, eccentric, formless.

It belongs to a tradition of poems of leave-taking in China and Japan. Buson provides an instance:

You go,
I stay;
two autumns

And Basho another:

Seeing people off,
Being seen off,—
autumn in Kiso

Goodbyes are powerful, and Americans, who say them all the time, don't seem to write about them very much. In *A Zen Wave,* Robert Aitken's book about Basho, he observes that the Japanese, customarily, wave until a departing guest has disappeared from sight. We are more likely to turn away before that happens, not so much erasing the other person as turning inward, toward our own separateness, and getting on with it. Buson doesn't do that; he lets the moment define itself, lets the distance speak. And, in imagining his own separateness, he imagines his friend's. That last image—two autumns—speaks absolutely of the way in which each of us is alone, but it also tends to multiply, expand: two autumns, dozens of autumns, a million autumns, worlds and worlds, and whether that fact is happy or unhappy, he doesn't say; he says it is. Basho makes something different but similar of the fact that parting is like the process of individuation. The second line of his poem in Japanese reads *okuritsu hate wa,* literally *okuri* (seeing off) *tsu* (now) *hate* (goal, outcome, upshot) *wa* (particle indicating the subject). In the version I quote, R. H. Blythe has, nicely, rendered *hate wa* as a dash; comings and goings resolve into a time and a place, the ongoing world without subject or object. Basho's insight moves us a step further than Buson's. Many worlds, many subjectivities become one world which includes, among other things, all the individual worlds. How sharply you feel that world emerging, how sharply the self dissolving into it, he leaves up to you.

Robert Aitken has written a fine, brief commentary on this poem:

Now being seen off; now seeing off—what is the upshot? Autumn in Kiso, rain in Manoa Valley, a gecko at the Maui zendo—*chi chi chichichi.*

Paul Gauguin asked: "Where do we come from? What are we? Where are we going?" You will find these words inscribed in French in the corner of one of his greatest paintings, a wide prospect of Tahiti, children, young adults, old people, birds, animals, trees, and a strange idol. What is the upshot after all? Paul Gauguin painted it very beautifully.

Snyder's "August on Sourdough" seems to say something like what Buson says: you go, I go. And in its evocation of space and movement something of what Basho says; it creates a wide, windy world whose center is no particular person. One understanding of it might come from looking at the personal pronouns, at the way American speech distinguishes the self as subject from the self as object. But another way that Snyder tries to discover what he means is rhythmically. *Chi chi chichichi.* One two onetwothree. What does the sound have to say about wholeness or endings or movement or separation? What rhythm heals? To ask these questions, we have to ask what rhythm is and how it engages us.

Some ideas first. I want to suggest that our experience of rhythm has three distinct phases. Clear enough that it implies the apprehension of a pattern. We hear

one two

and we are hearing a sound. When we hear

```
         one two
         one two
```

we are beginning to hear a rhythm. If we listen to something like this,

```
          one two
          one
          one two
       one two three
          one two
       one two three
          one two
          one
          one two
```

we attend to and can pick out three patterns of repetition:

one	one two	one two three
one	one two	one two three
one	one two	one two three
one	one two	one two three

   Part of the explanation for this is that we are pattern-
discerning animals, for whatever reason in our evolution-
ary history. We attend to a rhythm almost instinctively,
listen to it for a while, and, if we decide it has no special
significance for us, we can let it go; or put it away, not
hearing it again unless it alters, signaling to us—as it
would to a hunting or a grazing animal—that something
in the environment is changed. This process is going on in
us all the time, one way or another. It is the first stage,
wakeful, animal, alert, of the experience of rhythm. And it
is the place to which we are called by the first words of any
poem or story. *Once upon a time; how many dawns chill
from his rippling rest; it is a truth universally acknowl-*

edged . . .; fishbones walked the waves off Hatteras: it calls us to an intense, attentive consciousness. Probably that is what attracts some people to poetry, to writing generally, and it is probably what repels them, since the last thing many people want is to be conscious.

This threshold alertness is only the first phase of the experience of rhythm. The second includes the whole range of our experience of recurrent and varying sound. We enter, are made attentive, then something else begins to happen:

> one two
> one
> one two three
> one two
> one two three

or this variation on Herrick from a musician-poet, Nils Petersen:

> Whenas in silks
> Whenas in silks
> My Julia goes
> My Julia goes
> Then, then methinks (methinks)
> How sweetly flows
> Sweetly flows
> The liquefaction (faction) (faction)
> Of her clothes
>   her clothes her clothes

We move from attention to pleasure, from necessity to a field of play. The principle is recurrence and variation. The effect is hard to describe. Interplay, weaving, dialogue, dance: every phrase that comes to mind is a metaphor. This need to speak metaphorically suggests that rhythm is an idiom of the unconscious, which is why it seems an echo of many other human activities.

When we listen to a rhythm, especially an insistent rhythm, there is often a moment or more of compelled attention in which the play and repetition of the sounds seem—I am pulled toward metaphor again—to draw us in or overwhelm us. That kind of listening can lead to something like trance. It is the feeling out of which comes another set of metaphors—magic, incantation—and practices. We know that rhythm has always been a mnemonic device, that metrical compositions are usually easier to remember than non-metrical ones, that in ancient times all laws were expressed in incantatory rhythms, that the oldest Greek and Latin words for poetry were also the oldest words for law. This is part of the basis for the connection between memory and inspiration: *O musa, memora mihi,* the Aeneid begins. Far back rhythm, memory, trance are connected to authority and magical power.

An instance from the Plains Sioux, in Frances Densmore's translation:

> The whole world is coming
> A nation is coming
> A nation is coming

This song was made after the buffalo had been massacred by hide hunters. It is chant, magical invocation, designed to bring the herds down from Canada in the spring as they had always come.

> Eagle has brought the message to the tribe
> The father says so
> The father says so

It is rhythmic repetition moving toward magic. *Enchantment,* we say, *incantation,* singing the song inward. Often it is accompanied by a slight rocking of the body.

> From the north they are coming
> The buffalo are coming
> The buffalo are coming

At some point chant becomes hypnotic; it begins to induce the trance state, identified with possession.

> Crow has brought the message to the tribe
> The father says so
> The father says so

Its effect can begin to be a feeling of terror and confinement. In medieval Europe you could ward off the devil by repeating a small prayer three hundred or five hundred times. The medical histories of hysteria describe instances when the chanter, once begun, was unable to stop.

> The buffalo are coming
> The buffalo are coming
> The father says so
> The father says so

Repetition makes us feel secure and variation makes us feel free. What these experiences must touch in us is the rhythm of our own individuation. It's easy enough to observe in small children the force of these pulls between the security of infancy and the freedom of their own separateness. When my oldest child was two or so, we used to take walks. He had a zen carpenter's feeling for distance, running ahead of me in an abandoned waddle, coming to an abrupt stop when he felt he had come to the very edge of some magical zone of protection which my presence generated, and then gazing back at me over his shoulder with a look of droll glee. He knew he was right out there on the edge—the distance seemed to be about eleven or twelve squares of sidewalk. Sometimes he would take one more step, then another, looking back each time, and if I uttered a warning sound he would collapse in hilarity which seemed to be a celebration of his own daring. I was listening at the same time to Miles Davis, to how far he was willing to move away from the melody, to the way the feeling intensified the further away from it he got, as if he were trying to describe what it is like to get out there so far into the wandering hunger for the next note that it seemed at the same time exultant and explosively lonely and probably impossible to come back ever. I was also reading Theodore Roethke, the long poems with their manic inward-driven nursery-rhyme rhythms:

> The shape of a rat?
> It's bigger than that.
> It's sleek as an otter
> With wide webby toes.
> Just under the water
> It usually goes.

And it made me feel that there was not, in this, much difference between child and grown-up, between my son's impulses and the tidal pulls of adult life, the desire for merger, union, loss of self and the desire for freedom, surprise, singularity. I think it is probably the coming together of our pattern-discerning alertness with this pull between polarities in our psychic life that determines our feelings about rhythm.

It is important that we both want a rapt symbiotic state and don't want it; that we want solitariness and self-sufficiency and don't want it. Rhythmic repetition initiates a sense of order. The feeling of magic comes from the way it puts us in touch with the promise of a deep sympathetic power in things: heartbeat, sunrise, summer solstice. This can be hypnotically peaceful; it can also be terrifying, to come so near self-abandonment and loss of autonomy, to whatever in ourselves wants to stay there in that sound, rocking and weeping, comforted. In the same way, freedom from pattern offers us at first an openness, a field of identity, room to move; and it contains the threat of chaos, rudderlessness, vacuity. Safety and magic on one side, freedom and movement on the other; their reverse faces are claustrophobia and obsession or agoraphobia and vertigo. They are the powers we move among, listening to a rhythm, as the soul in the bardo state moves among the heavens and the hells, and they are what make the relation between repetition and variation in art dialectical and generative.

An example, from a metrical poem:

> A slumber did my spirit seal,
> I had no human fears;
> She seemed a thing who could not feel
> The touch of earthly years.
>
> No motion has she now, no force.
> She neither hears nor sees,
> Rolled round in earth's diurnal course
> With rocks and stones and trees.

In this poem of grief at the death of a young girl, Wordsworth brings us in the last lines to a small, majestic, orderly music in which we feel reconciled to the way the child has entered the natural universe. Like a cradle rocking, bringing us to rest. At least that is how I read the poem for a long time, until someone pointed out to me the randomness of the last sequence: rocks, stones, trees. What is the difference between a rock and a stone? Who knows? What difference could it make? Rocks and stones. She has passed into brute matter, into the huge, mute spaces that terrified

Pascal. For a while, with all the bad habits of education, I wondered which was the correct interpretation. I've come to see that the poem is so memorable and haunting because the two readings and feelings are equally present, married there, and it is the expressive power of rhythm that makes this possible.

First we hear: an order is insisted upon by the meter; then we listen, for that order is questioned immediately by the arrangement of the stanzas. Four beats in the first line, an insistent order; three beats in the second line, the same order but lighter, easier to live with. Four beats in the third line: the heavier order enters again, intensified slightly by the almost audible extra stress of "not feel." Three beats again in the fourth line, a lightening. The fifth line is interesting because the pause seems to promise an alteration in the pattern, to give us three beats, the lighter order, but no, after the pause we get two heavy stresses, "no force"; it almost says: were you wondering if "not feel" was two stresses? "Not feel" is two stresses. It is like a musical theme; we have begun to hear not just a play between three- and four-stress phrases, but a secondary drama of the four stresses tending toward a heavier and menacing five. In the sixth line we return to the three-stress pattern. In the seventh line the five stresses appear in full force, made large and dizzy by the long vowel sounds. They say, in effect, that from a human point of view an insistent order is equivalent to a chaos, and they are at the same time wondering, wonderful. In the last line we return to three stresses, the bearable rhythm, but we have already been made to hear the menace in the idea of order, so that last phrase, deliberate and random at once, leaves us with a deep and lingering uneasiness.

To speak of a sense of closure brings us to the third phase of rhythmic experience. Many things in the world have rhythms and many kinds of creatures seem to be moved by them but only human beings complete them. This last phase, the bringing of rhythmic interplay to a resolution, is the particular provenance of man as a maker. A rhythm is not a rhythmic form; in theory, at least, a rhythmic sequence, like some poetry readings, can go on forever, the only limits being the attention of the auditor and the endurance of the performer. Meter is that kind of sequence. The flow of blank verse suggests no natural stopping place of itself and most of the other metrical shapes, sonnets and the various stanzaic forms, are defined by their rhyme schemes. Daydream and hypnotic rhythm have it in common that their natural form is exhaustion. The resolution of rhythmic play, not just the coming down on one side or the other but the articulation of what ending feels like, is active making.

Think of the words you might want to use. *End:* to die. *Finish:* to be done with. *Conclude:* obligation over. *Complete:* to fulfill. *Consummate: really* to fulfill. *Close, terminate, arrive, leave off, release.* There are many senses of ending and they are drawn from our different experiences of it. There are rhythmic forms in nature—the day, a season, the life of a blossom. In human life, orgasm, the sentences in which we speak, falling asleep, the completion of tasks, the deaths we all see and the one death each of us must imagine. Many of our senses of ending are conventional—imagine the sound of a door opening: anticipation; of a door closing: finality. There are many possibilities of ending. In that way, each work of art is a three-line haiku. You go, I go—and the artist must provide the third line.

What hovers behind all this, I would guess, is a wish. Formally, the completion of a pattern imitates the satisfaction of a desire, a consummation, which is why orgasm is a preferred metaphor of conclusion. And because the material of poetry is language, it seems inevitable that an ending would also imitate the experience of insight. And because it is an ending, it will be death-obsessed. Sexual pleasure is a merging, a voluntary abandonment of the self; insight is a freeing, the central experience of our own originality. We don't know what death is. The wish behind the human play of artistic form is to know how these three are related: probably it is the hope that they are, or can be, the same thing. And there is another element to be added here, which belongs to the riddles of completion. When poet or reader listens through to the moment of resolution, it is over. The poet has not created until the thing is gone from his hands.

It's possible that what humans want from works of art are shapes of time in which the sense of coming to an end is also, as it very seldom is in the rest of life, a resolution. Hence the art formula common to television comedy and Wagner and the Shakespearean sonnet: tension, release; tension, release; tension, more tension, release. There is a large and familiar repertoire of formal techniques which produce this effect. It is probably a definition of a rigidifying art-practice that it has more answers than it has questions. In the early twentieth century, painting got rid of perspective, music of tonality, poetry of meter and rhyme so that they could tell what ending felt like again, and give it again the feel of making. It is this feeling of the made thing, of craft and of an event in time, that gives the poem— and the world—the feeling of historicity, of having been made by men, and therefore in movement, alive to our touch and to the possibility of change which the familiarity of convention is always deadening. The task is to listen to ourselves and make endings true enough to experience that they eliminate the ground for the old senses of completion or renew them.

So, there are three phases of the experience of rhythm: hearing it, developing it, bringing it to form. And real listening, like deep play, engages us in the issues of our lives. I want to look now at prosody, at ways of talking about how a rhythm is developed and brought to closure.

Some definitions. Metrical verse is a fixed pattern of stressed and unstressed syllables. In accentual verse, the number of strong stresses in a line is fixed, but the position of the stressed syllables is not and neither is the number or position of unstressed syllables. In free verse, neither the number nor the position of stressed and unstressed syllables is fixed. I have already remarked that meter is not the basis of rhythmic form. It is a way to determine the length of the line, but it is not, by itself, a way to shape a poem. For example, these lines by Yeats:

> When yóu aře óld aňd gréy aňd fúll ǒf sléep
> Aňd nóddiňg bý thě fíře, táke doẅn thĭs bóok,
> Aňd slówly̆ réad, aňd dréam ǒf thě sóft lóok
> Yoǔr eýes hǎd oňce, aňd óf thěir shádoẅs déep.

That is the metrical pattern. But what gives the passage the articulation of form is the pattern of pauses and stresses. It looks very different if we just indicate those:

> When you are OLD and GREY/ and FULL of SLEEP
> And NODding by the FIRE,/ TAKE DOWN this BOOK
> And SLOWly READ,/ and DREAM of the SOFT LOOK
> Your EYES HAD ONCE,/ and of their SHAdows DEEP.

It seems clear that the main function of the meter is to secure the lulling sound of the first line and a half. The sense of pattern is created by two- and three-stress phrases which tend to have thematic associations. The three-stress phrases, "take down this book," "dream of the soft look," "your eyes had once," carry the energy and urgency: the two-stress groups convey balance or resignation or fatality, "old and grey," "shadows deep." The three-stress phrase appears when it disrupts the balance of the first line and a half. The pattern looks like this:

$$2/2$$
$$2/3$$
$$2/3$$
$$3/2$$

The third line replays the theme; in the last line the pattern is reversed. Life and death, odd and even are the terms of play. Even, says the first line. Odd, says the second and third lines. Even, says the fourth line, rhyming with the idea that the shadows of desire in young eyes are the shadows of mortality.

In many modernist poems, technically metrical, the use of the effects of metrical rhythm is extraordinarily powerful—they feel hacked out, freshly made—but the metrical pattern as a whole counts for very little: the rhythmic articulation exists almost entirely in the pattern of stresses and pauses:

> Túrning and túrning in the wídening gýre
> The fálcon cánnot heár the fálconer;
> Thíngs fáll apárt; the céntre cánnot hóld;
> Mere ánarchy is loosed upon the world,
> The blóod-dimmed tide is loosed, and everywhere
> The ceremony of innocence is drówned;
> The bést lack áll convíction, while the wórst
> Are full of passionate inténsity.

It doesn't take a very refined analysis to see that this varies three- and four-stress phrases. If Yeats had written:

The blóod-dimmed tíde is loósed;
And everywhere the ceremony of innocence is drówned;
The bést láck áll convíction,
While the worst are full of passionate inténsity

the passage would not be less regular, but the sound has gone dead. The extra unstressed syllables in the second and fourth lines make them seem to sprawl out and the pattern of stresses feels leaden, fatal: 4,4,4,4. As it is, Yeats gets the fatality but also a sense of something broken, unbalanced: 4/1, 3; 4/1, 3. The inference to be drawn from this pattern is that at the level of form the difference between the strategies of free and metrical verse is not very great.

The difference lies, rather, in the stages of announcing and developing a rhythm. Every metrical poem announces a relationship to the idea of order at the outset, though the range of relationships to that idea it can suggest is immense. Free-verse poems do not commit themselves so soon to a particular order, but they are poems so they commit themselves to the idea of its possibility, and, as soon as recurrences begin to develop, an order begins to emerge. The difference is, in some ways, huge; the metrical poem begins with an assumption of human life which takes place in a pattern of orderly recurrence with which the poet must come to terms, the free-verse poem with an assumption of openness or chaos in which an order must be discovered. Another way to say this is to observe that most metrical poems, by establishing an order so quickly, move almost immediately from the stage of listening for an order to the stage of hearing it in dialogue with itself. They suppress animal attention in the rush to psychic magic and they do so by laying claim to art and the traditions of art at the beginning. The free-verse poem insists on the first stage of sensual attention, of possibility and emergence—which is one of the reasons why it has seemed fresher and more individual to the twentieth century. The prophetic poems of Yeats and the loose blank verse of the younger Eliot, by staying near to traditional prosodies, say in effect that there has been this order and it's falling apart, while Williams and the Pound of the *Cantos* say—to paraphrase

Robert Pinget—listen, there is no lost feast at the bottom of memory, invent.

The free-verse poem, by stripping away familiar patterns of recurrence and keeping options open, is able to address the forms of closure with the sense that there are multiple possibilities and that the poem has to find its way to the right one. Here is a simple example of how this might work. We can begin with a small poem of Whitman, "Farm Picture":

Through the ample open door of the peaceful country barn,
A sunlit pasture field with cattle and horses feeding.
And haze and vista, and the far horizon fading away.

As I hear it, there are six stresses in the first line, and a brief pause after "door"; in the second, six with a pause after "field"; in the third, six again with a pause marked by the comma. You could call this accentual verse. You could even argue that it's metrical, a relaxed mix of iambs and anapests. But that won't tell us why it feels complete. Notice the pattern:

> 3/3
> 3/3
> 2/4

The principle is that for a thing to be complete, it has to change. And the kind of change indicates how you feel about that fact. Suppose the poem ended "and haze and vista." It would be an ending and it would radically change the meaning of the poem. That is the possibility open to the poet who has not decided how many stresses each line should have. Let's look at the possible endings. They make four or five different poems:

Through the ample open door of the peaceful country barn,
A sunlit pasture field with cattle and horses feeding.
And haze, and vista.

Through the ample open door of the peaceful country barn,
A sunlit pasture field with cattle and horses feeding.
And haze and vista, and the far horizon.

Through the ample open door of the peaceful country barn,
A sunlit pasture field with cattle and horses feeding.
And haze and vista, and the far horizon fading.

Through the ample open door of the peaceful country barn,
A sunlit pasture field with cattle and horses feeding.
And haze and vista, and the far horizon fading away.

All of these poems seem to me plausible. Three of them,
at least, are interesting. The first poem is balanced: 3/3,
3/3, 1/1. To my ear, the last line is not excessively abrupt,
but it throws a terrific weight of disappointment or longing
onto what is not present, so that the balance of the last line,
thunk/thunk, seems an ironic echo of the amplitude of the
first two lines. (Though this hovers at the edge of something else because of that dialectical play in rhythm. A
little punctuation could make the poem feel like a gasp of
surprise such as Dr. Williams might feel:

Through the ample open door of the peaceful country barn,
A sunlit pasture field with cattle and horses feeding.
And haze, and vista!)

The second poem is also balanced: 3/3, 3/3, 2/2. It feels to
me too much so. If there is such a thing as sentimental
form, this is sentimental form. It invokes the idea of horizon, but prettily, so that there is no tension between the
solidity of the barnyard and the hazy vista. It is like bad

genre painting, nothing is problematic; distance is pretty, closeness is pretty. The third poem is unbalanced: 3/3, 3/3,2/3. The extra stress seems to evoke the asymmetry of what fades away and is lost. Three-stress phrases usually feel more open than two-stress phrases. (I think of Leonard Bernstein's remark: two is the rhythm of the body, three is the rhythm of the mind.) The first lines, two sets of three, reconcile those two rhythms, openness and the earth. The third line says unh-uh. We have to let go of the horizon in return for the presence and solidity of the earth. It is a melancholy poem. Whitman's poem is also balanced, but it contains the asymmetrical 2/4 line. Its feeling is most inclusive. The odd rhyme of "feeding" and "fading," which is an aspect of the theme of presence and absence, is muted and, though we take note of what is lost on the horizon, the rhythm is willing to include that loss in the solidity and presence of the scene.

The point of this should be obvious. All four, or five, poems say different things. A poet in a poem is searching for the one thing to be said, or the many things to be said one way. As soon as we start talking about alternative possibilities of form, we find ourselves talking about alternative contents. It is exactly here that the truism about the indissolubility of content and form acquires its meaning. The search for meaning in the content and shape in the rhythm are simultaneous, equivalent. That's why it doesn't matter too much which a writer attends to in composition, because the process attends to both. It is possible—the testimony on this seems pretty general—to pay attention consciously to one or the other exclusively; more often, writers experience a continual shifting back and forth between formal problems and problems of content, carrying the work forward at whichever level it wants to move. In the long run, though, no work can be alive, intelligent, imaginatively open, intense, at one level and not the other.

It should be clear by now that free-verse rhythm is not a
movement between pattern and absence of pattern, but
between phrases based on odd and even numbers of stresses:

I loáf and invíte my sóul,
I leán and loáf at my eáse, obseŕving a spéar of súm-
    mer graśs.

Three stresses in the first line, seven in the second with a
strong pause after *ease*. The pattern is 3, 3/4. The first two
clauses are almost equivalent. *I loaf and invite my soul*.
Then, *I lean and loaf at my ease*. Had he written *observing
a spear of grass,* all three phrases would be nearly equivalent and they would begin to build tension; instead he adds
summer, the leaning and loafing season, and announces
both at the level of sound and of content that this poem is
going to be free and easy.

The line comes into this and so does the stanza. It is with
them that we approach Pound's definition of rhythm, a
form carved in time, and Williams' notion of the variable
foot. Talking about the line as a "beat," as everyone who
has struggled with the idea has been compelled to admit,
doesn't make much sense if you are thinking of stress. But
looked at from the point of view of rhythm as I've tried to
describe it, I think it does. The metrical line proposes a
relationship to order. So does a three- or four-line stanza.
Imagine, it says, a movement through pattern. The stanza
is a formal proposal, Apollonian and clear. In this, it says,
I want to catch light or court a shaping spirit. Look at these
lines from Louis Zukofsky's "4 Other Countries":

La Gloire in the black	2
flags of the valley	2
of the	-
Loire	1

A lavender plough	2
in Windermere	1
The French blue	2
door	1
Of a gray	1
stone	1
house in	1
Angers	1
Walled farms	2
little lanes	2
of entry, orange-	2
red roofs	2

The rhythm of this passage is based on the strong three-beat phrase: *lavender plough in Windermere, French blue door, gray stone house, little lanes of entry, orange-red roofs;* it doesn't appear in the notation of the rhythm because Zukofsky has broken it across the line, everywhere, into units of one or two stresses and passed the whole through the balanced proposal of the four-line stanza. Three here is the beat of the bodily world and it is resisted and shaped otherwise by the rhythm the poet cuts in time, in imitation, I think, of the perceptions of travel. At the level of content it is straightforward description but it is given the quality of insight because the aural and visual imaginations are so freshly and attentively at work. The line, when a poem is alive in its sound, measures: it is a proposal about listening.

It should be fairly easy to turn now to a poem like Gary Snyder's "August on Sourdough" and listen to what's going on. The first thing to notice about it is that it is made from paired lines or half-lines which imitate and underscore its theme. *You hitched a thousand miles,* then *north from San Francisco; hiked up the mountainside,* then *a mile in the air.* Sets of two. The one break in this pattern comes in the next pair of lines: *the little cabin—one room—walled in glass.* A set of three with the poem's place of communion at its center. Two and three. You go, I go, what is the upshot? It is, when we look at the pattern of stresses, a transformation of the two stress rhythms into three stress rhythms:

YOU HITCHED a THOUsand MILES
        NORTH from SAN FranCISco
HIKED up the MOUNtainside   a MILE in the AIR
The LITtle CABin—ONE ROOM—
        WALLED in GLASS
MEAdows and SNOWfields,   HUNdreds of PEAKS.

Stress is relative and I have marked what I hear as the main stresses. The pattern looks like this:

$$
\begin{array}{c}
4 \\
3 \\
2/2 \\
2/2 \\
2 \\
2/2
\end{array}
$$

The base rhythm is the paired two-stress phrases. The variation comes in the one three-stress phrase and in the set of three two-stress phrases. The paired phrases with a pause in between insist on twoness, on the separateness of the two friends. There is just enough variety to convey a sense of movement, and the overall effect is balanced, relaxed. It is very deft work.

We LAY in our SLEEPing BAGS
        TALKing HALF the NIGHT;
WIND in the GUY CABLES   SUMmer MOUNtain
  RAIN.

This is the interlude in which the images and rhythm speak
of the communion of friends. It is a quiet expansion from
two- to three-stress phrases, and a different balance:

3

3

3/3

And then the parting:

NEXT MORNing I WENT WITH you
        as FAR as the CLIFFS,
LOANED you my PONCHo—   the RAIN aCROSS
  the SHALE—
YOU DOWN the SNOWfield
        FLAPping in the WIND
WAVing a LAST GoodBYE'   HALF-HIDden in
  the CLOUDS
To GO ON HITCHing   CLEAR to NEW YORK:
ME BACK to my MOUNtain   and FAR, FAR, WEST.

This is a more intricate restatement of the play between
two and three stresses, but it ends emphatically with a
rhythm based on threes. Two is an exchange, three is a
circle of energy, Lewis Hyde has said, talking about eco-
nomics. I would mark the primary pattern like this:

4

2

2/3

3/2

3/3
3/3
3/3

and that last phrase is carefully punctuated to sing it out: 1/1/1. It insists, finally on a rhythmic pairing of open three-stress elements. This is, formally, the solution it offers to the problems of identity and separation in partings and— as we've seen—in ending poems.

The articulation of rhythmic form, though, doesn't indicate what are for me the small miracles of feeling in the rhythm throughout. There are at least three musical phrases in the poem that are announced and then transmuted. One of them is *a mile in the air* which is echoed in *hundreds of peaks* and again in *as far as the cliffs,* and then changed to a three-stress cadence in *clear to New York.* (NEW YORK is a West Coast pronunciation of N'York—the emphatic *new* is a celebration of movement.) In the same way, *meadows and snowfields,* a playful pair of falling rhythms— MEAdows, SNOWfields—like the falling rhythms of nursery rhymes, Bobbie Shaftoe, Humpty Dumpty, is repeated in *loaned you my poncho* so that it has become a memory of playful reciprocity, and then it is transformed by the urgency of movement into *you down the snowfield.* Most brilliant and moving to me is the sudden iambic phrase, *the rain across the shale.* It is suggested in the first line, *you hitched a thousand miles,* echoed in *talking half the night* and *summer mountain rain.* And then, clearly, the old orderliness of iambic meter rises up to make us feel an order of nature older than us and steadier in which our comings and goings mean very little. "Hailstorm on the rocks at Stony Pass," Basho said. "The rain it raineth every day," Shakespeare said. "Rocks and stones and trees," said Wordsworth. The juxtaposition of rhythms and orders, *loaned you my poncho, the rain across the shale,* before the poem's open windy farewell is a lyrical hesitation, a moment of hearing really astonishing, I think, in its warmth, sharp pathos, and clear intelligence:

> Loaned you my poncho   the rain across the shale
> You down the snowfield . . .

It recapitulates the two worlds the poem speaks of, the little one, one room, walled in glass, and the big one, half-hidden in the clouds.

The freshness and life of this poem is not uncommon in the work of the 1950s when the younger poets were writing in the teeth of an institutionalized and deadening metrical facility. It was in those years, somewhere, that William Carlos Williams delivered a lecture to Theodore Roethke's students at the University of Washington, "The Poem as a Field of Action." "Imagism," he told them, "was not structural: that was the reason for its disappearance. . . . You can put it down as a general rule that when a poet, in the broadest sense, begins to devote himself to the *subject matter* of his poems, *genre,* he has come to the end of his poetic means." There is a wonderful sense of momentum in his talk and it is hard not to feel, though almost everyone writing now would claim him as a master, that that momentum has been lost. I think he identifies the symptom. Almost all the talk about poetry in the past few years has focused on issues of image and diction. There was a liveliness in the idea of hauling deep and surreal imagery into American poetry, but the deep image is no more structural than imagism: there was hardly any sense of what the rhythmic ground might be. Hence, stuff like this:

He played banana drums and dreamed of felt.
He discerned a tin angel in a caulking gun.
His bounced checks and their imaginative *noms de plume*
Glittered in the cash registers of abandoned motels.

etc. Five beats to the line. The imagery is unusual enough; the rhythm is absolutely conventional. The counterattack on this kind of writing has been that it should have a different content. So we have gotten an aggressive return to the conscious mind:

Pets are a creation of the industrial revolution.
And so is 'projective identification.'
You feed the useless animal to remind you of animals
While the terminology of relationship is elaborated.

One of these is writhing rebelliousness in the face of terminal ennui, the other is ironic intelligence in the face of same. The ennui is expressed by the simple, orderly, conformist, free-verse rhythms; that is the main message, and it can't be talked about if poetry is a matter of kinds of imagery and kinds of diction. Way below the content of a particular poem, the idea that rhythm is natural, bodily, spontaneous, has been transformed into the idea that it is simply a given, invisible or inevitable. What this expresses is a kind of spiritual death that follows from living in a world we feel we have no hope of changing.

I have it in mind that, during the Vietnam war, one of the inventions of American technology was a small anti-personnel bomb that contained sharp fragments of plastic which, having torn through the flesh and lodged in the body, could not be found by an X-ray. Often I just think about the fact that some person created it. At other times I have thought about the fact that the bomb works on people just the way the rhythms of poetry do. And it seems to me then that there really are technes on the side of life and technes on the side of death. Durable and life-giving human inventions—tragedy, restaurants that stay open late at night, holding hands, the edible artichoke—were probably half discovered and half invented from the materials the world makes available, but I think that they were also the result of an active and attentive capacity for creation that humans have, and that a poetry that makes fresh and resilient forms extends the possibilities of being alive.

(Antaeus)

Amy Herrick
Outerspace

O NE SATURDAY AFTERNOON ROBIN CALLS AND
says that her parents have been run over by a truck.
Sarah says that she will be there in a few minutes.
She bicycles down the middle of the street between heaps
of snow. The air is the color of gold. The trip should be
ordinary; she's made it hundreds of times. But everything,
let alone the fact that Robin claims her parents are dead,
is more and more unusual and beyond a simple explanation. She whizzes through the air, held aloft on a little
heartshaped seat by two spinning wheels, while dogs walk
past sporting hilarious coats. The street is filled, is running wild down to the vanishing point, with light and reflections of light.

At Robin's house, Robin's mother, Selma, opens the door
and guides and pokes her into the kitchen. Selma picks up
an apple and a banana. "It's murder," she says to Sarah
and looks up through the ceiling into Robin's room. "You
want to know what it is now? She says I should get ready.
She says she's going to get married."

Sarah puts her hands into her jacket pockets. Her pockets are filled with Di-Gel crumbs, bobby pins, used tissues,
bus transfers, peanuts, movie ticket stubs. She is amazed
at these evidences that she has had a past, at the idea of
time passing, of how sweet and imprecise a process it is,
that it could ever arrive at a point where Robin could succeed in annoying her mother by threats of marriage.

"Have an apple."

"No thank you."

"Well, have a banana."

"No, no thanks."

Selma sorrows over the fruit in her hands then looks again at Sarah. "Some salted almonds maybe? What's going to happen to you? You're so skinny. You'll vanish. Maybe you'd like some mother's tears. I have a whole pitcher in the refrigerator from all the grief that kid gave me this morning."

"Selma, you're a real card. Where is she? Is she upstairs?"

"Listen, you're going to go up and see her? Do me a favor. Ask her to go and visit her grandmother in the home. That's all I ask. It's not a big thing."

In Robin's room, Robin is asleep with her long dark hair fanned out across the pink bedspread. She is partially curled up like a huge shrimp. Between the top of her blue jeans and the hem of her shirt an area of soft white skin is exposed and the knobs of her big spine stick out. Sarah runs a fingernail down the bone until Robin turns her head and squints at her.

In this year they seem to understand each other perfectly. They barely need to talk. Wishing to make a point when they are in a crowd or with odious schoolmates or with Robin's parents, they need only look across at each other or turn a palm up or say a word.

The room is hot and still. Robin closes her eyes again and pulls out her lower lip.

"You'll spoil your appearance."

She lets go of her lip, but makes no answer.

"Your parents aren't dead," Sarah says.

Robin smiles. "It doesn't matter. I've decided that by the time we start college in September, I'll be married. It's February now so that gives me roughly six months."

The word *February* lies like a fairy's egg on Sarah's tongue, full of black seeds. She knows Robin to be a liar, but also very strongminded. Sarah is so nervous she could fly. She is looking for some ordinary fact to keep her in place.

"One solid fact, a true thing that you could say out loud, one little bell ringer, and then we could work forward from that and reconstruct the whole world," Robin says. She gets up and stretches and walks over to the window. "I wonder where outerspace begins."

"Should we work?" Sarah asks. "You wanna do some homework? It'll make Selma feel better."

"What's going to make Selma feel better is when she gets to drink some of my blood."

"You misinterpret her. You haven't got the right distance. She has a cuteness."

"Selma is a very, very heavy lady. Make no mistake. It's going to be her or it's going to be me."

"She's your mother. She's helpless in the face of it. She's training you for the big time."

"She's from outerspace. She's listening at the door right now."

"Ah no, Robin."

Sarah gets up and opens the door and Selma is standing there, innocently holding a pile of folded towels. "Laundry," she says. Sarah smiles at her pleasantly and closes the door.

"She washes the fruit with soap. I came downstairs the other day and there she was at the sink washing the fruit with a bar of soap. All right, listen, I'll go try to find some pencils and we'll do some math."

After Robin has left the room Sarah takes off her shoes and socks and goes over to the window and opens it up and the room gets very quiet. Suddenly first one and then another flash of white light flashes past her left ear. A sharp draft makes her shiver and she closes the window. A very wild, unfamiliar smell fills the room, something like licorice. Nervously she turns around to see what's behind her.

Obviously something from outerspace. Two pale blue, ball-shaped things are sitting on the carpet, one slightly larger than the other. They seem to be soft and porous like sponges. When they begin to roll around Sarah jumps up on the bed. They smell sweet and excited, actually very lovely. The smell gets stronger and stronger, wilder and wilder. They are about the size of laundry bags. They roll up and down the length of the room and then one hops onto the chair and then onto the desk. It rolls over to a wedge of lemon which is sitting beside an empty cup and saucer. In a second the other one is beside it and they are both sitting there attentively. The bigger one rocks slowly back and forth in meditation while the smaller one sits perfectly still. Suddenly the room begins to fill with something approximating the smell of lemons. Sarah's eyes smart and water although the smell is actually lighter than the odor of lemons, more complicated and faster. After a while this storm of lemons passes and the two blue balls roll over to the edge of the desk and drop onto the floor. They bounce a couple of times and come to a rest. Sarah feels that they are disappointed. The wild licorice smell is almost gone. Sarah tries to think what to do, but just then the smaller one gathers itself up for a big roll and bounces onto the foot of the bed. Sarah scurries up towards the pillow, her heart pounding in her ears. The ball follows her jauntily and comes to rest on one of her bare feet.

"Dear God," she thinks.

The thing is surprisingly light as if it were mostly air. The texture of it is silky. It doesn't feel bad on her foot. She stands extremely still hoping that it will not notice that she is alive. Almost immediately it begins to give off its weird, agitated, licorice smell again. The big ball takes a big roll, bounces onto the bed, and comes up and sits on her other foot. It, too, is excited. In a little while Sarah begins to detect subtle variations in the odor of each one. The smell of one gets stronger or higher or lower or a peculiar herbal fragrance comes and goes. And then the smell of the other gets weaker or lower or tinged with oregano. The courses of the two smells are running in a kind of counterpoint to each other. And then suddenly, how embarrassing, Sarah begins to smell her feet. The odor gets stronger and stronger and she just stands there feeling mortified until she realizes what is happening. The two of them are *imitating* the odor of her feet. They're trying to speak to her.

"Hey!" she says in protest and at the sound of her voice the spell of her feet is broken. For a moment the air is clear as a bell. Then two very distinct whiffs of terror pour from the aliens and they roll madly towards the window.

She jumps down from the bed and walks over towards them. They throw themselves wildly against the glass. A terrible smell of desperation and fear fills the room. When she tries to speak to them, the sound of her voice only frightens them more. Tears come into her eyes. She reaches forward gently and opens the window. The two light, light balls fling themselves out into the air and are picked up by a breeze. They revolve slowly upwards, obviously making for the sky.

"The trouble I am having," she tells Robin one day, "is that no one thing seems more particularly amazing than any other thing. I have absolutely no perspective. If the saucers from my coffee cups start flying around the room I am no more amazed than if somebody stops in the middle of the sidewalk and pulls up his socks. Everything is so dazzling."

They are lying in the grass in the early spring. The front of her, the part facing the sun, is warm. "What if the sun just suddenly exploded while we were lying here?" she suggests.

"What—that little thing?"

Here a big, purple, helium balloon with white stripes, carrying a basket, disentangles itself from out of the branches of a tree and swims into the clear blue arena of sky. Sarah gasps in astonishment, but Robin rakes her hand tragically through her black hair and states that nothing ever happens. Then she pulls out her lower lip and broods.

Sarah stares at her enchanted. How can anyone with their hair all stuck up around their head and their lip pulled out four inches still look so beautiful? "We have the whole summer coming to us and then college."

"The summer is the worst time. My mother knows no bounds. She has her nose in everything. She guesses everything."

"What does she guess?"

"Nothing. There's nothing to guess."

Sarah loves to listen to her. She could listen to her forever.

"Sarah, stop that. Stop appreciating me."

Sarah laughs.

"Let's do something."

Sarah would prefer to lie here in the grass for a long time and attempt to digest things.

"We'll be dead soon," Robin says admonishingly. "Plenty of people are dead right now."

Sarah puts her hands over her eyes for a moment. "Never leave me," she says. When she takes her hands away, the balloon is nearly overhead. Someone is watching them through binoculars.

"Imagine being burnt at the stake. Imagine how painful it would be," Robin suggests.

"If it happens to you just breathe really hard. The smoke will kill you fast and you won't feel a thing."

"It won't happen to me. Nothing exciting ever does happen to me."

"Listen, we better get out of here. That balloon is coming this way."

"What?"

"Come on."

Sarah forces her up and convinces her to climb into a nearby tree. It's one they've been up in before. Its leaves are still small, but there are thousands of them and they are sensitive and stiff at the girls' interruption. Once they are seated in the top, however, things calm down. They are inside the tree. It holds them in a strange jelly of yellow light. Sarah looks out over the tips of the other trees. The whole spring rests in the air between them like an elephant magically held aloft.

The balloon descends slowly and settles in the grass. A young man throws out an anchor and leaps over the side onto the earth and starts coming in their direction. When he gets to the spot where they had been lying in the grass he stops and looks all around him. He doesn't look up, but wanders over to the tree where they are hiding and stands right beneath them, chewing gum and humming a popular tune.

"Shhhh," Sarah cautions Robin, but Robin pulls a saltine out of her pocket and drops it onto the young man's head.

"Hey," Sarah protests, but in a moment he is snaking up the trunk and before they know it he has one foot in a low branch and he is flailing about for a place to grab hold. All the leaves are shaking and rustling and then the young man is crouched in a branch below them with sinister, doll-blue eyes.

Sarah doesn't like his looks. "Get out of this tree. This is our tree. Goodbye."

"You dropped a saltine on my head." He has a tiny, blonde mustache.

"A gift. Not an invitation. Get down, young man," Sarah says.

He looks at Robin and Sarah looks at her too. Robin's face has taken on new planes of thought and sneakiness.

It is swamped with afternoon light coming through the branches. "Young man, you've got a lot of nerve coming up here like this," she says. His smile is immediate, melancholy. She's warming him up somehow. "Young man, this is a private tree. You've got to go. It's nothing personal." She opens up her palms apologetically as if they were full of tiny, ripe bombs she had just picked.

"But I'm a tree surgeon," he says, pretending to be shy. "I had a phone call about this tree."

"No," she says to him, all sorrow and tenderness. "This tree is perfect."

"Perfect?" he whispers and looks around. Sarah looks around too and finds herself stopped by the individual force of each leaf, each fragment of sky between the leaves. The tree is full, like a cup, green and yellow. For a moment even this young man doesn't look bad, but hangs in the tree shining and looking at them longingly. Robin is tugging on her lip, all nerves. She is examining him as if she had made him herself.

Out of nothing everything becomes so beautiful sometimes, Sarah thinks, but then the young man says, "Would either of you like a foot rub?"

"Oh, go away," Sarah says, completely exasperated.

"You're tense," he says moving towards her foot.

She jerks it away. "GET THE HELL OUT OF THIS TREE."

The young man looks at Robin and she shrugs her shoulders. He climbs down the tree and drops to the ground and walks away.

"You wanted him to stay," Sarah says to Robin.

"I don't believe you're saying that to me. How can you say that to me?"

"You're the most incredible liar and deceiver."

Robin bows her head and smiles.

Sarah stays to dinner one night at Robin's house. Selma insinuates herself into every possible part of the kitchen. The plates, the bread, the meat, the broccoli fly through the air. Robin's father sits at a far end of the table, pleasantly quiet, and seems to dream. Robin and Selma keep a careful eye on him. At last everything comes to rest and Robin's mother sits down, the stones in the points of her eyeglasses gleaming and flickering.

In a while Robin's father makes a mistake. Having been eating an olive and having finished chewing and swallowing its meat, he decides recklessly to keep the pit in his mouth for a little extra time and suck on it. Selma notices this immediately and orders him to spit it out.

"Spit that out, Edward, before it gets stuck in your gullet and you choke to death."

Robin flushes angrily. "Leave him alone, mother, he's a grown man."

"A grown man, maybe, but a very absentminded type of person."

In shame and confusion Robin's father bends his head over his hand and spits out the pit. Selma extends a small, empty dish and Robin's father drops the pit into it submissively. Selma slides the dish to her side of the table.

"So any handsome ones, Sarah?"

"Handsome whats?"

"Handsome boyfriends."

"Who said anything about boyfriends?"

Robin's father seems to resume his dreaming easily. He takes a bite and chews it and chews it.

"There's more to life than being handsome, mother."

"No kidding. I think I know that."

Robin's father seems to catch some words accidentally as if they were feathers that had just drifted down from somewhere and gotten caught in his hair. He looks around and stares at them. Sarah finds herself also caught up in the suspense.

"I'm glad to know that you realize looks are not so important," he says to Robin.

Sarah gets the distinct impression that they are all small children at a tea party.

Robin's mother pulls out her lower lip sulkily.

"Don't, mother, you'll spoil your appearance and then who will kiss you?"

"Are you going to visit your grandmother tomorrow?"

"Tomorrow I can't."

"And why can't you?"

"Because Sarah and I have to study for a history exam." Which is the first Sarah has heard of it.

"Don't you understand that your grandmother is dying?"

"We're all dying."

"You're so smart." Selma beings to weep.

"Oh, mother, she's not dying yet, she's just old. And anyway she doesn't even recognize me when I go to visit her."

"And when she's dead tomorrow then what will you say?"

"She won't be. But I promise you that I will go on Sunday."

They look to Robin's father for a judgment, but he's dreaming. His hands lie still upon the table, his food mostly untouched. He's gone away, gone down a rabbit hole, smiling gently into the air.

One morning Sarah sits up and squints out the window. The summer sits on people's heads like big old-fashioned hats. Men, on their way to work, appear to bear haberdashery trimmed with birds, spangles, flowers, feathers, and thin veils. The light is as substantial as a thin rain. It runs down the gutters into the drains in small streams. Crouching children sail twigs and paper boats in it.

By the time she gets downstairs the light has broken into the kitchen; windows have all been flung open; doors flap mysteriously on their hinges in the still air. No one else is around. She is light-headed with hunger, but cannot eat anything. Everything she touches turns to gold. Flowers swill noisily in the garden beneath the window. Robin appears in the doorway backed up by the sweet, droning, buzzing noise of bees carousing.

"Thank God you're here," Sarah says. "It's murder."

"You're my best friend," Robin says, ignoring her.

"Don't say that. What a terrible thing to say. Look me in the eye."

Robin's eyes are all ready to trip people up. The green iris is much too big and flickers with little, glinting, yellow specks like banana peels in the distance. "You've got to cover for me. I'm counting on you. Don't ask me to explain."

"No need to explain," Sarah says miserably.

"I want you to go away somewhere where you won't be recognized. Come back in a couple of hours. Then if anybody asks you tell them you went to the nursing home with me to visit my grandmother and that's what you tell my mother the next time you see her."

"I don't want to."

"It doesn't matter. You'll do it out of loyalty to me."

"Is he handsome?"

"No, no. Very ugly." She opens her arms up wide so that they can both easily imagine how rare it is in the vast heavens around them to find a really magnificent and true ugliness.

Sarah goes out into the park with a book under her arm. Strolling, trying to act casual, she conceals herself in some bushes. She tries to remember if summer has been like this before. A dog sniffs her out and sits down with her amicably. She stares at him in amazement. Surely a dog is just as wild a thought as sponges from outerspace. The dog is spangled green and gold from the light coming through the bushes. She longs to take something for granted. She holds out her bare foot and the dog comes forward sweetly and smells it with great care until a kind of mutual ecstasy is attained. All of her bare skin is twelve times awake; the light, the imperceptible wind, the startling cold dog nose slide over her like thousands of tiny trolley cars.

One day, towards the end of summer, they approach Robin's house and great billows of smoke fill the air.

"A fire," Sarah says. "Someone's house is on fire."

"I know. It's mine. I set fire to the curtains before we left."

"You couldn't have."

Fire engines fly by. One, two, three, four. Firemen cling tightly to the sides, dressed in raincoats and rubber boots, ready for rain. One by one the engines go down into a big pothole and spring out of it, winged and clattering. A fireman's hat flies off. From out of nowhere knots of running children appear. The clamor of sirens and high voices goes up and up into the bright, stretching, blue sky. Sarah smells something burning.

"I couldn't take it anymore. Now my father will not be able to wander into the livingroom anymore to stare at me sentimentally. I've had it. My mother believes in war."

"You can't just burn people's houses down. You have to show them. You have to talk to them."

"Oh no, you don't understand. I had to do it."

"Oh no, I do understand. I understand you perfectly, you goofball, remember?"

They round the corner to Robin's block. The smoke pours from someone else's kitchen window down the street. The fire trucks are parked hastily, giving everything a festive air. The hedges are thick with little, glossy red berries. Adults wait straight up and down with their arms folded while the children, in another plane, lower down, fool around, zoom in and out of legs. Buoyant with ladders and axes, the whole fire department surrounds the house, until at last a fireman, perhaps the chief, breaks in the front door and the crowd lets out a single sigh. Other firemen rush in and then finally one reappears holding aloft a pot that had been left burning on the stove. The children begin to throw the red berries at one another and one child proudly wears the fire hat that blew away.

To the wedding Sarah wears a yellow dress. It happens early in the morning on a clear, amberous, late summer day.

Afterwards they all descend to a huge dining room to eat and dance. She is seated at the bride's table and watches Robin cautiously. Sarah has lugged up with her out of childhood many explanations for things and today she tries some here and tries some there, but none seems to go. Robin is dressed in white and is horribly pale. She keeps drinking the sweet wine and pays no attention when some-one lets doves go from a wicker cage. "Nice looking boy," people whisper of the groom and when he asks her to dance, Sarah, witless, embarrassed, full of intimations of her own perpetual lack of poise, accepts. She tries to ignore his sinister, doll-blue eyes and tiny, gold mustache while they twirl clumsily around and around.

"Relax," he says.

"What are you saying? How can you say such a thing?"

"It's easy," he says. "Watch how I do it. I'll say it again. Watch." He mouths the word slowly.

"Do you know what you've done? She's very, very diffi-cult."

"The moment I saw her in that tree, I knew she was the one."

"In trees, well yeah. But you have to see the thing in a broader perspective."

"She has only the nicest things to say about you."

She stares at him in disgust. Prig. Murderer.

"Take it easy. What you need is a good massage and your

back cracked." He pokes at her spine.

"Don't."

They continue to dance, looking over from time to time at Robin who seems a distant point traveling slowly and constantly away from them into outerspace.

When they sit down she is gone. Sarah eats another piece of white wedding cake slowly, swallowing the little silver balls whole. Suddenly Selma appears from behind a great pink and white bowl of chrysanthemums and says, "Robin is asking for you. She wasn't feeling well and is across the hall lying down."

She is lying down on the floor with her face over a waste-paper basket, throwing up. Sarah falls on her knees beside her and holds back her damp dark hair. In the sun a pleasant musty smell rises from the carpet. Robin groans and asks for a tissue. When she has wiped her mouth she asks Sarah if she will ever forgive her.

"For what?" Sarah asks stiffly and Robin ignores her and says, "And will you always be my friend?"

"You know that I will."

"Do you still love me?"

"Yes."

Robin groans and throws up again. Afterwards Sarah stretches out on the carpet beside her and they lie quietly for a while listening to the accordion music from across the hall.

Sarah cannot begin to imagine getting married. If lying here in the sun she tries it on for size, it hangs hugely about her, white and, in its stiff folds, giving off a fragrance she has never smelled before.

"I cannot imagine how you could have done this."

"Done what?"

"Gotten married. I mean even come close to considering it. What a perfect act of imagination. You must have your reasons. Did you tell me? I think about it and I can hardly breathe. It's so amazing." This is not what Sarah wished to say.

Robin turns on her furiously and says, "Will you stop telling me how damn amazing everything is! Everything is not so damn amazing. Getting married is a perfectly ordinary thing to do." Robin groans and turns away to weep into the carpet.

Do they understand each other perfectly? Do they hardly need to speak? When Robin's new husband enters the room full of concern, Sarah leaves quietly.

Robin has gone to the Poconos for her honeymoon. Sarah will soon be leaving for college. One night she has a brief visit from the sponges who draw her to her open window by perfectly imitating the smell of blue cheese. They are sitting in the big elm like nightingales and once they have her attention they switch to something sweeter, an unrecognizable smell, planetary, which suggests that they are glad to see her and would like to repay her for her previous kindness. She is careful not to speak, not to make any noise that will frighten them. She leans her elbows upon the window sill and examines the night sky. She briefly considers asking them to murder Robin's new husband, but discards the thought casually. Instead, as an answer, a greeting, she holds out an old, souvenir balsam pillow from Cape Cod and the smaller sponge hops over to the window and tugs it gently out of her hand with a tiny, blue paw which she hadn't noticed before. There is no need to say a word. The sponge takes off into the sky followed by the bigger one. Both look blue and edible against the white moon.

The next day she goes to visit Robin's grandmother. An attendant points out an old lady sitting with a tangle of purple yarn in her lap. She is trying to wind it up, but is only making it worse. Sarah sits down next to her quietly and introduces herself. "Hello, Mrs Binder, I'm Robin's friend, Sarah."

"This is murder," the old woman says without looking up.

The air is pungent, composed of many smells.

"I brought you some flowers, Mrs Binder."

"Don't exaggerate." She eyes the flowers from the side of her head like a bird.

Sarah brings the flowers back to herself uncertainly. "I'm a friend of your granddaughter's, Mrs Binder. A friend of Robin's."

The old woman turns to her at last, but is unable to find her and looks instead at something farther away, something long ago and suspended in the air. "Hello," she says and smiles. The smile is a big success, drawing attention to her big ears and a papery white light behind her skin. Oldness, Sarah thinks. The ball of yarn lies still in the old lady's lap. "My friend Eleanor?" she asks.

"No, Mrs Binder, my name is Sarah."

"Come here," she says.

Sarah gets right up out of the chair and kneels down in front of the old lady.

"Why did you come?"

"Your granddaughter Robin has just gotten married and couldn't visit you herself because she is on her honeymoon. I came in her place."

"Liar."

The flowers whisper in Sarah's lap. She looks around the room for some real horror, for some proof of the brevity of life and its underlying mortal ordinariness.

"Nevermind." Mrs Binder holds out her hand imperiously. Her hand is small, strong, bluish, and dirty. The little gold wedding band looks out of place to Sarah, from another world. She puts the flowers in her arms. Robin's grandmother brings them up to her face so hard she knocks some petals off and they flutter into her lap with the yarn. She looks at Sarah over her bouquet coquettishly. "You're a sweet one. Always were." Her whole body trembles with laughter and she strains downwards to kiss the kneeling Sarah. Sarah stretches up to help her. The kiss slips uncer tainly off her chin.

"Here, let me help you with this," Sarah says and takes the yarn from the old lady's lap and sits down with it. "Robin will be back on Sunday," Sarah says as she winds.

"Onions?"

"No. Sunday."

"Delicious."

An old man rises from his chair and floats over to them. He looks at Sarah and his face breaks up into a big smile, another big deal. "Hello! Hello! I haven't seen you in about a hundred years."

"Give him two dollars," Robin's grandmother whispers.

Sarah touches him timidly on the shoulder and he floats away again easily.

Now Sarah tries one more time. She looks around the room bravely. A tiny lady in a wheelchair looks at her and begins to sing a scale of notes. "One, two, three, four, five!" She sings like a bird inside a hedge.

"Listen, Eleanor," Robin's grandmother whispers, "we've got to make a plan."

Sarah looks at her and draws her breath in sharply. Mrs Binder is pulling her lower lip out thoughtfully while she tries to come up with a plan. Everything, Sarah thinks in amazement, is ordinary. No matter fails to shed light on any other matter or fails to bear resemblance to any other thing you might remember or dream of.

The old lady lets go of her lip and takes Sarah's hand. "You've always been my best friend, Eleanor." She looks into Sarah's eyes. "Let's meet in Asbury Park at three. And wear your blue coat. It's your best color."

Sarah agrees to Asbury Park at three. She finishes winding up the ball of wool and places it in the old lady's lap with the flowers.

When her mother takes her to buy a winter coat, she se-
lects a blue one. She wears it all that first year around
campus, shedding as much light on things as she is able,
looking her best.

(The Kenyon Review)

Denis Johnson
The Incognito Lounge

The manager lady of this
apartment dwelling has a face
like a baseball with glasses and pathetically
repeats herself. The man next door
has a dog with a face that talks
of stupidity to the night, the swimming pool
has an empty, empty face.
My neighbor has his underwear on
tonight, standing among the parking spaces
advising his friend never to show
his face around here again.
I go everywhere with my eyes closed and two
eyeballs painted on my face. There is a woman
across the court with no face at all.

*

They're perfectly visible this evening,
about as unobtrusive as a storm of meteors,
these questions of happiness
plaguing the world.
My neighbor has sent his child to Utah
to be raised by the relatives of friends.
He's out on the generous lawn
again, looking like he's made
out of phosphorus.

*

The manager lady has just returned
from the nearby graveyard, the last
ceremony for a crushed paramedic.
All day, news helicopters cruised aloft
going whatwhatwhatwhatwhat.

She pours me some boiled
coffee that tastes like noise,
warning me, once and for all,
to pack up my troubles in an old kit bag
and weep until the stones float away.
How will I ever be able to turn
from the window and feel love for her?—
to see her and stop seeing
this neighborhood, the towns of earth,
these tables at which the saints
sit down to the meal of temptations?

*

And so on—nap, soup, window,
say a few words into the telephone,
smaller and smaller words.
Some TV or maybe, I don't know, a brisk
rubber with cards nobody knows
how many there are of.
Couple of miserable gerbils
in a tiny white cage, hysterical
friends rodomontading about goals
as if having them liquefied death.
Maybe invite the lady with no face
over here to explain all these elections:
life. Liberty. Pursuit.

*

Maybe invite the lady with no face
over here to read my palm,
sit out on the porch here in Arizona
while she touches me.
Last night, some kind
of alarm went off up the street
that nobody responded to.
Small darling, it rang for you.
Everything suffers invisibly,
nothing is possible, in your face.

The center of the world is closed.
The Beehive, the 8-Ball, the Yo-Yo,
the Granite and the Lightning and the Melody.
Only the Incognito Lounge is open.
My neighbor arrives.
They have the television on.

It's a show about
my neighbor in a loneliness, a light,
walking the hour when every bed is a mouth.
Alleys of dark trash, exhaustion
shaped into residences—and what are the dogs
so sure of that they shout like citizens
driven from their minds in a stadium?
In his fist he holds a note
in his own handwriting,
the same message everyone carries
from place to place in the secret night,
the one that nobody asks you for
when you finally arrive, and the faces
turn to you playing the national anthem
and go blank, that's
what the show is about, that message.

*

I was raised up from tiny
childhood in those purple hills,
right slam on the brink of language,
and I claim it's just as if
you can't do anything to this moment,
that's how inextinguishable
it all is. Sunset,
Arizona, everybody waiting
to get arrested, all very
much an honor, I assure you.
Maybe invite the lady with no face

to plead my cause, to get
me off the hook or name
me one good reason.

The air is full of megawatts
and the megawatts are full of silence.
She reaches to the radio like Saint Therese.

*

Here at the center of the world
each wonderful store cherishes
in its mind undeflowerable
mannequins in a pale, electric light.
The parking lot is full,
everyone having the same dream
of shopping and shopping
through an afternoon
that changes like a face.

But these shoppers of America—
carrying their hearts toward the bluffs
of the counters like thoughtless purchases,
walking home under the sea,
standing in a dark house at midnight
before the open refrigerator, completely
transformed in the light. . . .

*

Every bus ride is like this one,
in the back the same two uniformed boy scouts
de-pantsing a little girl, up front
the woman whose mission is to tell the driver
over and over to shut up.
Maybe you permit yourself to find
it beautiful on this bus as it wafts
like a dirigible toward suburbia
over a continent of saloons,
over the robot desert that now turns

purple and comes slowly through the dust.
This is the moment you'll seek
the words for over the imitation
and actual wood of successive

tabletops indefatigably,
when you watched a baby child
catch a bee against the tinted glass
and were married to a deep
comprehension and terror.

(Antaeus)

Bill Knott
The Closet
(...after my Mother's death)

Not long enough after the hospital happened
I find her closet lying empty and stop my play
And go in and crane up at three blackwire hangers
which quiver, airy, released. They appear to enjoy

Their new distance, cognizance born of the absence
Of everything else. The closet has been cleaned out
Full-flush as surgeries where the hangers could be
Amiable scalpels though they just as well would be

Themselves, in basements, glovelessly scraping uteri
But, here, pure, transfigured heavenward, they're
Birds, whose wingspans expand by excluding me. Their
Range is enlarged by loss. They'd leave buzzards

Measly as moths: and the hatshelf is even higher!—
As the sky over a prairie, an undotted desert where
Nothing can swoop sudden, crumple in secret. I've fled
At ambush, tag, age: six, must I face this, can

I have my hide-and-seek hole back now please, the
Clothes, the thicket of shoes, where is it? Only
The hangers are at home here. Come heir to this
Rare element, fluent, their skeletal grace sings

Of the ease with which they let go the dress, slip,
Housecoat or blouse, so absolvingly. Free, they fly
Trim, triangular, augurs leapt ahead from some
   geometric

God who soars stripped (of flesh, it is said): catnip

To a brat placated by model airplane kits kids
My size lack motorskills for, so I wind up glue-scabbed,
Pawing glaze skins, second fingernails fun to peer in as
Frost-i-glass doors . . . But the closet has no windows,

Opaque or sheer: I must shut my eyes, shrink within
To peep into this wall. Soliciting sleep I'll dream
Mother spilled and cold, unpillowed, the operating-
Table cracked to goad delivery: its stirrups slack,

The forceps closed—often I'll see mobs of obstetrical
Personnel kneel proud, congratulatory, cooing
And oohing and hold the dead infant up to the dead
Woman's face as if for approval, the prompted

Beholding, tears, a zoomshot kiss. White-masked
Doctors and nurses patting each other on the back,
Which is how in the Old West a hangman, if
He was good, could gauge the heft of his intended. . .

Awake, the hangers are sharper, knife-'n'-slice, I jump
Gropelessly to catch them to twist them clear,
Mis-shape them whole, sail them across the small air
Space of the closet. I shall find room enough here

By excluding myself; by excluding myself, I'll grow.

(originally printed in a different form in *Ironwood*)

Richard Leigh
Madonna

SEVENTY MILES TO THE EAST, THE SUBURBS BEGIN, AS if acid had been spilled over the landscape. And then Belfast itself, where the banshee, incarnate in sirens, howls nightly—a pall of smoke and petrol fumes veiling dawn's smelted sky, a gray haze of pulverized concrete and mortar, a misty tapestry woven of violence, resentment and fear, stitched with tangles of barbed wire. Boarded-up shops, barricaded thoroughfares, streetcorners bristling with patrols, gutted buildings whose vacant windows gape like eyes in faces shocked insensate. Shattered glass sprinkles the mud with sharp diamond scintillas, venomous slogans straggle along soot-bleakened walls, occasional rusty stains on the pavement mark the sites of the more recent atrocities. And amid the yellowing newspapers, the empty tins and beer bottles, the discarded mattresses, the broken toys and spent cartridge cases that litter the alleys, ragged skeins of children's voices weave themselves with shrill vindictiveness into the city's indefatigable murmur. Nurtured on bitter gall of hatred, gangs of grimy urchins clamber like monkeys about the fire escapes, seethe through the passageways between the tenements, stalk each other in the shadow of the huddled houses. Eyes glittering eagerly, they watch the dark-green armored cars—mechanized scorpions—rumble by; and behind their vehement masks, they dream of when they too, like their fathers and elder brothers, will be old enough to wield rifles instead of sticks, to hurl grenades instead of stones. For in this urban miasma, there is no innocence.

But that is in Belfast itself. Here, seventy miles to the west, lies a green parenthesis ostensibly unscarred by social and historical enmity. Here one might be at the core of an emerald—a rain-rinsed crystal, a luminous prism faceted with sparkling silver dew. Fairy-tale valleys cradle isolated cottages, white farmhouses, a sleepy little gingerbread town, its church a quaintly kneaded hymn of antiquated stone. Dream-soft hills reverberate into the distance, taking no cognizance of the border—the line of rigid demarcation drawn and patrolled by man across his own movements, his own freedom, his own yearning. Foliage fringes the roadsides with a hushed cathedral-like solemnity, a cool dark-vaulted basilica that exudes pastoral peace. Somnolent meadows accommodate the timeless tableau of drowsily browsing livestock, as well as two snipers sprawled prone in the sedge. Silence imposes a lyrical dominion, closing imperturbably around sporadic rifle shots, flatly reverberative over the dormant fields. And when the rain begins again, the greenness itself becomes fluid, as if the entire verdant world were dissolving, liquefying into the green sap from which it coalesced. One might then expect to see it created anew—moist, shining, freshly painted in resonantly visible hues.

There is nothing radiant about it for the man in the cottage, however—the man in the black woolen pullover with the cold black tubular barrel of an America-made automatic rifle in his lap. From where he crouches behind the slats of the boarded window, he is conscious only of death's composed blank gaze upon him, unwinking, impassive, indifferent. Granted, that gaze is familiar enough to Liam Dougherty. He has confronted it for ten of his twenty-eight years now, in half the slums of Londonderry and Belfast. At first he did so with romantic and vainglorious audacity—the audacity of a youth asserting himself, intoxicated by his newly acquired capacity to kill. At first he was prone to flamboyant self-dramatization—avatar of ancient legendary heroes stalking a mythical landscape, pitted in epic combat against his country's hereditary foes. At first death beckoned to him like a seductive woman shrouded in mysterious veils; and he flirted, he courted her, he half solicited her with a thrilling intensification of his manhood. But that was only at first. Later, death assumed a more grisly countenance—the visage of a scabrous old hag—and Liam Dougherty became a veteran, a professional murderer. In death's presence, he has now learned to cauterize his sensibility, as well as his exalted self-esteem. And now it is with a cool and brisk efficiency, a meticulous workmanlike precision, that he performs his assigned task. A fortnight ago, this task was to detonate a bomb in a Belfast pub, a tavern habitually patronized by the Royal Ulster Constabulary. During the ensuing public outcry, during the dragnet of searches and arrests, Liam Dougherty was transferred from the city, ordered to rural surroundings where his face would be unknown. As he huddled fetus-like in the boot of his comrades' car, he briefly lamented the two young women—one of them his sister's age—who had died in the explosion, together with their fiancés. Yet despite this transient regret, he did not doubt that their lives—like those of the six soldiers and policemen previously credited to his marksmanship—served to further the progress of his cause. He repents none of them, regarding such misfortunes as merely distasteful aspects of a necessary job. Nevertheless, he feels uneasy, peering between the gnawed wooden boards that seal the cottage's windows, immersing him and the sparse furnishings in a damp, wine-colored gloom. For Liam Dougherty is an urban creature, unaccustomed to silence and solitude; and in silence and solitude, death is no longer familiar. Amid the human detritus of the city, death was knowable, imaginable, almost predictable—as punctilious as a good civil servant. Here—in this impersonal green vegetation—there is something disturbing, even something uncanny, about its possible imminence.

The man in the toolshed four hundred yards distant is also uneasy. For him, too, the last few hours have been a

species of wrestling match—he and death circling each
other warily, seeking an opening, an instant's careless-
ness, a momentary lowering of the guard. Like Liam
Dougherty, Colin Bishop wears a black woolen pullover.
Instead of an automatic rifle, however, his fingers fondle a
more conventional weapon, standard Army issue but fitted
with a special sniper's scope; and in his pocket he
carries the distinctive badge of the Special Air Service.
Like Liam Dougherty, Colin Bishop is a professional murderer—albeit less experienced in his trade, for he is only
twenty-three years old. On the other hand, he has attained
his status with the aid of a government's resources and
most advanced technology; he is a triumph of modern psychological engineering, methodically trained and programmed as a sentient weapons system. Nevertheless, his
hatred is less abstract, more personal and therefore more
human than Liam Dougherty's. It stems from a year ago,
when—a rubicund-faced corporal in a country regiment—
he was posted, along with his unit, from the Rhine to the
streets of Belfast. At that time he had felt only fear and
wild incomprehension, had wondered in anguish why he,
the son of a Birmingham estate agent, should be plunged
into Ireland's insane feuds. At that time he looked forward
only to demobilization, to marriage with the sister of a
mate in his battalion, to a home in the Birmingham suburbs and a place in his father's firm. Cynically deriding his
anxiety, his comrades scoffed at the "silly saint-soaked isle."
And then Colin Bishop's mate—bleeding across the pavement, a sniper's bullet in the belly—was stoned and clubbed
to death by a band of children. And Colin Bishop made a
vow, which led him, a week later, to apply for candidacy in
the Special Air Service. In the months of arduous discipline that followed, his fears, his self-doubts, his uncertain-
ties, were systematically anesthetized. Nevertheless, Colin
Bishop now feels uneasy. As if in quest of reassurance, his
fingers stray to the badge in his pocket—the badge that

certifies his position in the Army's most elite and prestigious corps. Yet despite the drills that have steeled his muscles and honed his reflexes, there is something disturbing, even something uncanny, about the silence and the solitude.

Neither Liam Dougherty nor Colin Bishop has accorded much notice to the countryside, except as an arena of tactical possibilities—of features affording more or less concealment or vulnerability, more or less advantage or disadvantage, more or less favorable opportunity to strike. Nor, for that matter, has either man seen the other—not even as a target, still less as another man. Each dimly senses the other's presence, as animals scent the ozone that precedes a storm. But for both there is only one real presence, one real witness and adversary, which each, in the lonely solitude of his skull, vainly endeavors to imagine—a spurt of flame from the foliage, the frenzied sting of a searing coal in brain or entrails, an all-enveloping blackness whence no cry will ever issue, of pain, of rage, of hatred, of longing or of despair.

In the town, morning arrives like a beggar, swathed in tattered rags of mist, and the clop of hooves on the cobbles mingles with the jingle of harness, the clatter of milk pails, the rumble of vegetable carts. A few citizens are already visible, a few workmen and farmhands filing along the sidewalks, splashing their faces in the dawn. A few cars inch timidly through the narrow thoroughfares, as if sensing their anachronistic displacement. Drowsily bucolic, the hour still resonates in the belfry, lapping with lethargic metallic waves over the crooked leaded roofs, over the muffled shops and houses, over the somnolent main street— which, several hundred yards beyond, slithers across a bridge into open country, struggles up a tree-shagged hill, vanishes into the whitening sky.

At the end of the street, embedded in time as in a quag-

mire, stands a dilapidated squat stone building, a typical
Council edifice. Every night it is visible above the river,
shaped out of the darkness by the tireless amber glow of
its windows, which now flash signals from the rising sun.
This structure shelters the headquarters of a charitable
institution, non-political in its objectives, dedicated to a
compassionate cause. To the lonely, the frightened, the desperate, the potentially suicidal, it offers counseling services, advice, solace, the comfort of a human voice; and in
a country still fettered to the spirit if not the letter of a
once-omnipresent priesthood, the telephones on its worn
desks perform a function akin to the confessional. Through
these black bakelite instruments, abscesses of inarticulate
misery are eased by the lancet and balm of speech. Through
these instruments, anguish, coerced into words, assumes
less daunting, more human proportions. Through these
instruments, guilt—real or imagined—stammers falter-
ingly toward atonement and absolution.

Before one of these instruments sits a woman in her
early thirties, with the high-strung fastidiousness of a
thoroughbred mare and gentle gray-blue eyes—dream-
bright eyes to which unusually large and dark pupils impart a mournful, wistfully haunted depth. She sits with
relaxed yet upright formality, an innate sense of decorum;
and her posture, as well as her manners and gestures,
reflect a practiced and demure grace which, like a cuirass,
both encumbers and becomes her. Although tastefully and
expensively dressed, she is not ostentatiously so; nor is
there much calculated provocation in her crisp frothy frock,
whose charm is distinctly conservative, even prim. She is
obviously not a local resident—she is too elegant, too gracious, too patently patrician, despite her self-deprecating
modesty. Nevertheless, her presence has become familiar
to the townspeople. Among themselves they may query the
motives for her self-effacing work, but they gratefully accept it.

Yet she is shy, prone to underestimate herself, to doubt her capacities for the task she has assumed. When the telephone rings—as it does now—she jumps slightly, the composed poise of her face giving way to a poignant vulnerability, a disheveled girlish fluster; and her eyes—the eyes of a startled doe—dilate in momentary alarm. Her accent, too, betrays her—an English accent with the faintly nasal urbanity characteristic of her class, the brisk, insistently cheerful and precise enunciation. Her voice is somewhat breathless, issuing from the upper registers of her throat—a voice unaccustomed to its own sound, unaccustomed to sustained exercise. After a moment, however, it grows steadier, deeper, more certain of itself, welling no longer from disquiet but from a primordial feminine affinity, an archaic comprehension of motherhood, of suffering and grief.

Most callers prefer to remain anonymous, but the one now on the line readily volunteers her name: Mrs. Cathleen Flint, widowed by "the troubles," residing a half mile west of town. She wishes to speak about Fergus, her five-year-old son. Having stated that much, she falls silent.

Courteous, patient, encouraging, the young woman at the telephone cajoles her to continue.

In the first place, Mrs. Flint declares, Fergus has disappeared—has not been home all night, has not been seen since the previous afternoon. She has already rung the police, who, however, are occupied. Someone has reported terrorists in the area. And terrorists apparently take precedence over a lost child.

The woman at the telephone tries to be reassuring. She is sure Fergus will turn up, she says. It is not unusual for five-year-old boys to sham precocious flights from home, to indulge their natural longing for mystification, for independence and adventure. In any case, she will undertake to ring the police herself, to report the child's absence and demand appropriate action.

Mrs. Flint expresses her gratitude, then pauses once more, her silence a tautening wire in the hollow depths of the receiver. There is something else, she begins haltingly. To tell the truth, she is worried about Fergus. No, not just about his disappearance. About other things too. About the boy's balance, one might say—the boy's mind. He had been a difficult birth, so much so that he had nearly killed her. And shortly before his death eight months ago, her husband had hinted that Fergus was not quite right in the head. At the time she had angrily denied this possibility, but now she must grant it a certain credence. Though how can you tell when a child is not right in the head?

You can't, the woman at the telephone replies gently. Not really. It may be that Fergus is different from other children—more sensitive perhaps, more creative, more nervous. But this does not imply anything wrong.

Yes, Fergus is different, Mrs. Flint sighs. Very different. Too different for a body not to notice it. Is it normal for a five-year-old boy never to speak unless goaded, and then to say only yes or no? Is it normal for such a boy never to smile, never to laugh, never to play with other children, never to show any interest in things? Is it normal, one can't but wonder, for a boy to sit awake all night, every night, with a strange expression on his face that gives one the shivers—the expression of an animal sniffing the wind, or bemused by the moon?

The woman at the telephone chooses her words carefully, judiciously, as though picking her way through a thorn-hedge. Not typical perhaps, but not necessarily abnormal either. In any case, it would be rash to draw a premature conclusion. Ideas in psychology have greatly changed, and one can't nowadays think in terms of oversimplified labels and categories. She would advise Mrs. Flint to seek a professional opinion—the opinion of a specialist experienced in such matters. If Mrs. Flint so wishes, she herself will make inquiries and recommend someone . . .

An abrupt click, then a peculiar stillness—peculiar, the young woman realizes, because she can no longer hear Cathleen Flint's labored breathing. There is no background hum or static. Not even a dial tone. And yet Cathleen Flint did not hang up, she realizes. The line has simply gone dead.

For some moments, she contemplates the receiver in her hand. At last she replaces it, waiting expectantly for another ring. From behind the gabled rooftops of the house opposite, the sun's rim sears the eastern sky, sifts brazenly through the window, fills the room with a haze of lazily swirling dust motes, kindles to golden filigree a loose wisp of the woman's honey-hued hair. In one corner, a horsefly drones sonorously, sizzles like grease on a grill. On the desk, the telephone gleams with black opaline intensity, but remains mute.

In the musty half-light behind her yellow shutters, Cathleen Flint stands beside a table littered with framed photographs and empty whiskey bottles, peering perplexedly into her captious telephone receiver. She is a pallid, exhausted-looking woman of twenty-five, emaciated, slatternly, with prominent cheekbones, lank straw-colored hair and lusterless apathetic eyes—eyes extinguished by sustained exposure to horror. For Cathleen Flint has witnessed a generous spectrum of horror from her house beside the road—three firemen slaughtered, a constable dragging his body through the dust with blood sluicing from the bullet holes in his knees. And two pregnant girls, flogged, tarred and feathered, with prickly gray-shaven scalps, who incurred their punishment for the crime of falling in love—as if passion could be regulated by politics, could be dammed and diverted to circumvent the appeal of

lonely young British soldiers. But despite what she has
witnessed, a modicum of effort would suffice to render
Cathleen Flint pretty, if not indeed attractive. She has not
made such effort for eight months.

For a moment longer, she remains motionless, glaring at
the receiver with accumulating exasperation, as if she in-
tends to wring its neck. Impatiently she replaces it, then
picks it up again and again listens. There is no dial tone,
no background static, nothing but silence without echo.
Once more she bangs the instrument down and shambles
to the window, exposing her pinched and haggard features
to a wan shaft of sunlight that seeps through the bleared
pane. Outside, the world is green. But grief is also green.
And memory is green. Memory of eight months before,
when the shattering roar of a revolver wrenched her headlong from the bedroom to the same window, her nightgown
tangled between her knees. Ten minutes earlier, her husband—a postman and part-time policeman—had kissed
her, donned his cap and disappeared out the door. When
she next saw him, he lay in the garden, a crater of bleeding
flesh where his eye had been, bright, garish, incongruously
red against the green landscape as a spilled splash of paint.
Standing beside her in his yellow cardigan, Fergus had
remained oblivious to her scream, his luminous green eyes
opaque, inscrutable and unsmiling.

Frowning into the sunlight, Cathleen Flint surveys the
surrounding serenity—the hushed peace of pastures, of
cowpats steaming in the misty residue of rain, of green
hills undulating to the horizon's rim. A streak of wandering wind arrows through the vast green amphitheater,
ripping the reeds and rushes, ruffling the petticoats of the
willows. Across the road, the toolshed sways imperceptibly,
a tenuous conclave of huddled staves. Beyond it, tall grass
beards an abandoned cottage, its boarded windows like
bandaged eyes. As if returning from some immeasurable
distance, Cathleen Flint's gaze sharpens, focuses to a pin-

point of intensity—probing the vista for the shrill yellow lilt of her son's cardigan. The greenness remains unbroken, however, save in the garden—where, from among festoons of bracken, a few fragile flowers brandish the challenge of snowdrop innocence.

At last, Cathleen Flint turns from the window, plods back to the telephone on the table with a self-abashed hope moistening her eyes. She has never spoken of her grief to anyone, never verbalized her fears about her son—sole legacy of the man she loved. She has never imagined she could possibly express such things; and yet the sound of the strange English voice, another woman's voice, made it not only easy, but comforting. Once more she lifts the receiver, once more she hangs up, rolling her gaze toward the ceiling in rueful despair. Then she sighs and, with trembling fingers, pours a tumbler of whiskey. The bottle clinks against the glass like a coin dropped in a mausoleum.

Framed in the rear door of the cottage, Liam Dougherty squints in appraisal of a severed strand of wire—sagging level with the roof a few minutes before, now dangling, nudged by damp puffs of wind. Depositing his clippers on a shelf beside the entrance, he returns to his post at the boarded-up window overlooking the road. From here he can once more survey the terrain before him, marred only by a toolshed some four hundred yards distant and, a little further beyond, by a dirty-white clapboard house with rickety gate, desiccated garden and flaking ocher shutters. Foolish of him perhaps, but that building had made him nervous. If someone within had heard him, for example, had glimpsed his presence and rung the authorities . . .

Liam Dougherty begins to pace tensely, accompanied by his misshapen shadow. Despite his precautions, he is still uneasy, still scents the proximity of death; and he still wonders why it should be more disturbing here than in Londonderry or Belfast. He has not yet discerned that death

in the city is both unique and human—an interruption of
a well-regulated rhythm, an intrusion which must, of necessity, draw attention to itself. Here death is neither unique
nor human, is not isolated by man's arrogant sense of drama
from the context in which it occurs. Here death is but a
pulse of a natural cycle, with a pervasive and ineluctable
logic of its own—the immutable logic of seed, flower, fruit,
husk, loam and seed. Here death is neither a climax nor
an interruption, but a manifestation of order, pattern and
coherence—an index of meaning rather than of chaos, an
integral component in a harmonious plan. Here death is
omnipresent—in the mute apocalypse of the sunset, the
interlocking meshwork of animal existence, the expiring
sighs of swooning leaves, the soundless shriek of a twig
tumbling end over end to the forest floor. Here death is
placid, organic, devoid of malice or hatred, interwoven with
life and with creation. Liam Dougherty—a man sustained
by malice and hatred—stands apart from life and creation;
and in consequence, he must perforce find death strangely
alien, strangely cold and inimical. It is not surprising that
the silence should make him jittery, abrading his already
raw nerves. It is not surprising that a rustle, a patter of
rapid footfalls, a twig snapped in the ditch beside the road,
should vibrate for him like the clangorous tolling of a gong.
It is not surprising that a lilt of yellow in the underbrush
should galvanize him to a rigid and strained attention, his
eyes peering down the barrel of his weapon, out through
the gnawed boards. The road, he knows, has been sealed
off by soldiers. Any movement on it he must assume to be
hostile.

In the precarious shelter of the toolshed, Colin Bishop
has also attained an attenuation of tension; but from where
he crouches, he enjoys a slightly better prospect of the road.
With an audible exhalation of relief, he perceives another
human presence, even though it is that of a child—a wisp-
ish waiflike child in a yellow cardigan, with triangular

fox-shaped face and a conflagration of flame-colored hair. To Colin Bishop, the diminutive apparition is oddly fascinating, oddly preternatural—for a moment, at any rate, before professional considerations usurp the foreground of his consciousness. There are other soliders, he knows, posted within range of the road. Some of them may not see it clearly; and the accidental death of a child would seriously embarrass the Army, would attract adverse publicity from the media, would ignite the wrath of the countryside and incite reprisals. Uncertainly, Colin Bishop hesitates, calculating whether to break radio silence, to warn his unseen comrades and, in so doing, to betray his own position—to risk, if not his life, at least the escape of his quarry. Fingering the portable transmitter at his belt, he gingerly caresses the knobs; but before his vacillation can resolve itself, he is spared all need for decision. From the cottage windows four hundred yards distant, a viper's tongue of flame flickers repeatedly, accompanied by a blurred mechanical stutter, like that of a pneumatic drill. In the ditch beside the road, Fergus Flint—a weightless rag doll in his yellow cardigan—reels violently sidewards, spins, flops suddenly into the mud and twitches with convulsive spasms, as though pummeled by invisible blows.

In the precarious shelter of the toolshed, Colin Bishop is paralyzed with horror and revulsion—for a moment, at any rate. A convenient blunder, he concludes with a certain grim satisfaction, kneeling, bracing his rifle stock against his shoulder, squinting into the ruby-tinged scope. Such blunders can be strategically exploited, blazoned through the media; for even atrocities are valuable commodities here, the vital currency not only of propaganda but of public relations as well. In the red glass, an X superimposes itself on the magnified slats of the cottage, between which a tubular black barrel is visible. Very calmly, Colin Bishop squeezes his trigger, jerks with the recoil of the weapon, winces at the vicious reverberative crack that rebounds deafeningly from the shed's moldering walls. And before the echoes have subsided, he fires again. A pause, while the eddies of sound sift and settle, while the ringing in his ears vibrates tremulously into silence. Colin Bishop then lowers his rifle, detaches the portable transmitter from his belt. Through months of rigorous training, all rashness, all impetuosity, all imprudent haste have been drilled out of him. In accordance with established procedure, he now radios for support; and only when it arrives will he advance, flanked by well-armed comrades. Together they will surround the target, inch their way carefully forward to appraise his handiwork.

In the cottage, behind the boards that bar the window, Liam Dougherty lies on his side, doubled upon his pain, curled like a fetus about to be born into death. In the shattered scaffolding of his chest, a coal rages with rapacious frenzy, while a terrifying coldness seeps numbingly up his legs, a thick and viscous liquid icily congealing. From his rent lungs, his breath issues in ragged gasps, raucous as wind through ruined houses. Blindly, the dying man's hand fumbles toward his wound, touches a warm and bubbling stickiness. When he stares at his stiffening fingers through a red haze of agony, they too are red, but wetly shining as well. With his other hand, Liam Dougherty gropes into the flap pocket of his trousers, claws out a fragmentation grenade with a three-second fuse. Raising it to his whitening lips, he extracts the pin with his teeth, still holding down the lever; then he rolls over onto his belly, clamping the primed explosive between his flesh and the floor. Behind the glazed opacity filming his eyes, consciousness is almost extinguished—little more now than a roaring blackness, riven by jagged red lightning bolts of torment. But before too long, Liam Dougherty nevertheless realizes, the soldiers will surely find him. When they lift his body, they will not even have time to be surprised.

In the mud of the ditch, Fergus Flint lies motionless amid motionless puddles, which hold, prisoned in their shimmering surface, the mirrored image of the sky. Around him a canopy of foliage drapes itself serenely, a taut green-silver cocoon with only a single aperture for the trill of a lark. After some moments, he opens one luminous green eye, his elfin shoulders wracked by uncontrollable giggles. After another pause, he raises his head and peers gleefully down the length of his cardigan, frayed and tattered by bullets, soaked wet-brown by the slime; and although he cannot see it, the same slime spatters his neck, streaks his triangular fox-shaped face, dampens the conflagration of his flame-colored hair. Again Fergus Flint giggles, sitting upright and, with the sleeve of one arm, wiping his mouth and nose. Then he clambers to his feet, scrambles with simian dexterity from the ditch and scampers away toward the cottage, a muted lilt of yellow receding into the sedge.

His transmitter arrested in his hand, Colin Bishop watches from the toolshed, more astonished than relieved. Inconceivable that the man in the cottage could have missed at such short range; inconceivable that the boy should be both alive and apparently unscathed. But Colin Bishop cannot know, any more than the boy's mother, that Fergus Flint is not human, not mortal at all. Fergus Flint is the spawn of fog and fire, an emanation of the gray vapors of the dawn, of the storm above dim haunted shores, of the shifting shadows of the woods, of the elemental earth itself—and as ancient, as primordial. Progeny of the Little People, Fergus Flint is a changeling, substituted for his stillborn counterpart five years before; and the midwife, turning from a dead child to a feverishly tossing mother, had whirled round in disbelief at his cry. For five years he has inhabited his fragile boot of flesh, his tenuous semblance of humanity. For five years he has been an enigma—a flickering and elusive existence ungovernable as the moods of a rose, which breathes with the waxing and waning of

the moon. On his thirteenth birthday, Fergus Flint will
disappear, return to the spume whence he came, dissolve
into the morning mist, the drifting scud of cloud-wrack,
the disconsolate gray sifting of the wind. Until that time,
however, he will retain his present form but will be immortal, immortal as the earth itself; and like the earth itself,
he is invulnerable to man's infinite resourcefulness in de-
struction. Invulnerable in body, at least; for though Fergus
Flint may be proof against bullets, he, like the earth itself,
is susceptible to impalpable taints and infections—to the
toxins with which man's gratuitous violence pollutes air,
soil and soul. Like the earth itself, Fergus Flint is innocent;
but such innocence may yet be sullied, warped, twisted
into unprecedented forms of malevolence. Like the earth
itself, Fergus Flint is a perpetual witness; but horror scars
its witnesses as well as its victims, and from the house
beside the road Fergus Flint has seen many horrors. By
dint of such horrors, he is learning to participate in man's
incomprehensible games; and in these games, as in anything else, there are certain conventions. When one is struck
by bullets, for example, one falls.

One falls for a moment at least, imitating the perishable
mortality one feigns; then one tires of the game and proceeds to explore more consequential mysteries, like that of
death. Framed now in the rear door of the cottage, Fergus
Flint's green gaze drinks in Liam Dougherty's prostrate
and contorted body, the bulging and sightless eyes, the
mouth frozen round a soundless curse still echoing down
the corridors of eternity. It also drinks in the glistening
pool of blood, a muddy red mire from which sinuous ten-
drils worm their way to rust over the dusty floor. Fergus
Flint kneels, cautiously extends his hand, dips it into the
warm wet stickiness. With a grimace of distaste he quickly
recoils, wiping his fingers on his cardigan. And then, for
the first time in his incarnate life, Fergus Flint laughs—

an eerie and unpleasant laugh, which dribbles maliciously from his lips beneath his luminous green eyes.

In the squat stone building near the bridge, the young woman at the telephone has waited in vain for Cathleen Flint to ring again. She has already checked her own telephone, assured herself it is in working order. She has already informed the police—preoccupied though they were— of Fergus Flint's absence. At the stove in the kitchen behind her, she has also lit the gas, placed a teakettle on the boil. Producing a silver fountain pen from her purse, she had then bent her head over her log-book, had begun to transcribe her inconclusive dialogue with Cathleen Flint; and as she reconstructed it in memory, she had heard, somewhere to the west, a mechanical stutter, followed by two sharp claps—slightly muffled but still reverberative over the sun-flecked fields and hills. Elsewhere, perhaps, the nature of such sounds might be indeterminate, irrelevant; but in this country one neither ignores nor mistakes their origin. To the young woman at the telephone, they are all the more alarming for the direction from which they issued. Now, with her ringed and manicured fingers, she is thumbing through the directory for Cathleen Flint's number.

Scribbling a hasty note of it, she turns back to the telephone, listens to the dry plastic of the dial gnawing into the silence. A pause, a confused sequence of clicks, a hollow electronic monotone. The young woman replaces the receiver, then tries again, obtaining the same result. Again she hangs up; and when she lifts the receiver for the third time, she dials the operator. She is having trouble getting through, she states briskly, yet politely, in the clipped and authoritative voice she reserves for dealing with plodding bureaucracies. Would the operator please try 823?

That number, the operator replies a minute later, seems

to be out of order. Perhaps there is a fault on the line. She will report it as soon as possible.

The young woman sits motionless, her poised, finely chiseled features etched in a mask of impatient and frustrated anxiety, her palms pressed together in an arrowhead between her knees—as though mutely pleading, on behalf of an unknown child, for grace, for reprieve, for mercy. After a moment she rises from her seat, peers out the window into the cobbled road, where the houses huddle against one another like frightened animals; then, with a crisply sibilant seething of her frock, she glides into the kitchen, turns off the gas on the stove. At last she broods her way back to the desk, sits down, bends her head over her logbook. Beneath her fingers the pale gold nib of the fountain pen scuttles across the page, leaving an illegible blue scrawl in its wake.

A thump, a rustle, a creak of footfalls in the corridor causes her to start. When a middle-aged woman appears in the doorway, the tension in her face melts into a gracious welcoming smile—a smile, however, which the worry in her blue-gray eyes betrays. Hurriedly, she rises from the desk, offering her seat to the newcomer, the volunteer scheduled to relieve her at her post before the telephone. As the newcomer sags into the vacant chair, the young woman bustles into the kitchen to prepare a cup of tea for her colleague.

A quiet night, she declares, the words, mingled with steam, wafting back over her shoulder—no visits, only a few routine calls, except for one this morning. Her voice vibrant with solicitude, she describes her dialogue with Cathleen Flint, the shots she heard, the vagaries of the telephone.

Yes, the older woman replies from the desk, she also heard the shooting. Apparently there are terrorists in the area. The road to the west is sealed off, and the security forces—the Army as well as the police—have set up road-blocks.

The young woman tugs open a cabinet above the stove, extracts a teacup and saucer. She is concerned about Cathleen Flint, she confesses. And Cathleen Flint's little boy.

The woman at the desk shrugs dully, her creased face expressionless. They shouldn't be in any particular danger, she replies after a pause. In any case, there is nothing one can do but wait.

The young woman returns from the kitchen, carefully lowers teacup and saucer to the desk; and through the film of steam, she searches her colleague's gaunt, seamed features. Their futility evokes recollection of a fortnight ago, of what, in dejected admission, the organization's director confided to her: that he was worried, that staff morale was low, that all sense of purpose was being eroded by apathy, monotony, hopelessness. It was apparent, the young woman replied, nodding gravely, sympathetically. What the staff needed was something new, something which imparted meaning to their activity, which endowed that activity with significance: a broader context, a broader frame of reference, a broader perspective and dimension for a depressing and thankless job. Perhaps, she now muses, she should have voiced the suggestion which then occurred to her: that she herself meet with some of the staff, talk to them, introduce them to certain psychological techniques and exercises she has learned in London. At the time she shrank from this proposal, shrank from what it would have entailed—a commitment to speak in public, to assume a role of leadership, to place herself in the glaring spotlight of strange people's scrutiny. The prospect still daunts her, still distresses her, still makes her heart trip a little too light and a little too fast; she is too inarticulate, she tries to remind herself, too incompetent, too lacking both in ideas and the capacity to present them. Nevertheless, and despite her misgivings, she feels a passionate, almost desperate need to *do* something—something which, she now concedes with nervous reluctance, she alone is equipped to do. Biting her lip, she belts herself into her beige raincoat, bids her colleague a cheerful yet preoccupied and fretful goodbye. There is no alternative, she sighs to herself, stepping out into the brazen glare of sunlight which gilds the dust above the road. Yes, she resolves with timorous determination, she will submit to the ordeal she so dreads; she will speak to the director when she next sees him, will offer to do what she can for staff morale.

On the bridge two hundred yards distant, Fergus Flint scarcely notices the squat stone building, the door that swings open in its bleak facade, the willowy young woman who emerges in a beige raincoat. As though it were seared into his luminous green gaze, he sees only the grisly image of Liam Dougherty's crumpled body. Granted, Fergus Flint has seen such things before—three firemen slaughtered, a constable writhing like a half-crushed insect down the road, the gory visage of his own mortal father gaping sightless at the sky. Such things are hardly novel to Fergus Flint; but in some obscure fashion, each, as it occurs, is more disturbing than the last. He cannot, of course, formulate his discomfort in thoughts, still less in language. Nonetheless, he is oppressed by the inchoate awareness that death—hitherto an integral and vital pulsation of his world, his reality—has been violated, rendered incomprehensibly unnatural. It is no longer an organic rhythm but something artificial and mechanical, something arbitrarily imposed—as if man, having already denied himself a life of his own, were now abdicating all claim to a death of his own as well, accepting the death haphazardly decreed by others. Death, Fergus Flint now dimly perceives, has ceased to be necessary, ceased to be a strand in the cyclical tapestry he inhabits. It has been made superfluous, pointless; and this, to Fergus Flint, is alarming—a disruption of inherent order, a harbinger of fragmentation and chaos. Like an animal quailing before a forest fire, Fergus Flint is wildly afraid, afraid to the point of panic. But because he aspires to human games, he feels compelled to conceal his fear; and as human beings do, he conceals it, with involuntary protectiveness, behind a reflex of mirth—mirth which, in any other consciousness, would be tantamount to hysteria. Perhaps it is the same aspiration to human games that has drawn him from the blood-soaked cottage to the town. In any event, it is this aspiration which—when a shattering explosion rends the western sky—impels him to fling himself, headlong and seemingly stricken, onto the cobbles at the foot of the bridge.

At the stunning impact of the blast, the young woman in the raincoat lurches dizzily, staggers, clutches the doorknob behind her for support. As her gaze careens in terror down the road, she sees a child fall at the foot of the bridge—a frail wraith-like child in a soiled yellow cardigan, with a conflagration of flame-colored hair; and as the echoes roll over the rooftops, he lies motionless, a hideous red stain across his chest. Before she has knowingly made any decision, the woman is stumbling forward, her raincoat billowing like a bell about her long gazelle's legs, her heels resounding with stark and brittle urgency on the damp cobbles. Before the agitated air grows still, she is kneeling breathlessly beside Fergus Flint, fearfully touching his elfin body, cradling his mud-caked head in her lap. As she smooths his disheveled hair, her face is an agonized mask, shaped by the force of her anguish, while a speechless insurrection of tears threatens to overbrim her eyes. Above her the air still resonates tumultuously, a vibration clamorous as a beehive.

Enfolded in her arms, Fergus Flint opens one luminous green eye, his diminutive shoulders wracked by convulsive giggles. For an instant the woman in the raincoat is bewildered, baffled to speechless rigidity. She cannot, of course, know the nature of the being she seeks to succor. Nevertheless, she is a woman—whose mission, therefore, as she instinctively recognizes and accepts, is to heal, to restore, to reconcile, to hold things together, or at least to try. And she is also a mother, discerning in the waif she clasps a child like all other children—like all the victimized children of the world pawned heedlessly to men's games beneath the cold, implacable stars. On finding Fergus Flint unharmed, she does not question. With a gasp, a choked sob of unutterable relief, she crushes him passionately to her, pressing his head against her breast.

From the enveloping warmth of her embrace, Fergus Flint stares quizzically up into her eyes—eyes still bruised with barely suppressed tears, which are now, however, tears of joy. And of something else as well, something Fergus Flint has never seen before, not even in the face of his mother. In Cathleen Flint's face he has seen many things—misery, hope, possessiveness, disillusion, voracious maternal solicitude. He has even, on occasion, seen an approximation of love, but never the kind of love that now illumines the face above him—an aching and grieving beauty directed at him yet at the same time transcending him, radiating through him and for him, out to the ravaged land he embodies. Extending his tiny arms, Fergus Flint wraps them impulsively round the woman's neck, buries his fox-shaped face in the folds of her coat.

"I was afraid," he whimpers. "But not so much anymore . . ."

From the west arises the banshee wail of a siren, threading itself with despairing lament into an inflamed sky. On the cobbles at the foot of the bridge, the young woman embraces the child more tightly, gazing wistfully over his shoulder into the distance—as if seeking some beacon and some promise, as if mirroring, over a limitless expanse of sorrow, some unimaginable vista beyond.

Although she cannot know it, she has humanized the inhuman. But who will humanize the men?

(previously unpublished)

William Logan
The Country of the Imagination

The black dogs come down from the passes
Where mendicants eat flies off the faces
Of the dead. It is not a religious spring,

Even in the country of the imagination.
In the meanest world, the success of adjacent
Mornings is measured by a swollen light

Unmarked by death. A red sun succeeds
The uneven rim of atmosphere. By noon
Willows stand dying along the concrete

Irrigation ditch, once a rough creek.
The leaves rattle their silvery, mothlike
Undersides. The real religious find

Their followers speaking stringent languages,
Whose vocabulary cannot guess the intention
Of the straw-haired woman sweeping a frieze

Of grasshoppers from her porch, or the
Awkward dead in dry grass, or the men
Burning the nesting field. Language

Banishes the behavior of its times.
Evenings, across acres of plowed field,
A scruffy peacock cries. Leashed to a

Splintered stake, it squawks demands
Within a reduced geometry, and pecks
A stony meal under transplanted bamboo.

In the imagination it no longer exists.

(Shenandoah)

Thomas Lux
If I Die Before I Wake

If I die before I wake
I pray the Lord my soul to take . . . .
From a common enough
and non-denominational child's prayer.
Not too unlike a lullaby, it's a simple
pledge in verse before hitting
the dark night after night
and one line ringing maybe
a few times in the mind: *If I die*
before I wake. O the generations
of insomniacs created,
the nite-light industry booming!
But let's face it: Prayer is good,
especially for children.
They should understand some things
so they might appreciate
them. Like: the buzzards and the bees,
what those stone visors mean,
poking up, on lawns behind fences,
in rows, whitish dominoes . . . .
They should know: it's a sleepy journey
to a half-promised land
and you never wake at all.

(Pequod)

Howard Nemerov
Insomnia I

Some nights it's bound to be your best way out,
When nightmare is the short end of the stick,
When sleep is a part of town where it's not safe
To walk at night, when waking is the only way
You have of distancing your wretched dead,
A growing crowd, and escaping out of their
Time into yours for another little while;

Then pass ghostly, a planet in the house
Never observed, among the sleeping rooms
Where children dream themselves, and thence go down
Into the empty domain where daylight reigned;
Reward yourself with drink and a book to read,
A mystery, for its elusive gift
Of reassurance against the hour of death.
Order your heart about: *Stop doing that!*
And get the world to be secular again.

Then, when you know who done it, turn out the light,
And quietly in darkness, in moonlight, or snowlight,
Reflective, listen to the whistling earth
In its backspin trajectory around the sun
That makes the planets sometimes retrograde
And brings the cold forgiveness of the dawn
Whose light extinguishes all stars but one.

(Salmagundi)

Katha Pollitt
Parthians

*For the Parthians threw their darts as they fled . . . and it is,
indeed, a cunning practice.*

-PLUTARCH

Dust and gray dunes. Ribbed bed of an ancient sea.
What do the black birds cry who roost in these thorns?

For years we have tracked you
by evidence of your absence:

a gold ring caught on a branch, a charred
kitchen of stones that says, last night you were here.

Old ones,
emptyhanded in the blue

horizon's freedom, that dull rubbish you
walked off from is our fate.

Wait
for us. Speak to us.

Each night we sleep
in your camp of the night before

and dream of pitched battle:
that gash and grapple, how we promise to love it,

it would be an embrace, it would be a way of knowing.
But we are trapped in your past,

the arrows that destroy us
float casually backward, as at a foolish regret,

and a new morning heats its terrible metals.
Yet we go on,
we go on,
as though if we could just move fast enough

we'd break through the flaw in time
that keeps us locked in parallel dimensions.

Beautiful mirages! In the distance
glimmer what green oases, what cool leaves?

Your tents stand shimmering, as though seen through
water.

(Antaeus)

Mark Rudman
Log
(Journey to "Four Corners")

Ubiquity of the sign
"Bridge Freezes Before Road Surface."

America. Empty stadiums at dawn.
Beer mugs
soldered to men's fists
in Akron poolhalls.

109 miles of high tension wire
between here and Toledo.
Hills shaped like whales
and hills leveled for strip mining.
Hills like walled fortresses.
I must have forgotten the insignia
for "Mack" trucks was a bulldog
in convict's stripes.

Towns unlikely to appear in nightmares
race past "a mile a minute." Get
across the road woodchuck
I mutter to the creature
frozen in my path: downshift:
he goes back and the "Mack"
passes grazing my left elbow.
Over the Black River.

Whirlpools. Gulleys. Trucks.
I pass one sprawled like a toppled

elephant in the ditch
where the discarded shards of machines,
beehives of rust,
are scattered like relics.

Driving into the light side by side
puts the lust in us, our bodies
rustle under cool mottled motel sheets
and sleep comes any number of times.
The sky is constant at our departures.

Dawn rain. Crows
throw no shadow on the gray road
where the mashed collie lay.
Charcoal clouds swirl down.
Smoke spirals in thick
sulphurous braids.
Infernal air here,
ahead there is only
the outline of a man,
pipes and wires bent into this white,
animistic shape that multiplies
and stretches endlessly
as I drive into the light.

Searching for clearings
behind the eye,
silos multiply,
grain elevators rise
at the speed of light.

When our early, silent meditations
to the grave and airy
"Music for 18 Musicians"
dissipate in the bad hour, before noon,

I'm startled by the symmetry of cow and calves
in the trailer I dawdle behind
hungry. Crossing

another State Line,
surrounded by Illinois cornfields
where I used to hide in childhood foxholes,
it all comes back—twenty years ago
the stalks were pliant, stiff,
rough green fibers, unwoven,
and winds that chafed my face
and dazed me. Now
harvesters groan to the edge,

shadows scatter over the fields
and freed from the glare I look up
relieved to see
cloud patches overhead
and wonder if they give
the only shade around here
in the raging, treeless air.

A vast meadow flared
outside our Best Western Motel.
And dusk held at the horizon's edge
long after stars had burst through.

Nebraska flatlands. I am
struck by the absolute
division of the sky by one
darkening cloud: the rest
is an abyss of air. Time passes,
to all evidence, invisibly,
like the sky
that had no direction to go in
and hurled rain hard on our heads

and made us take refuge here,
in the desert air,
where the mountains are snow-capped
in summer.

Ubiquity of the sign
"D.H. Lawrence Shrine."
The roads in the hills outside
Taos are muddy, rutted,
and the wheels churn
the car to a standstill.

Feet deep in the clayey soil
we wade upward.
Lawrence's death certificates
hang on the wall like trophies.
I wondered what could appease
the spirits of the place

when a white cat,
standing sentinel on Frieda's headstone
upended an urn,
and all the ashes fell out
and scattered
and when I saw the cat again
its tail was entirely ashen.

Shapes in this light steady me.
Snow. Oval. Dome. Silo.
Shadows lengthen and stay.
But not for long.

(Pequod)

Alan Shapiro
Rain

for my Grandmother

Nobody troubled you
that last night, no one came.
No daughter visited
whose unrelenting care
accused you of your deep
need to have her there:
child now to your own child,
only your needling her
(she could do nothing right)
kept clenched your pride, yet left you
needing her that much more.
Not even your ex-husbands
appeared, as they always did
the moment you were sleeping,
to rummage through your purse
and drawers for every cent
you still imagined yours;
you'd feel their fast hands pass
like shadows over your skin,
still passionate because,
you'd cry, "You bastards can't
forget how good I was."
But seeing no one leave
that night before you woke,
there was, for once, no need
for your complaining, "Go
piss on my back, but don't

tell me it's raining."
                              That night,
all this was past.
                         Mildly,
just to yourself, you spoke
for a while about the weather
held in your window where,
twenty four years ago,
your stroke had put it:
                              Now
you could hear rain, all right,
outside, troubling you,
though casually, the way
a mother loves small trouble
for the care it lets her show:
mother and child, together—
nobody else was there—
lover and loved, you told
yourself. "Be sure to wear
your coat. It's not that cold
tonight, but you never know.
Be sure to button up
for me, before you go."

                                   (Ploughshares)

Peter Taylor
The Gift of the Prodigal

HERE'S RICKY DOWN IN THE WASHED RIVER GRAVEL of my driveway. I had my yardman out raking it before 7 A.M.—the driveway. It looks nearly perfect. Ricky also looks nearly perfect down there. He looks extremely got up and cleaned up, as though *he* had been carefully raked over and smoothed out. He is wearing a three-piece linen suit, which my other son, you may be sure, wouldn't be seen wearing on any occasion. And he has on an expensive striped shirt, open at the collar. No tie, of course. His thick head of hair, parted and slicked down, is just the same tan color as the gravel. Hair and gravel seem equally clean and in order. The fact is, Ricky looks this morning as though he belongs nowhere else in the world but out there in that smooth spread of washed river gravel (which will be mussed up again before noon, of course—I'm resigned to it), looks as though he feels perfectly at home in that driveway of mine that was so expensive to install and that requires so much upkeep.

Since one can't see his freckles from where I stand at this second-story window, his skin looks very fair—almost transparent. (Ricky just misses being a real redhead, and so never lets himself get suntanned. Bright sunlight tends to give him skin cancers.) From the window directly above him, I am able to get the full effect of his outfit. He looks very masculine standing down there, which is no doubt the impression his form-fitting clothes are meant to give. And Ricky *is* very masculine, no matter what else he is or isn't. Peering down from up here, I mark particularly that where his collar stands open, and with several shirt buttons left carelessly or carefully undone, you can see a triangle of darker hair glistening on his chest. It isn't hard to imagine just how recently he has stepped out of the shower. In a word, he is looking what he considers his very best. And this says to me that Ricky is coming to me *for* something, or *because of* something.

His little sports car is parked in the turnaround behind this house which I've built since he and the other children grew up and since their mother died. I know of course that, for them, coming here to see me can never really be like coming home. For Rick it must be like going to see any other old fellow who might happen to be his boss and who is ailing and is staying away from the office for a few days. As soon as I saw him down there, though, I knew something was really seriously wrong. From here I could easily recognize the expression on his face. He has a way, when he is concerned about something, of knitting his eyebrows and at the same time opening his eyes very wide, as though his eyes are about to pop out of his head and his eyebrows are trying to hold them in. It's a look that used to give him away even as a child, when he was in trouble at school. If his mother and I saw that expression on his face, we would know that we were apt to be rung up by one of his teachers in a day or so or maybe have a house call from one of them.

Momentarily Ricky massages his face with his big right hand, as if to wipe away the expression. And clearly now he is headed for the side door that opens on the driveway. But before actually coming over to the door he has stopped in one spot and keeps shuffling his suède shoes about, roughing up the smooth gravel, like a young bull in a pen. I almost call out to him not to *do* that, not to muss up my gravel, which even his car wheels haven't disturbed—or not so much as he is doing with his suède shoes. I *almost* call out to him. But of course I don't really. For Ricky is a man twenty-nine years old, with two divorces already and no doubt another coming up soon. He's been through all

that, besides a series of live-ins between marriages that I
don't generally speak of, even.

For some time before coming on into the house, Ricky
remains there in that spot in the driveway. While he stands
there, it occurs to me that he may actually be looking the
place over, as though he'd never noticed what this house is
like until now. The old place, on Wertland Street, where he
and the other children grew up, didn't have half the style
and convenience of this one. It had more room, but the room
was mostly in pantries and hallways, with front stairs and
back stairs and third-floor servants' quarters in an age
when no servant would be caught dead living up there in
the attic—or staying anywhere else on the place, for that
matter. I am not unaware, of course, how much better that
old house on Wertland was than this one. You couldn't have
replaced it for twice what I've poured into this compact and
well-appointed habitation out here in Farmington. But its
neighborhood had gone bad. Nearly all of Charlottesville
proper has, as a matter of fact, either gone commercial or
been absorbed by the university. You can no longer live
within the shadow of Mr. Jefferson's Academical Village.
And our old Wertland Street house is now a funeral parlor.
Which is what it ought to have been five years before I left
it. From the day my wife, Cary, died, the place seemed like
a tomb. I wandered up and down the stairs and all around,
from room to room, sometimes greeting myself in one of
Cary's looking glasses, doing so out of loneliness or out of
thinking *that* couldn't be *me* still in my dressing gown and
slippers at midday, or fully dressed—necktie and all—at 3
A.M. I knew well enough it was time to sell. And, besides, I
wanted to have the experience at last of making something
new. You see, we never built a house of our own, Cary and
I. We always bought instead of building, wishing to be in
an established neighborhood, you know, where there were
good day schools for the girls (it was before St. Anne's

moved to the suburbs), where there were streetcars and buses for the servants, or, better still, an easy walk for them to Ridge Street.

My scheme for building a new house after Cary died seemed a harebrained idea to my three older children. They tried to talk me out of it. They said I was only doing it out of idleness. They'd laugh and say I'd chosen a rather expensive form of entertainment for myself in my old age. That's what they *said*. That wasn't all they *thought*, however. But I never held against them what they thought. All motherless children—regardless of age—have such thoughts. They had in mind that I'd got notions of marrying again. Me! Why, I've never looked at another woman since the day I married. Not to this very hour. At any rate, one night when we were having dinner and they were telling me how they worried about me, and making it plainer than usual what they thought my plans for the future were or might be, Ricky spoke up—Ricky, who never gave a thought in his life to what happened to anybody except himself—and he came out with just what was on the others' minds. "What if you should take a notion to marry again?" he asked. And I began shaking my head before the words were out of his mouth, as did all the others. It was an unthinkable thought for them as well as for me. "Why not?" Ricky persisted, happy of course that he was making everybody uncomfortable. "Worse things have happened, you know. And I nominate the handsome Mrs. Capers as a likely candidate for bride."

I *think* he was referring to a certain low sort of woman who had recently moved into the old neighborhood. You could depend upon Rick to know about her and know her name. As he spoke he winked at me. Presently he crammed his wide mouth full of food, and as he chewed he made a point of drawing back his lips and showing his somewhat overlarge and overly white front teeth. He continued to

look straight at me as he chewed, but looking with only one
eye, keeping the eye he'd winked at me squinched up tight.
He looked for all the world like some old tomcat who's found
a nasty morsel he likes the taste of and is not going to let
go of. I willingly would have knocked him out of his chair
for what he'd said, even more for that common look he was
giving me. I knew he knew as well as the others that I'd
never looked at any woman besides his mother.

Yet I laughed with the others as soon as I realized they
were laughing. You don't let a fellow like Rick know he's
got your goat—especially when he's your own son and has
been in one bad scrape after another ever since he's been
grown and seems always just waiting for a chance to get
back at you for something censorious you may have said to
him while trying to help him out of one of his escapades.
Since Cary died, I've tried mostly just to keep lines of com-
munication with him open. I think that's the thing she
would have wanted of me—that is, not to shut Rick out, to
keep him talking. Cary used to say to me, "You may be the
only person he can talk to about the women he gets involved with. He can't talk to me about such things." Cary
always thought it was the women he had most on his mind
and who got him into his scrapes. I never used to think so.
Anyway, I believe that Cary would have wished above all
else for me to keep lines open with Rick, would have wanted
it even more than she would have wanted me to go ahead
in whatever way I chose with schemes for a new house for
my old age.

Because the house was *our* plan originally, you see, hers
and mine. It was something we never told the children
about. There seemed no reason why we should. Not talking
about it except between ourselves was part of the pleasure
of it, somehow. And that night when Ricky came out with
the speculation about my possibly marrying again, I didn't
tell him or the others that actually I had already sold the

Wertland Street house and already had blueprints for the new house here in Farmington locked away in my desk drawer, and even a contractor all set to break ground.

WELL, MY NEW HOUSE WAS FINISHED THE FOLlowing spring. By that time all the children, excepting Rick, had developed a real enthusiasm for it. (Rick didn't give a damn one way or the other, of course.) They helped me dispose of all the superfluous furniture in the old house. The girls even saw to the details of moving and saw to it that I got comfortably settled in. They wanted me to be happy out here. And soon enough they saw I was. There was no more they could do for me now than there had been in recent years. They had their good marriages to look after (that's what Cary would have wished for them), and they saw to it that I wasn't left out of whatever of their activities I wanted to be in on. In a word, they went on with their busy lives, and my own life seemed busy enough for any man my age.

What has vexed the other children, though, during the five years since I built my house, is their brother Ricky's continuing to come to me at almost regular intervals with new ordeals of one kind or another that he's been going through. They have thought he ought not to burden me with his outrageous and sometimes sordid affairs. I think they have especially resented his troubling me here at home. I still go to the office, you see, two or three days a week— just whenever I feel like it or when I'm not playing golf or bridge or am not off on a little trip to Sarasota (I stay at the same inn Cary and I used to go to). And so I've always seen Ricky quite regularly at the office. He's had every chance to talk to me there. But the fact is, Rick was never one for bringing his personal problems to the office. He has always brought them home.

Even since I've moved, he has always come *here*, to the house, when he's really wanted to talk to me about something. I don't know whether it's the two servants I still keep or some of the young neighbors hereabouts who tell them, but somehow the other children always know when Ricky has been here. And they of course can put two and two together. It will come out over Sunday dinner at one of their houses or at the Club—in one of those little private dining rooms. It is all right if we eat in the big dining room, where everybody else is. I know I'm safe there. But as soon as I see they've reserved a private room I know they want to talk about Ricky's latest escapade. They will begin by making veiled references to it among themselves. But at last it is I who am certain to let the cat out of the bag. For I can't resist joining in when they get onto Rick, as they all know very well I won't be able to. You see, often they will have the details wrong—maybe they get them wrong on purpose—and I feel obliged to straighten them out. Then one of them will turn to me, pretending shocked surprise: "How ever did you know about it? Has *he* been bringing his troubles to *you* again? At his age you'd think he'd be ashamed to! Someone ought to remind him he's a grown man now!" At that point one of the girls is apt to rest her hand on mine. As they go on, I can hear the love for me in their voices and see it in their eyes. I know then what a lucky man I am. I want to say to them that their affection makes up for all the unhappiness Ricky causes me. But I have never been one to make speeches like that. Whenever I have managed to say such things, I have somehow always felt like a hypocrite afterward. Anyway, the talk will go on for a while till I remember a bridge game I have an appointment for in the Club lounge, at two o'clock. Or I recall that my golf foursome is waiting for me in the locker room.

I've never tried to defend Rick from the others. The things he does are really quite indefensible. Sometimes I've even found myself giving details about some escapade of his that the others didn't already know and are genuinely shocked to hear—especially coming from me. He was in a shooting once that everybody in Farmington and in the whole county set knew about—or knew about, that is, in a general way, though without knowing the very thing that would finally make it a public scandal. It's an ugly story, I warn you, as indeed, nearly all of Ricky's stories are.

He had caught another fellow in bed with a young married woman with whom he himself was running around. Of course it was a scandalous business, all of it. But the girl, as Rick described her to me afterward, was a real beauty of a certain type and, according to Rick, as smart as a whip. Rick even showed me her picture, though I hadn't asked to see it, naturally. She had a tight little mouth, and eyes that—even in that wallet-sized picture— burned themselves into your memory. She was the sort of intense and reckless-looking girl that Ricky has always gone for. I've sometimes looked at pictures of his other girls, too, when he wanted to show them to me. And of course I know what his wives have looked like. All three of his wives have been from good families. For, bad as he is, Ricky is not the sort of fellow who would embarrass the rest of us by *marrying* some slut. Yet even his wives have tended to dress themselves in a way that my own daughters wouldn't. They have dressed, that is to say, in clothes that seemed designed to call attention to their female forms and not, as with my daughters, to call attention to the station and the affluence of their husbands. Being the timid sort of man I am, I used to find myself whenever I talked with his wife— whichever one—carefully looking out the window or looking across the room, away from her, at some inanimate object or other over there or out there. My wife, Cary, used to say that Ricky had bad luck in his wives, that each of them turned out to have just as roving an eye as Ricky himself. I can't say for certain whether this was true for each of them in the beginning or whether it was something Ricky managed to teach them all.

Anyway, the case of the young married woman in whose bed—or apartment—Ricky found that other fellow came near to causing Ricky more trouble than any of his other escapades. The fellow ran out of the apartment, with Rick chasing him into the corridor and down the corridor to a door of an outside stairway. It was not here in Farmington, you see, but out on Barracks Road, where so many of Rick's friends are—in a development that's been put up on the very edge of where the horse farms begin. The fellow scurried down the outside stairs and across a parking lot toward some pastureland beyond. And Rick, as he said, couldn't resist taking a shot at him from that upstairs stoop where he had abandoned the chase. He took aim just when the fellow reached the first pasture fence and was about to climb over. Afterward, Rick said that it was simply too good to miss. But Rick rarely misses a target when he takes aim. He hit the fellow with a load of rat shot right in the seat of the pants.

I'll never know how Rick happened to have the gun with him. He told me that he was deeply in love with the young woman and would have married her if her husband had been willing to give her a divorce. The other children maintain to this day that it was the husband Rick meant to threaten with the gun, but the husband was out of town and Rick lost his head when he found that other fellow there in his place. Anyhow, the story got all over town. I suppose Ricky himself helped to spread it. He thought it all awfully funny at first. But before it was over, the matter came near to getting into the courts and into the paper. And that was because there was something else involved, which the other children and the people in the Barracks Road set didn't know about and I did. In fact, it was something that I worried about from the beginning. You see,

Rick naturally took that fellow he'd blasted with the rat shot to a doctor—a young doctor friend of theirs—who removed the shot. But, being a friend, the doctor didn't report the incident. A certain member of our judiciary heard the details and thought perhaps the matter needed looking into. We were months getting it straightened out. Ricky went out of town for a while, and the young doctor ended by having to move away permanently—to Richmond or Norfolk, I think. I only give this incident in such detail in order to show the sort of low company Ricky has always kept, even when he seemed to be among our own sort.

His troubles haven't all involved women, though. Or not primarily. And that's what I used to tell Cary. Like so many people in Charlottesville, Rick has always had a weakness for horses. For a while he fancied himself a polo player. He bought a polo pony and got cheated on it. He bought it at a stable where he kept another horse he owned— bought it from the man who ran the stable. After a day or so, he found that the animal was a worthless, worn-out nag. It couldn't even last through the first chukker, which was humiliating of course for Ricky. He daren't try to take it onto the field again. It had been all doped up when he bought it. Ricky was outraged. Instead of simply trying to get his money back, he wanted to have his revenge upon the man and make an even bigger fool of *him*. He persuaded a friend to dress himself up in a turtleneck sweater and a pair of yellow jodhpurs and pretend just to be passing by the stall in the same stable, where the polo pony was still kept. His friend played the role, you see, of someone only just taking up the game and who thought he *had* to have that particular pony. He asked the man whose animal it was, and before he could get an answer he offered more than twice the price that Rick had paid. He even put the offer into writing—using an assumed name, of course. He said he was from up in Maryland and would return in two days' time. Naturally, the stableman telephoned Ricky as

soon as the stranger in jodhpurs had left the stable. He said
he had discovered, to his chagrin, that the pony was not in
as good condition as he had thought it was. And he said
that in order that there be no bad feeling between them he
was willing to buy it back for the price Ricky had paid.

Ricky went over that night and collected his money. But
when the stranger didn't reappear and couldn't be traced,
the stableman of course knew what had happened. Rick
didn't return to the stable during the following several
days. I suppose, being Ricky, he was busy spreading the
story all over town. His brother and sisters got wind of it.
And I did soon enough. On Sunday night, two thugs and
some woman Ricky knew but would never identify—not
even to me—came to his house and persuaded him to go
out and sit in their car with them in front of his house. And
there they beat him brutally. He had to be in the hospital
for five or six days. They broke his right arm, and one of
them—maybe it was the woman—was trying to bite off
the lobe of his left ear when Ricky's current wife, who had
been out to some party without the favor of his company,
pulled into the driveway beside the house. The assailants
shoved poor Ricky, bruised and bleeding and with his arm
broken, out onto the sidewalk. And then of course they sped
away down the street in their rented car. Ricky's wife and
the male friend who was with her got the license number,
but the car had been rented under an assumed name—the
same name, actually, as some kind of joke, I suppose, that
Ricky's friend in jodhpurs had used with the stablekeeper.

Since Ricky insisted that he could not possibly recognize
his two male assailants in a lineup, and since he refused
to identify the woman, there was little that could be done
about his actual beating. I don't know that he ever con-
fessed to anyone but me that he knew the woman. It was
easy enough for me to imagine what *she* looked like. Though
I would not have admitted it to Ricky or to anyone else, I

would now and then during the following weeks see a woman of a certain type on the streets downtown—with one of those tight little mouths and with burning eyes—and imagine that she might be the very one. All we were ever able to do about the miserable fracas was to see to it finally that the stable was put out of business and that the man himself had to go elsewhere (he went down into North Carolina) to ply his trade.

THERE IS ONE OTHER SCRAPE OF RICKY'S THAT I MUST mention, because it remains particularly vivid for me. The nature and the paraphernalia of this one will seem even more old-fashioned than those of the other incidents. Maybe that's why it sticks in my mind so. It's something that might have happened to any number of rough fellows I knew when I was coming along.

Ricky, not surprising to say, likes to gamble. From the time he was a young boy he would bet on anything at home. He would often try to inveigle one of the other children into making wagers with him on how overdone his steak was at dinner. He always liked it very rare and when his serving came he would hold up a bite on his fork and, for a decision on the bet, would ask everyone what shade of brown the meat was. He made all the suggestions of color himself. And one night his suggestions got so coarse and vile his mother had to send him from the dining room and not let him have a bite of supper. Sometimes he would try to get the other children to bet with him on the exact number of minutes the preacher's sermon would last on Sunday or how many times the preacher would use the word "Hell" or "damnation" or "adultery." Since he has got grown, it's the races, of course, he likes—horse races, it goes without saying, but also such low-life affairs as dog races and auto races. What catches his fancy above all else, though, is the chicken fights we have always had in our part of the country. And a few years ago he bought himself a little farm a dozen miles or so south of town, where he could raise his own game chickens. I saw nothing wrong with that at the time. Then he built an octagonal barn down there, with a pit in it where he could hold the fights. I worried a little when he did that. But we've always had cockfights hereabouts. The birds are beautiful creatures, really, though they have no brains, of course. The fight itself is a real spectacle and no worse than some other things people enjoy. At Ricky's urging, I even went down to two or three fights at his place. I didn't bet, because I knew the stakes were very high. (Besides, it's the betting that's illegal.) And I didn't tell the other children about my going. But this was after Cary was dead, you see, and I thought maybe she would have liked my going for Ricky's sake, though she would never have acknowledged it. Pretty soon, sizable crowds began attending the fights on weekend nights. Cars would be parked all over Ricky's front pasture and all around the yard of the tenant house. He might as well have put up a sign down at the gate where his farm road came off the highway.

The point is, everyone knew that the cockfights went on. And one of his most regular customers and biggest bettors was one of the county sheriff's right-hand men. I'm afraid Rick must have bragged about that in advertising his fights to friends—friends who would otherwise have been a little timid about coming. And during the fights he would move about among the crowd, winking at people and saying to them under his breath, "The deputy's here tonight." I suppose it was his way of reassuring them that everything was all right. I don't know whether or not his spreading the word so widely had anything to do with the raid, but nevertheless the deputy was present the night the federal officers came stealing up the farm road, with their car lights off and with search warrants in their pockets. And it was the deputy who first got wind of the federal officers' approach. He had one of his sidekicks posted outside the barn. Maybe he had somebody watching out there every night that he came. Maybe all along he had had a plan for his escape in such an emergency. Rick thought so afterward. Anyhow, the deputy's man outside knew at once what those cars moving up the lane with their lights off meant. The deputy got the word before anyone else, but, depend upon Ricky, he saw the first move the deputy made to leave. And he was not going to have it. He took out after him.

The deputy's watchman was prepared to stay on and take his chances. (He wasn't even a patrolman. He probably only worked in the office.) I imagine he was prepared to spend a night in jail if necessary, and pay whatever fine there might be, because his presence could explain one of the sheriff's cars' being parked in the pasture. But the deputy himself took off through the backwoods on Ricky's property and toward a county road on the back of the place. Ricky, as I've said, was not going to have that. Since the cockfight was on his farm, he knew there was no way out of trouble for himself. But he thought it couldn't, at least, do him any harm to have the deputy caught along with everybody else. Moreover, the deputy had lost considerable amounts of money there at the pit in recent weeks and had insinuated to Ricky that he suspected some of the cocks had been tampered with. (I, personally, don't believe Ricky would stand for that.) Ricky couldn't be sure there wasn't some collusion between the deputy and the feds. He saw the deputy's man catch the deputy's eye from the barn doorway and observed the deputy's departure. He was right after him. He overtook him just before he reached the woods. Fortunately, the deputy wasn't armed. (Ricky allowed no one to bring a gun inside the barn.) And fortunately Ricky wasn't armed, either, that night. They scuffled a little near the gate to the woods lot. The deputy, being a man twice Rick's age, was no match for him and was soon overpowered. Ricky dragged him back to the barn, himself resisting—as he later testified—all efforts at bribery on the deputy's part, and turned in both himself and his captive to the federal officers.

Extricating Ricky from that affair and setting matters aright was a long and complicated undertaking. The worst of it really began for Ricky after the court proceedings were finished and all fines were paid (there were no jail terms for anyone), because from his last appearance in the federal courthouse Ricky could drive his car scarcely one block through that suburb where he lives without receiving a traffic ticket of some kind. There may not have been anything crooked about it, for Ricky is a wild sort of driver at best. But, anyhow, within a short time his driving license was revoked for the period of a year. Giving up driving was a great inconvenience for him and a humiliation. All we could do about the deputy, who, Ricky felt sure, had connived with the federal officers, was to get him out of his job after the next election.

The outcome of the court proceedings was that Rick's fines were very heavy. Moreover, efforts were made to confiscate all the livestock on his farm, as well as the farm machinery. But he was saved from the confiscation by a special circumstance, which, however, turned out to produce for him only a sort of Pyrrhic victory. It turned out, you see, that the farm was not in Ricky's name but in that of his young tenant farmer's wife. I never saw her, or didn't know it if I did. Afterward, I used to try to recall if I hadn't seen some such young woman when I was down watching the cockfights—one who would have fitted the picture in my mind. My imagination played tricks on me, though. I would think I remembered the face or figure of some young girl I'd seen there who could conceivably be the one. But then suddenly I'd recall another and think possibly it might be she who had the title to Ricky's farm. I never could be sure.

W HEN RICKY APPEARED OUTSIDE MY WINDOW JUST now, I'd already had a very bad morning. The bursitis in my right shoulder had waked me before dawn. At last I got up and dressed, which was an ordeal in itself. (My right hip was hurting somewhat, too.) When finally the cook came in, she wanted to give me a massage before she began fixing breakfast even. Cary would never have allowed her to make that mistake. A massage, you see, is the worst thing you can do for my sort of bursitis. What I wanted was some breakfast. And I knew it would take Meg three-quarters of an hour to put breakfast on the table. And so I managed to get out of my clothes again and ease myself into a hot bath, groaning so loud all the while that Meg came up to the door twice and asked if I was all right. I told her just to go and get my breakfast ready. After breakfast, I waited till a decent hour and then telephoned one of my golf foursome to tell him I couldn't play this afternoon. The two other members of the foursome had already called him and said they also had bursitis and couldn't play today. It's this damp fall weather that does us in worst. All you can do is sit and think how you've got the whole winter before you and wonder if you'll be able to get yourself off to someplace like Sarasota.

While I sat at a front window, waiting for the postman (he never brings anything but circulars and catalogues on Saturday; besides, all my serious mail goes to the office and is opened by someone else), I found myself thinking of all the things I couldn't do and all the people who are dead and that I mustn't think about. I tried to do a little better— that is, to think of something cheerful. There was lots I

could be cheerful about, wasn't there? At least three of my
children were certain to telephone today—all but Ricky,
and it was sure to be bad news if he did! And a couple of
the grandchildren would likely call, too. Then tomorrow
I'd be going to lunch with some of them if I felt up to it.
Suddenly I thought of the pills I was supposed to have
taken before breadfast and had forgotten to: the Inderal
and the potassium and the hydrochlorothiazide. I began to
get up from my chair and then I settled down again. It
didn't really matter. There was no ailment I had that could
really be counted on to be fatal if I missed one day's dosage.
And then I wholeheartedly embraced the old subject, the
old speculation: How many days like this one, how many
years like this one lay ahead for me? And finally, irresist-
ibly, I descended to lower depths still, thinking of past
times not with any relish but remembering how in past
times I had always *told* myself I'd someday look back with
pleasure on what would seem good old days, which was an
indication itself that they hadn't somehow been good
enough—not good enough, that is, to stand on their own
as an end in themselves. If the old days were so damned
good, why had I had to think always how good they would
someday seem in retrospect? I had just reached the part
where I think there was nothing *wrong* with them and
that I ought to be satisfied, had just reached that point at
which I recall that I loved and was loved by my wife, that I
love and am loved by my children, that it's not them or my
life but *me* there's something wrong with!—had just reached
that inevitable syllogism that I always come to, when I was
distracted by the arrival of Saturday morning's late mail
delivery. It was brought in, it was handed to me by a pair
of black hands, and of course it had nothing in it. But I took
it upstairs to my sitting room. (So that even the servant
wouldn't see there was nothing worth having in it.) I had
just closed my door and got out my pills when I heard
Ricky's car turn in to the gravel driveway.

He was driving so slowly that his car wheels hardly disturbed the gravel. That in itself was an ominous phenomenon. He was approaching slowly and quietly. He didn't want me to know ahead of time what there was in store for me. My first impulse was to lock my door and refuse to admit him. I simply did not feel up to Rick this morning! But I said to myself, "That's something I've never done, though maybe ought to have done years ago, no matter what Cary said. He's sure to send my blood pressure soaring." I thought of picking up the telephone and phoning one of the other children to come and protect me from this monster of a son and from whatever sort of trouble he was now in.

But it was just then that I caught my first glimpse of him down in the driveway. I had the illusion that he was admiring the place. And then of course I was at once disillusioned. He was only hesitating down there because he dreaded seeing me. But he was telling himself he *had* to see me. There would be no other solution to his problem but to see his old man. I knew what he was thinking by the gesture he was making with his left hand. It's strange how you get the notion that your children are like you just because they have the same facial features and the same body build and make the same gestures when talking to themselves. None of it means a thing! It's only an illusion. Even now I find myself making gestures with my hands when I'm talking to myself that I used to notice my own father making sometimes when we were out walking together and neither of us had spoken a word for half an hour or so. It used to get on my nerves when I saw Father do it, throwing out his hand almost imperceptibly, with his long fingers spread apart. I don't know why it got on my nerves so. But, anyhow, I never dreamed that I could inherit such a gesture—or much less that one of my sons would. And yet there Ricky is, down in the driveway, making the same gesture precisely. And there never were three men with more different characters than my father and me and my youngest child. I watch Ricky make the gesture several times while standing in the driveway. And now suddenly he turns as if to go back to his car. I step away from the window, hoping he hasn't seen me and will go on off. But, having once seen him down there, I can't, of course, do that. I have to receive him and hear him out. I open the sash and call down to him, "Come on up, Ricky."

He looks up at me, smiles guiltily, and shrugs. Then he comes on in the side entrance. As he moves through the house and up the stairs, I try to calm myself. I gaze down at the roughed-up gravel where his suède shoes did their damage and tell myself it isn't so bad and even manage to smile at my own old-maidishness. Presently, he comes into the sitting room. We greet each other with the usual handshake. I can smell his shaving lotion. Or maybe it is something he puts on his hair. We go over and sit down by the fireplace, where there is a fire laid but not lit in this season, of course. He begins by talking about everything under the sun except what is on his mind. This is standard procedure in our talks at such times. Finally, he begins looking into the fireplace as though he were watching low-burning flames. I barely keep myself from smiling when he says, "I've got a little problem—not so damned little, in fact. It's a matter that's got out of hand."

And then I say, "I supposed as much."

You can't give Ricky an inch at these times, you see. Else he'll take advantage of you. Pretty soon he'll have shifted the whole burden of how he's to be extricated onto your shoulders. I wait for him to continue, and he is about to, I think. But before he can get started he turns his eyes away from the dry logs and the unlit kindling and begins looking about the room, just as he looked about the premises outside. It occurs to me again that he seems to be observing my place for the very first time. But I don't suppose he really is. His mind is, as usual, on himself. Then all at once his eyes do obviously come to focus on something over my shoulder. He runs his tongue up under his upper lip and then under his lower lip, as though he were cleaning his teeth. I, involuntarily almost, look over my shoulder. There on the library table behind me, on what I call my desk, are my cut-glass tumbler and three bottles of pills—my hydrochlorothiazide, my Inderal, and my potassium. Somehow I failed to put them back in my desk drawer earlier. I was so distracted by my morbid thoughts when I came upstairs that I forgot to stick them away in the place where I keep them out of sight from everybody. (I don't even like for the servants to see what and how much medicine I take.) Without a word passing between us, and despite the pains in my shoulder and hip, I push myself up out of my chair and sweep the bottles, and the tumbler, too, into the desk drawer. I keep my back to Ricky for a minute or so till I can overcome the grimacing I never can repress when these pains strike. Suddenly, though, I do turn back to him and find he has come to his feet. I pay no special attention to that. I ease myself back into my chair, saying, "Yes, Ricky." Making my voice rather hard, I say, "You've got a problem?" He looks at me coldly, without a trace of the sympathy any one of the other children would have shown—knowing, that is, as he surely does, that I am having pains of some description. And he speaks to me as though I were a total stranger toward whom he feels nothing but is just barely human enough to wish not to torture. "Man," he says—the idea of his addressing *me* that way!—"Man, you've got problems enough of your own. Even the world's greatest snotface can see that. One thing sure, you don't need to hear *my* crap."

I am on my feet so quick you wouldn't think I have a pain in my body. "Don't you use that gutter language with me, Ricky!" I say. "You weren't brought up in some slum over beyond Vinegar Hill!" He only turns and looks into the fireplace again. If there were a fire going I reckon he would have spat in it at this point. Then he looks back at me, running his tongue over his teeth again. And then, without any apology or so much as a by-your-leave, he heads for the door. "Come back here, Ricky!" I command. "Don't you dare leave the room!" Still moving toward the closed door, he glances back over his shoulder at me, with a wide, hard grin on his face, showing his mouthful of white teeth, as though my command were the funniest thing he has ever heard. At the door, he puts his big right hand on the glass knob, covering it entirely. Then he twists his upper body, his torso, around—seemingly just from the hips—to face me. And simultaneously he brings up his left hand and scratches that triangle of dark hair where his shirt is open. It is like some kind of dirty gesture he is making. I say to myself, "He really is like something not quite human. For all the jams and scrapes he's been in, he's never suffered any second thoughts or known the meaning of remorse. I ought to have let him hang in some noose of his own making years ago. I ought to have let him hang," I say to myself, "by his own beautiful locks."

But almost simultaneously what I hear myself saying aloud is "Please don't go, Rick. Don't go yet, son." Yes, I am pleading with him, and I mean what I say with my whole heart. He still has his right hand on the doorknob and has given it a full turn. Our eyes meet across the room, directly, as they never have before in the whole of Ricky's life or mine. I think neither of us could tell anyone what it is he sees in the other's eyes, unless it is a need beyond any description either of us is capable of.

Presently Rick says, "You don't need to hear my crap."

And I hear my bewildered voice saying, "I do . . . I do." And "Don't go, Ricky, my boy." My eyes have even misted over. But I still meet his eyes across the now too silent room. He looks at me in the most compassionate way imaginable. I don't think any child of mine has ever looked at me so before. Or perhaps it isn't really with compassion he is viewing me but with the sudden, gratifying knowledge that it is not, after all, such a one-sided business, the business between us. He keeps his right hand on the doorknob a few seconds longer. Then I hear the latch click and know he has let go. Meanwhile, I observe his left hand making that familiar gesture, his fingers splayed, his hand tilting back and forth. I am out of my chair by now. I go to the desk and bring out two Danlys cigars from another desk drawer, which I keep locked. He is there ready to receive my offering when I turn around. He accepts the cigar without smiling, and I give it without smiling, too. Seated opposite each other again, each of us lights his own.

And then Ricky begins. What will it be this time, I think. I am wild with anticipation. Whatever it will be, I know it is all anyone in the world can give me now—perhaps the most anyone has ever been able to give a man like me. As Ricky begins, I try to think of all the good things the other children have done for me through the years, and of their affection, and of my wife's. But it seems this was all there ever was. I forget my pains and my pills and the cancelled golf game, and the meaningloo mail that morning. I find I can scarcely sit still in my chair for wanting Ricky to get on with it. Has he been brandishing his pistol again? Or dragging the sheriff's deputy across a field at midnight? And does he have in his wallet perhaps a picture of some other girl with a tight little mouth, and eyes that burn? Will his outrageous story include her? And perhaps explain her fascination or perhaps not explain it, leaving her a blessed mystery? As Ricky begins, I find myself listening not merely with fixed attention but with my whole being. . . . I hear him beginning. I am listening. I am listening gratefully to all he will tell me about himself, about his life, about any life that is not my own.

(The New Yorker)

Jean Thompson
Remembering Sonny

MOTHERS HATED HIM. HE WASN'T THE HOOD TYPE, with tattoos and a knife in his boot and a frozen sneer. If he had been, the mothers could have at least defined what they objected to, though it's still doubtful the daughters would have been convinced. Nor was he too good-looking, which would have been another cause for suspicion. No, as it was, they would encounter Sonny in their kitchens, scrambling eggs, or helping little brother put the batteries in his ray gun, the most innocent and pastoral of situations, and Sonny would grin and say Good afternoon, Mrs. So and So, and the mothers would be struck cold. For they could tell he didn't ever mean a word he said, not to them, not to the daughters. And furthermore, he knew the mothers saw through him and he didn't care. His manners were a charade, one of their own weapons used against them.

(Fathers, of course, noticed nothing. They shook hands with him and remembered him as Johnny or Sammy or simply as one of those cars which was always blocking the drive.)

Well what's wrong with him? the daughters demanded, and the mothers were forced to use words like smart-aleck and dishonest. Which were entirely too vague. The daughters stamped their feet and said, You just don't want me to go out with anyone. You don't want me to have any fun at all. The daughters, of course, recognized Sonny's insincerity towards the mothers, even recognized that it was turned against themselves, but they weren't above using the mothers' confusion to best advantage. So Sonny would smile his too-tight smile, which made his face look narrow and foxy, and say, Good evening, Mrs. So and So, and usher the daughters out into the lurid unsafe night.

Alice's mother went so far as to come to her room once as she was dressing to go out with him and say in a rapid, rehearsed voice, Sonny is just not a nice boy, and maybe the others aren't nice boys either but at least they care about you and Sonny doesn't, so if he asks you say no. Her mother didn't look at her when she spoke; she seemed to address her recital to the poster above Alice's head. The poster showed Jimi Hendrix against a billowing formless background of purple, orange, and painful green, the one unequivocal adolescent note in Alice's Early American bedroom.

Alice, who was both embarrassed and resentful, nevertheless refrained from saying, What do you mean? Which would have been simply intolerable for her mother to answer. Instead she said OK, and waited, dryly, tapping a comb against the dresser so her mother could see she was intruding.

Alice thought that this episode was one reason her mother never said anything about Sonny's death, though she must have known about it. Her mother had wanted Sonny to be, if not quite dead, at least thoroughly absent. Perhaps she felt indirectly guilty. If she mentioned his death with regret Alice could accuse her of hypocrisy. If her words contained the faintest hint that his end was somewhat inevitable, or just-as-well, Alice would seize on it. Either way, the memory of that incident would shimmer between them, its embarrassment resurrected.

Therefore, nothing was ever said. By that time Alice no longer lived at home and the threat of Sonny was replaced by other threats and finally her mother was convinced that everything she had ever warned about had already happened anyway. So there was no real reason to mention him. Alice herself didn't think of him incessantly. Though since he had died at the rather ridiculous age of nineteen she

felt, as she grew older, a sense of obligation. Not just to
remember him as he was but to imagine him as he might
have been with the silliness and mistakes outgrown.

Besides, there was a certain pleasure in having a dead
lover. In songs and movies, after all, it was the very essence
of romance. A part of her despised such morbid sentimen-
tality and tried to keep her feelings genuine and uncom-
plicated. But sooner or later she would find herself thinking not of Sonny but of herself, how interesting her
melancholy was, how poignant, how attractive. Sternly she'd
force her attention back to Sonny. But she was like a Puri-
tan trying to avoid the subtle sin of Pride and finding it
instead at every turn. If she thought of his death, for example, she inevitably thought of how she had learned of it,
what effect the news had on her, and so on.

What kind of person was she, she'd ask herself in a fit of
disgust. Hadn't she cared about Sonny at all? Yet she knew
her self-loathing was exaggerated too. Finally she was forced
to accept her memories and the accompanying histrionics.
After all, she had been very young when she'd known him.
It was inevitable that some of those embarrassing younger
attitudes should survive, twined around the memory of
Sonny like vines around a stump.

So remembering Sonny was more complicated than it
first appeared, because it meant remembering herself too.

The last time she saw him they'd spent all night skidding from one Chicago freeway to another in Sonny's brand-
new van. It was a powder-blue Dodge with a windshield so
large it was like flying an airplane, Sonny said, pounding
on the dash, though of course he'd never flown an airplane.
Alice thought it was more like driving a Greyhound bus,
you were so high up and the seat pitched you forward into
that slick bubble of glass. But she didn't say anything because Sonny was so perfectly happy and besides, she'd never
driven a Greyhound either.

An April night, very black and frosty, wind shredding

the new leaves. A shrill unsettled night, more like Hallowe'en than spring. In the back was a friend of Sonny's who was already out of the service. His name was Graham, she didn't know if that was his first or last name, and he kept getting tangled in the wires for the speakers. Or else he'd kneel between the two front seats to be part of the conversation, and every time Alice turned around his face would be about two inches from hers.

He had very round blue eyes and he kept grinning at her with this really *feverish* enthusiasm, Alice thought. The grin made his face look like a china plate that's been cracked and the pieces put back together wrong.

Once, when Sonny took a turn so fast it sent Graham somersaulting against the back door, Alice leaned over and asked, What did you do, sell me to this guy?

It's a trade. I'm getting two blankets and some venison.

Sonny, I'm serious, what the hell have you been telling him?

Aw, he's just so horny he's cross-eyed. Be nice to him.

I will not, said Alice, loud enough to be heard over the music. I won't be any nicer than I feel like being.

But Sonny was singing along with the tape, ignoring her. Graham was back in his place between the seats. She caught a whiff of body heat from him, a close, muddy kind of heat.

Old Sonny sure wishes this was an airplane, huh? The grin prodded her.

He sure does. Experimentally, she smiled. Graham's breath thickened. His eyes seemed to squirm. Good God, Alice thought, and pretended to rummage through the box of tapes so she wouldn't have to look at him.

The highway at night was a separate glamorous country of speed and loneliness, whispering of accidental death. The pavement hummed beneath the van's wheels. Shallow headlights swung past them on the opposite side of the road. They drove first west, then south out of the city, then doubled back into the intricate concrete ugliness of Chicago. Alice watched the landscape. A single farmhouse would materialize from the darkness, or a whole new outcropping of subdivision bathed in pink sodium vapor. They passed so quickly it was hard to imagine yourself actually there, standing in some spot you fixed your eyes on. For a moment she played that game with herself, trying to penetrate the frail lighted windows and their promise of mystery.

Of course, it was also true that there was not much else for them to do. Eventually what had been a whole range of possibilities went flat, so that by ten o'clock Alice said, trying not to sound querulous, Sonny, is there anyplace we can go?

Sonny shrugged and said I dunno, then, unexpectedly, We'll stop at my folks' crib. Again they reversed directions.

They were traveling a section of lighted road, the tall poles delicate and menacing, like giant insects in a science fiction movie. Stripes of numb light blinked over them in quick succession. Alice watched Sonny's face jump in and out of darkness. Every so often she could persuade herself he was good-looking.

Certainly if you were talking to a girlfriend, someone who didn't know him, you could make him sound OK, in fact she had often done so. 'He has green eyes,' she'd say, emphasizing this as something especially intriguing and subtle, and the girlfriend would be impressed. His eyes were tilted at the corner and Sonny had a habit of narrowing them even further so they expressed nothing but irony. 'His hair,' Alice might add, 'is reddish-brown, you know,' waving her hand vaguely, 'chestnut-colored.' Though just plain brown would have done, and Sonny wore it trimmed too short in back and too long in front, a peculiar compromise with his father and later with the Navy.

He had been too skinny, still a boy in spite of his booming voice and large-knuckled hands and black sprouting

whiskers. She tried to be loyal, and she imagined him as
he might have grown. After all, she herself had developed
breasts and finally learned how to fix her hair. Yet she had
to admit she felt something of the survivor's secret gloat-
ing, grateful she hadn't been stuck in adolescence like a
gawky Peter Pan.

Sonny's parents' house was expensive and dull, like everything in the suburbs, she thought. His parents weren't
home. It seemed they were never home, though maybe
Sonny only brought people over in their absence. Alice had
never once met them, and she formed her ideas of them
from their empty house. The sign his mother clipped to the
refrigerator: Think sex, not food! His father's fussy-looking
humidor stand. Their bedroom, as neat and noncommittal
as something in a Holiday Inn. It was the sort of house
which at Christmas displays a white aluminum tree in the
picture window, decked with blue lights and blue glass
balls.

Graham was saying, Some spread, man, as they walked
up the path between careful, vaguely Japanese arrangements of stones and dwarf evergreens creaking in the wind.
Sonny just grunted. Any reference to his parents' money
seemed to discomfit him, and it surfaced in cynicism. So
that now, unlocking the front door, he said, Think of it as
one of those period rooms in a museum. Middle-class interior, late twentieth-century American.

The living room carpet was white and frosty in the darkness, its clean expanse rather intimidating. Sonny flipped
on a light and sauntered across to the kitchen. Graham
was at her elbow saying God *damn*, wish I had an apartment as big as this one room, huh? And while she felt sorry
for him in an impersonal way, she wanted to watch Sonny.
He was slamming cupboard doors, letting the water run
full blast in the sink. Whenever he was in this house he
seemed to be acting out an exaggerated contempt.

Now that they were out of the van Alice could see how short Graham was, no taller than herself, really, so she drew herself up, rocking a little on her heels. Yes, it is pretty big, she agreed, staring down at him. His grin flickered and he joined Sonny in the kitchen.

Sonny didn't get along with his own parents any more than he got along with the parents of his girlfriends. Nor had he lived long enough for rebellion against them to become less important, as it had for everyone else. In addition, the disagreements had been particularly violent. So that when Alice read the newspaper account of his father's remarks at the dedication of the flag pole (if that wasn't irony enough) with its standard words like sadness, duty, sacrifice, inspiration, she felt not just anger but distaste.

Granted, what could you expect him to say? 'My son often disappointed me. I would like to think that we loved each other in spite of our troubles, but I can't be sure. The ties among family members are often made legitimate simply by enduring over time, and we never had that time. Sonny would have laughed himself sick at the sight of this flag pole. I thank you.'

No, you couldn't expect much honesty, let alone eloquence, from people at such times. But Alice remembered Sonny showing up at her house with a swollen jaw, the inside of his mouth still bleeding, saying, The old man did that, his voice a mixture of fury and queer pride at how bad things really were now. And Alice had fussed and exclaimed over it more than was necessary, until Sonny was a little embarrassed. The night before, he said, he'd ridden the train back and forth to the city until dawn because he had no place else to go. That night she snuck him in the back door after her parents were asleep.

She was thinking of that time as Sonny emerged from the kitchen with a bucket of ice, vodka, and a pitcher of orange juice. She wanted to mention it, in an off-hand and conspiratorial fashion, something that would re-establish their shared past. But Sonny began singing in his exaggerated, operatic baritone, all tremolo and lushness:

Do you remember Sweet Alice, Ben Bolt
Sweet Alice, the girl from the town?
Who laughed with delight when you gave her
your smile
And trembled with fear at your frown

It never failed to annoy her. Why do you always sing me that dopey song? she demanded.

Because you're so sweet.

Bullshit. I bet it's not even a real song.

She watched him set the ice down carelessly on the top of the piano and mix the drinks. Here, he said, handing one to Graham. Take your medicine quietly and we won't have to give you the injection.

An injection could be interesting, said Graham, winking at Alice. Now that she was sitting down he seemed to have recovered some of his self-assurance.

Bend over and show us your best profile, then.

Aw Sonny. He was embarrassed again.

Madame. Sonny bowed and gave her a glass.

Thank you, Rufus.

Ole Rufus, he be happy to sarve you all, Miz Alice, don't ya'll pay me no nevah mind.

Please Sonny, spare us.

But he was off on one of his routines, on his knees in the white carpet, swaying back and forth with his hands clasped in front of him: Ah spect when ah stand befo dat hebbenly throne, de Lawd he 'member ole Rufus, de Lawd he not fergit his chillun. Miz Alice, Ah be hearin dem bands o angels fore long, 'deed, Ah spect ole Rufus not see de sun rise tomorry. Effen only ah be 'lowed to spen this yere las Chrissmus Eve wif mah wife an lil chile . . . Aarrgh.

Alice had nudged him with her foot and he sprawled face down in the carpet. They were both laughing now, more than the joke deserved. Graham looked from one to the other, smiling expectantly, trying to edge in on things. After a minute he cleared his throat and said, Hey Sonny, what's downstairs?

Oh, the stereo, said Sonny, righting himself. The pool table, my dad's aquarium . . . the etchings. He said this last in a silky, theatrical tone. Graham gave him a look.

How bout it, he said, standing so close to Alice's chair that their knees almost touched. Want to listen to some records? He'd retrieved his grin, though one corner of it looked downright agonized. She had no doubt that this was all Sonny's doing.

I'll be there in a minute, she said, and smiled. Which left him no choice but to go downstairs by himself. They heard his feet echoing forlornly on the cold basement tiles.

She turned to Sonny. You ought to be ashamed of yourself.

Who, me?

Don't play dumb. Alice crossed the room to the piano and rubbed at the spilled water with her sleeve. She only managed to smudge the dark oiled surface.

Aw, I just thought maybe—

I know what you thought. She wasn't as mad as she was pretending to be, and in pretending she was threatening to overdo it a little.

Sonny got up and put his arms around her from behind. Don't be pissed off. He's not such a bad guy.

He runs with a bad crowd, she said, struggling against his hold, struggling to preserve her pose of anger. Having Sonny trying to appease her was an unaccustomed pleasure.

OK, so forget about Graham. I'm sorry. He turned her around, pressing against her.

You're really sorry?

Sorry I brought him along. He's in our way.

Mm, she said, not wanting to concede his meaning.

Sweet Alice, he crooned. She sagged against him, passive now. Downstairs they heard the stereo click on, and the sound of a Stones record came funneling up the stairs.

Poor guy, said Alice. Maybe we should go down.

Yeah.

But they stood, swaying together while the raucous music beat against them. Sonny was getting more and more insistent. His breath enveloped her. Finally Alice drew his hands away and said, When you going back, Sonny?

Tomorrow night I fly to San Francisco. Then I've got a few days before they ship me out.

Maybe it's just as well. She spoke with her face muffled in his flannel shirt. Her nostrils filled with the smells of wool, perfume, and cold air, a blend which reminded her treacherously of countless nights spent in cold parked cars.

Thanks a lot.

No, I mean your flying tomorrow, I mean . . . Why was she trying to talk about it? You could never talk Sonny out of anything, and once you were discussing it, both *yes* and *no* became possibilities. But it was too late.

There's always tonight.

You can't be serious.

Why not?

It's . . . She wasn't sure, in spite of everything, why she didn't want to sleep with him, or rather, she marveled at the fact that she still might want to. Finally she managed, It'd be too complicated.

What could be less complicated than a sailor's last night ashore?

Damn it, Sonny. I don't think you really want to either. Otherwise you might try to be a little more *winning*.

Sonny grinned. What if I wore my uniform?

You're impossible.

How long's it been?

Years.

Come on. Before I went in.

A year, then. All I have to do, she thought, is walk downstairs. All I have to do is stop talking. But she couldn't resist adding, I don't like the idea of you just gaily dropping in every shore leave and expecting all the goodies.

He raised his arms in astonishment. So what should I do, take you with me?

Oh come on, first you try to pawn me off on Popeye there, then you just casually take the notion to screw me. It doesn't mean anything to you, I don't know why you pursue it.

Because you want me to.

Sure, I'm really leading you on.

Sure. He caught her round the waist and set his full weight against her until she nearly toppled backwards. Sonny, stop! she demanded, but she only breathed it, and she knew by her lack of protest that she was assenting. He led her backwards into the bedroom and closed the door. It was always like this, she thought as she lay back on Sonny's unfresh sheets, they never made anything easy for each other. Warm air whispered continually from invisible vents. Once she thought she heard feet on the basement stairs, but if so they turned and retreated.

Sonny was motionless, his shoulder jutting against her chin. Sonny. She reached up and tugged his hair. We better get dressed.

He sat up, and in the blue-white dimness of the room his nakedness looked meager, his backbone too knobby and pronounced. She waited for him to look at her or say something.

Hey, she said finally. Is anything wrong?

He shrugged and reached for his shirt. Nothing. She followed him into the living room, where he snapped off the light and lay back on the couch. Downstairs another record was playing, though softer than before.

She stood, not knowing what to do. Should we go see what Graham's up to?

No. I don't really want to go look at my father's acquireeum.

Alice sat on the opposite end of the couch. What had gone wrong? This was one reason she hadn't wanted it to happen, because of this inevitable separation afterwards, the feeling that she'd failed in some obscure but fundamental way, otherwise why would he go from wanting her to despising her? Why couldn't he be happy now? It would be years before she learned the aftermath of love could be anything but silence and cruelty. If she didn't say something, she thought, she'd start crying with the misery of it all. So, she asked, what's it like over there, Sonny? hating the false bright sound of her voice.

What.

You know, the Navy, the war and all.

He looked impatient. It's not bad.

Well, tell me about it.

Not enough time for that.

She persisted. How about the war?

We don't see much of it. You know the Seabees? We work with them, mostly, construction and transport stuff.

The recital seemed to bore him. He scuffed at the couch with his heel. She knew if she kept asking him things he'd only get more and more abrupt. So she sat in silence. There seemed to be no way she could reach him.

Eight months later Sonny lay dying in a Japanese hospital from burns received in a boiler explosion. Even then there was no feeling that it was the war which killed him. The war was something people went to, like going to work or school. The war hadn't killed him, the boiler had, a sort of industrial accident that could happen anywhere, the sort of death that the war produced almost casually and which wasn't really supposed to count.

She knew none of the details. News reached her through letters from friends who knew as little as she did, through obscenely noncommittal paragraphs clipped from the suburban newspaper. Alice did not cry but that first night she lay on her bed and tried to evoke the delirium of pain, the raw, bacon-like scabs, the starched and acid air of the hospital, the gauze, the poisonous yellow ointment, as if by imagining it she could somehow lift the pain from Sonny, though by then he was beyond it all.

Sometime that night she woke, fighting sleep as if it were an unwholesome drug, something thick she had to swim through. In her dream they were making love, though the dream was not so much erotic as semaphoric, a series of brisk, disconnected pictures. Looking up at Sonny's face in the grainy and uncertain light she saw he was straining not to come, not to cry out. It was all right, she urged, go ahead, go ahead, and when he showed her his wounds she was overcome by tenderness, and finally they were able to weep together freely.

But in that glossy and astringent living room there had been no real premonition of these things, only her desperation at his silence. What else did he want from her? Why did they always end up so unhappy for no reason? She felt clumsy and ashamed. Were people meant to be like this? A part of her recoiled in weariness at the thought of love, the grasping and losing that might last a whole lifetime. Sonny, please, she said finally. Don't be like this. It drives me crazy.

What do you want me to do?

Just don't act like you hate me. She was starting to get teary now, and she struggled to keep it out of her voice. That would be the worst thing she could do.

He sat up a little straighter, though he still looked out the window, not at her. I don't hate you, Al.

Are you upset because of Graham?

Yeah, sort of. He hasn't had much of a night.

It'll be OK, she said, though she didn't entirely believe it. He'll understand.

He didn't acknowledge her, and said instead, Sometimes I think I'm the most fucked-up shit in the world, you know?

What do you mean?

But he shook his head, and she knew he wouldn't say any more. She reached over and squeezed his hand. Hey. Just tell him I seduced you.

She saw him smile faintly, and she could tell things were all right, or at least as all right as they could be. Still friends? she asked.

Sure.

They sat once more in silence and she was wary but content. In the oblique light from the kitchen Sonny's face was slack and rather tired. Somehow that moment seemed like the true end of the evening for her, though things had gone on. After a while Graham clumped back up the stairs, embarrassment making his feet sound thick and awkward. They'd sat in the van, still parked in Sonny's driveway, and smoked grass and listened to music for a time until Sonny drove her home.

She couldn't remember the last thing Sonny said to her, couldn't even remember if they'd kissed good-bye. Probably not, since Graham was there. No, she'd walked up to the door by herself in the black shrill unsettled night and waved to him and that was that.

Or was it? Again she willed herself to evoke that silent moment in the darkness, tried to make it like a clear piece of glass, a place from which you could view both past and future. The imbecile vision of a flagpole set in sparkling cement intruded on her for a moment but she brushed it aside. She would make her own monuments. And now her memory threw her a scrap, something Sonny said when he heard Graham (whose unhappiness, she saw now, was not just a comic grace note to the evening) clumping up the stairs. Ah now, said Sonny, and she could see him prodding himself back into his old antic irony, ah now, let's have some more fun.

(Kansas Quarterly)

Linda Vavra
Baby Poem 4

My mother does the dishes
looks out over the yard
where moonlight picks out
a trunk, a branch.
She hums to herself.
Flecks of soap bloom
on her hands and disappear. When she finishes

she goes to my father,
watching cars out the window,
gathers him up in her arms.
His legs hang, his head is larger
than her shoulder, balanced in the curve.
She carries him as though he were so light,
a bird, a pan of water
taken into a sickroom
placed at the foot of the bed.

At first he wants to say
I can walk by myself. Or
I'm too heavy
trying to rise out of her arms
toward the ceiling, the strange bent shadow
of his head coming to meet him.
But something in him likes being carried,
the sway of his legs,
her mouth like a small window
over his face.
The room looks different from her arms,
she's so tall,
bends to fit the door,

stands by the bed   rocking him
crooning

oh oh see the moon
oh oh see the stars

(Field)

C. K. Williams
From My Window

Spring: the first morning when that one true block of
    sweet, laminar, complex scent arrives
from somewhere west and I keep coming to lean on the
    sill, glorying in the end of the wretched winter.
The scabby-barked sycamores ringing the empty lot
    across the way are budded—I hadn't even noticed—
and the thick spikes of the unlikely urban crocuses have
    already broken the gritty soil.
Up the street, some surveyors with tripods are waving
    each other left and right the way they do.
A girl in a gymsuit jogged by awhile ago, some kids
    passed, playing hooky, I imagine,
and now the paraplegic Vietnam vet who lives in a half-
    converted warehouse down the block
and the friend who stays with him and seems to help him
    out come weaving towards me,
their battered wheelchair lurching uncertainly from one
    edge of the sidewalk to the other.
I know where they're going—to the "Legion"; once, when
    I was putting something out, they stopped,
both drunk that time, too, both reeking—it wasn't ten
    o'clock—and we chatted for a bit.
I don't know how they stay alive—on benefits most likely.
    I wonder if they're lovers.
They don't look it. Right now, in fact, they look a wreck,
    careening haphazardly along,
contriving as they reach beneath me to dip a wheel from
    the curb so that the chair skewers, teeters,
tips, and they both tumble, the one slowly, almost
    gracefully sliding in stages from his seat,
his expression hardly marking it, the other staggering

over him, spinning heavily down,
to lie on the asphalt, his mouth working, his feet shoving
    weakly and fruitlessly against the curb.
In the store-front office on the corner, Reed and Son, Real
    Estate, have come to see the show:
gazing through the golden letters of their name, they're
    not, at least, thank god, laughing.
Now the buddy, grabbing at a hydrant, gets himself erect
    and stands there for a moment, panting.
Now he has to lift the other one, who lies utterly still, a
    forearm shielding his eyes from the sun.
He hauls him partly upright, then hefts him almost all
    the way into the chair but a dangling foot
catches a support-plate, jerking everything around so
    that he has to put him down,
set the chair to rights and hoist him again and as he does
    he jerks the grimy jeans right off him.
No drawers, shrunken, blotchy thighs; under the thick
    white coils of belly blubber
the poor, blunt pud, tiny, terrified, retracted, is almost
    invisible in the sparse genital hair,
then his friend pulls his pants up, he slumps wholly back
    as though he were, at last, to be let be,
and the friend leans against the cyclone fence, suddenly
    staring up at me as though he'd known
all along that I was watching and I can't help wondering
    if he knows that in the winter, too,
I watched, the night he went out to the lot and walked,
    paced rather, almost ran, for how many hours.
It was snowing, the city in that holy silence, the last we
    have, when the storm takes hold,
and he was making patterns that I thought at first were
    circles then realized made a figure eight,
what must have been to him a perfect symmetry but
    which, from where I was, shivered, bent,
and lay on its side: a warped, unclear infinity, slowly, as

the snow came faster, going out.
Over and over again, his head lowered to the task, he
    slogged the path he'd blazed
but the race was lost, his prints were filling faster than he
    made them now and I looked away,
up across the skeletal trees to the tall center-city
    buildings, some, though it was midnight,
with all their offices still gleaming, their scarlet warning-
    beacons signaling erratically,
against the thickening flakes, their smoldering auras
    softening portions of the dim, milky sky.
In the morning, nothing; every trace of him effaced, all
    the field pure white,
its surface glittering, the dawn, glancing from its glaze,
    oblique, relentless, unadorned.

(The Paris Review)

Tobias Wolff
Next Door

I WAKE UP AFRAID. MY WIFE IS SITTING ON THE EDGE of my bed, shaking me. "They're at it again," she says.

I go to the window. All their lights are on, upstairs and down, as if they have money to burn. He yells, she screams something back, the dog barks. There is a short silence, then the baby cries, poor thing.

"Better not stand there," says my wife. "They might see you."

I say, "I'm going to call the police," knowing she won't let me.

"Don't," she says.

She's afraid that they will poison our cat if we complain.

Next door the man is still yelling, but I can't make out what he's saying over the dog and the baby. The woman laughs, not really meaning it, "*Ha! Ha! Ha!,*" and suddenly gives a sharp little cry. Everything goes quiet.

"He struck her," says my wife. "I felt it just the same as if he struck me."

Next door the baby gives a long wail and the dog starts up again. The man walks out into his driveway and slams the door.

"Be careful," says my wife. She gets back into her bed and pulls the covers up to her neck.

The man mumbles to himself and jerks at his fly. Finally he gets it open and walks over to our fence. It's a white picket fence, ornamental more than anything else. It couldn't keep anyone out. I put it in myself, and planted honeysuckle and bougainvillea all along it.

My wife says, "What's he doing?"

"Shh," I say.

He leans against the fence with one hand and with the other he goes to the bathroom on the flowers. He walks the length of the fence like that, not missing any of them. When he's through he gives Florida a shake, then zips up and heads back across the driveway. He almost slips on the gravel but he catches himself and curses and goes into the house, slamming the door again.

When I turn around my wife is leaning forward, watching me. She raises her eyebrows. "Not again," she says.

I nod.

"Number one or number two?"

"Number one."

"Thank God for small favors," she says, settling back. "Between him and the dog it's a wonder you can get anything to grow out there."

I read somewhere that human pee has a higher acid content than animal pee, but I don't mention that. I would rather talk about something else. It depresses me, thinking about the flowers. They are past their prime, but still. Next door the woman is shouting. "Listen to that," I say.

"I used to feel sorry for her," says my wife. "Not any more. Not after last month."

"Ditto," I say, trying to remember what happened last month to make my wife not feel sorry for the woman next door. I don't feel sorry for her either, but then I never have. She yells at the baby, and excuse me, but I'm not about to get all excited over someone who treats a child like that. She screams things like *"I thought I told you to stay in your bedroom!"* and here the baby can't even speak English yet.

As far as her looks, I guess you would have to say she's pretty. But it won't last. She doesn't have good bone structure. She has a soft look to her, like she has never eaten anything but doughnuts and milk shakes. Her skin is white. The baby takes after her, not that you would expect it to take after *him,* dark and hairy. Even with his shirt on you can tell that he has hair all over his back and on his shoulders, thick and springy like an Airedale's.

Now they're all going at once over there, plus they've got the hi-fi turned on full blast. One of those bands. "It's the baby I feel sorry for," I say.

My wife puts her hands over her ears. "I can't stand another minute of it," she says. She takes her hands away. "Maybe there's something on TV." She sits up. "See who's on Johnny."

I turn on the television. It used to be down in the den, but I brought it up here a few years ago when my wife came down with an illness. I took care of her myself—made the meals and everything. I got to where I could change the sheets with her still in bed. I always meant to take the television back down when my wife recovered, but I never got around to it. It sits between our beds on a little table I made. Johnny is saying something to Sammy Davis, Jr. Ed McMahon is bent over laughing. He is always so cheerful. If you were going to take a really long voyage you could do worse than bring Ed McMahon along.

"Sammy," says my wife. "Who else is on besides Sammy?"

I look at the television guide. "A bunch of people I never heard of." I read off their names. My wife hasn't heard of them either. She wants to know what else is on. " '*El Dorado,*' " I read. " 'Brisk adventure yarn about a group of citizens in search of the legendary city of gold.' It's got two-and-a-half stars beside it."

"Citizens of what?" asks my wife.

"It doesn't say."

Finally we watch the movie. A blind man comes into a small town. He says that he has been to El Dorado and that he will lead an expedition there for a share of the proceeds. He can't see, but he will call out the landmarks one by one as they ride. At first people make fun of him, but eventually all the leading citizens get together and

decide to give it a try. Right away they get attacked by
Apaches and some of them want to turn back, but every
time they get ready the blind man gives them another
landmark, so they keep going.

Next door the woman is going crazy. She is saying things
to him that no person should ever say to another person. It
makes my wife restless. She looks at me. "Can I come
over?" she says. "Just for a visit?"

I pull down the blankets and she gets in. The bed is just
fine for one, but with two of us it's a tight fit. We are lying
on our sides with me in back. I don't mean for it to happen
but before long old Florida begins to stiffen up on me. I put
my arms around my wife. I move my hands up onto the
Rockies, then on down across the plains, heading south.

"Hey," she says, "No geography. Not tonight."

"I'm sorry," I say.

"Can't I just visit?"

"Forget it. I said I was sorry."

The citizens are crossing a desert. They have just about
run out of water, and their lips are cracked. Though the
blind man has delivered a warning, someone drinks from
a poisoned well and dies horribly. That night, around the
campfire, the others begin to quarrel. Most of them want
to go home. "This is no country for a white man," says one,
"and if you ask me, nobody has ever been here before." But
the blind man describes a piece of gold so big and pure that
it will burn your eyes out if you look directly at it. "I ought
to know," he says. When he is finished, the citizens are
silent: one by one they move away and lie down on their
bedrolls. They put their hands behind their heads and look
up at the stars. A coyote howls.

Hearing the coyote, I remember why my wife doesn't feel
sorry for the woman next door. It was a Monday evening,
about a month ago, right after I got home from work. The
man next door started to beat the dog and I don't mean just
smacking him once or twice. He was beating him, and he

kept beating him until the dog couldn't even cry any more; you could hear the poor creature's voice breaking. It made us very upset, especially my wife, who is an animal lover from way back. She gives to all the funds. Finally it stopped. Then, a few minutes later, I heard my wife say "Oh!" and I went into the kitchen to find out what was wrong. She was standing by the window, which looks into the kitchen next door. The man had his wife backed up against the fridge. He had his knee between her legs and she had her knee between his legs and they were kissing, really hard, not just with their lips but rolling their faces back and forth one against the other. My wife could hardly speak for a couple of hours afterwards. Later she said that she would never waste her sympathy on that woman again.

It's quiet over there. My wife has gone to sleep and so has my arm, under her head. I slide it out and open and close my fingers, considering whether to wake her up. I like sleeping in my own bed, and there isn't enough room for both her and me. Finally I decide that it won't hurt either of us to change places for one night.

I get up and fuss with the plants for a while, watering them and moving some to the window and some back. I trim the coleus, which is starting to get leggy, and put the cuttings in a glass of water on the sill. All the lights are off next door except the one in their bedroom window. I think about the life they have, and how it goes on and on, until it seems to be the life they were meant to live. Everybody is always saying how great it is that human beings are so adaptable, but I don't know. A friend of mine was in the Navy and he told me that in Amsterdam, Holland, they have a whole section of town where you walk through it and from the street you can see women sitting in rooms. If you want one of them you just go in and pay and they close the drapes. This is nothing special to the people who live in Holland. In Istanbul, Turkey, my friend saw a man walking down the street with a grand piano on his back.

Everyone just moved around him and kept going. It's awful, what we get used to.

I turn off the television and get into my wife's bed. A sweet, heavy smell rises off the sheets. At first it makes me dizzy but after that I like it. It reminds me of gardenias.

The reason I don't watch the rest of the movie is that I can already see how it will end. The citizens will kill each other off, probably about ten feet from the legendary city of gold, and the blind man will stumble in by himself, not knowing that he has made it back to El Dorado.

I could write a better movie than that. My movie would be about a group of explorers, men and women, who leave behind their homes and their jobs and their families—everything they have known. They cross the sea and are shipwrecked on the coast of a country which is not on their maps. One of them drowns. Another gets attacked by a wild animal, and eaten. But the others want to push on. They ford rivers and cross an enormous glacier by dog sled. It takes months. On the glacier they run out of food, and for a while there it looks like they might turn on each other, but they don't. Finally they solve their problem by eating the dogs. That's the sad part of the movie.

At the end we see the explorers sleeping in a meadow filled with white flowers. The blossoms are wet with dew and stick to their bodies, petals of columbine, clematis, blazing star, baby's breath, larkspur, iris, rue—covering them completely, turning them white so that you cannot tell one from another, man from woman, woman from man. The sun comes up. They stand and raise their arms, like white trees in a land where no one has ever been.

(Antaeus)

Charles Wright
Lost Souls

From the bad eye and early morning
                                        you raise me
Unshuttered from the body of ashes
                                        you raise me
Out of the dust and moth light
                                memory
Into the undertow of my own life
                                        you make me remember

———

I never dreamed of anything as a child.
I just assumed it was all next door,
                                or day-after-tomorrow at least,
A different shirt I'd put on when the time was right.

It hasn't worked out that way.

My father wrote out his dreams on lined paper,
as I do now,
And gave them up to the priest
                                for both to come to terms with.
I give you mine for the same reason,

To summon the spirits up and set the body to music.

———

   The last time I saw George Vaughan,
He was standing in front of my father's casket at the
laying out,
One of the kindest men I've ever known.

When I was 16, he taught me the way to use a
  jackhammer,
                  putting the hand grip
Into my stomach and clinching down,
Riding it out till the jarring became a straight line.

He taught me the way a shovel breathes,
And how the red clay gives away nothing.
He took my hand when my hand needed taking.

And I didn't even remember his name.

———

One evening in 1957 I found myself outside of
  Nashville,
                face down on the ground,
A straw in my mouth, the straw stuck deep
In the ginned heart of a watermelon,
                     the faces of five friends
Almost touching my face
As we sucked the sweet gin as fast as we could.

Over the green hinge of the Cumberland Plateau
The eyelash dusk of July was coming down
                effortlessly, smooth as an oiled joint.
Agnes rolled over and looked up at the sky.
Her cousin, our host, rolled over and looked up at the sky.

What a life, he said. Jesus, he said, what a life.

———

Nobody needs to remember the Kingsport Times-News
In the summer of 1953,
                but I do,

Disguised to myself as a newspaperman on my slow way
To the city jail to check the drunk tank,

                              full summer and after supper,
Korea just over, the neon of Wallace's News and Parks-
   Belk
Lying along the sidewalk like tear sheets of tinted plastic,
Across Center and down to Freels Drug,

                          then left, and then left again
Into the blowing shadow and light
Under the elm trees,
The world and its disregard in the palm of my hand.

Nobody needs to remember the smell of bay rum
And disinfectant,

                the desperate grey faces
Of dirt farmers caught in the wrong dark at the wrong
   time,
Bib overalls sour with sweat and high water,
Brogans cracked and half broken,

                   the residue
Of all our illuminations and unnamed lives . . .
At least I thought that then.
And nobody needs to remember any of that,

                        but I do.

———

What *does* one do with one's life? A shelf-and-a-half
Of magazines, pictures on all the walls
Of the way I was, and everyone standing next to me?
This one, for instance for instance for instance . . .

Nothing's like anything else in the long run.
Nothing you write down is ever as true as you think it
   was.

But so what? Churchill and I and Bill Ring
Will still be chasing that same dead pin-tail duck
                              down the same rapids in 1951
Of the Holsten River. And Ted Glynn
Will be running too.
                    And 1951 will always be 1951.

————

   A little curtain of flesh, Blake said,
For his own reasons . . .
And I had mine to draw it last night on the Wasatch
   Range
And pull it back as the sun rose
                              over the north fork
And blue weave of the Cumberlands.
It was June again, and 1964 again,
                              and I still wasn't there
As they laid her down and my father turned away,
I still imagine, precisely, into the cave of cold air
He lived in for eight more years, the cars
Below my window in Rome honking maniacally
                    O still small voice of calm . . .

(Field)

Patricia Zelver
Unglued

ELAINE BABCOCK WAS TWENTY-NINE YEARS OLD. She was tall, with full breasts and wide hips. Her large blue eyes had a serious little girl's expression. It was not the expression of the kind of little girl who is shrewd and conniving and knows what side her bread is buttered on, thereby reaping honors and rewards; it was the expression of a little girl who obliges so quietly and unobtrusively that nobody notices her at all. She wore her hair, which had once been very light, and now had darkened, in the same long straight style she had worn it when she married Tom Babcock, eleven years ago. It had never occurred to her to change her hair style.

Elaine had met Tom when she was a typist in the Planning Office of the City of Fremont, and she was still living with her folks. Tom was a Junior Executive with Superdog, a national Fast Food Franchise. Superdog's headquarters were in L.A., but Tom's job kept him on the road, and, because he loved Elaine and was lonely without her, she accompanied him, all expenses paid. This was part of Tom's agreement with Superdog, who had a high regard for his abilities.

Superdog, according to Tom, was a Name and Know How. If someone wanted to start a Superdog, his credit and references were checked out in the Home Office; if they checked out okay Tom would be sent in to arrange the deal. Tom had the Know How. He would approve or disapprove the prospective site. If he approved, he would assist the new owner-to-be through the bureaucratic maze of zoning laws and city council meetings and help convince the City Fathers and their staff to grant a Use Permit.

Superdog had an excellent reputation. It made a point of

hiring local help and buying from local wholesalers. Its advertising on the billboards and on TV encouraged family business. Superdog adhered strictly to the local health codes and, in every way, was super clean and super respectable. For these reasons, and, also owing to Tom's sincere and pleasing and efficient manner, the Use Permit was almost always granted. Then Tom gave the new owner a training course in Superdog management. Following this, the contract for the franchise was signed and the owner was presented with the Superdog architectural plans; the big Superdog neon sign, and the Superdog trays and paper napkins and plastic spoons and forks, with the Superdog logos on them.

Tom's territory covered most of the West—sometimes the big cities, but usually small cities and towns. Tom would rent a car at the airport and settle Elaine in a nice motel out on the highway. The downtown hotels were almost always seedy and rundown. Tom always chose a motel with a swimming pool and a kitchenette. He liked to swim before breakfast, and he liked to make his own breakfast and have a homecooked dinner on weeknights with Elaine. Elaine had never learned to drive, so Tom bought the groceries. He made the dinners, too. He enjoyed messing around in the kitchen after work and was an accomplished cook. After dinner, on weeknights, they watched TV together. Tom enjoyed the 6 o'clock news and sporting events. At least three times a week, sometimes four, they had sex. Tom was extremely complimentary to Elaine on her sexual behavior.

"Still waters run deep," he told her. "Nobody would guess what a tiger you are in bed."

Once he called her a "living doll," another time, "dynamite."

Elaine puzzled a little over these compliments. She always complied with Tom's sexual desires, but he required noth-

ing special in this line—"Missionary Style" being his favorite position, except when his back bothered him, when
he preferred a position he called "Spoons." Since Elaine
took pleasure in pleasing, she was as satisfied as Tom. But
a living doll? She was not a living doll, nor was she dynamite.

Certainly there was nothing tigerish about her. It was
just Tom's way of talking, she decided. He picked up expres-
sions like this in his line of work, and, being the kind of
man who always felt the need to comment, and wishing to
show his regard, it did not occur to him that they were not
quite suitable forms of endearment for her. But what would
be a suitable form of endearment? When she tried to think
of one she became aware of Tom's problem, and being aware
of the problem she felt a peculiar discomfort when he com-
plimented her in this manner, as if he were reaching out
for something that was not there.

On weekend nights they had dinner out. Tom liked to
keep up on the other fast food franchises. He had made a
check list, which helped him rate these restaurants, as to:

Service—Fast, Friendly, Efficient
Atmosphere—Cheerful, Comfortable, Clean, Attractively-deco-
rated
Clientele—Teenagers, Families, Businessmen, Mixed
Location—Central Business District, Major Arterial, Shopping
Center
Food Quality—A. B. C. D.

In this way, he could compare these other franchises to
Superdogs. While they ate, he would make out the report,
often asking for Elaine's opinion. Did it bother her if the
mustard dispenser was used by everyone? What did she
think of the decor? Did she like the old-fashioned checked
granny gowns the waitresses wore, or did she prefer more
modern-type uniforms? How would she rate the food quality? And so forth.

Tom often invited her opinions about the Superdog commercials on TV, too. The commercials were made in L.A. by a national advertising firm; they were the same on every program, except for the address of the local Superdog, which was printed on the screen below the commercial. Tom had nothing to do with this advertising side of the business, but he took a deep interest in everything related to Superdog, and wanted to know what she thought about each new one, when it appeared, and how she compared it to the commercials for the other franchises.

Elaine was pleased that he had respect for her opinions. She was not, she knew, as clever or as quick as Tom, but she gave careful consideration to his questions, reflecting a long time before responding. She set a high value on honesty and it was important to her to give truthful and objective replies.

After dinner, they sometimes attended a movie. Once Elaine pointed out that, if they waited, they could see the same movie, free, on TV, but Tom was not as patient as she, and preferred them freshly released. Moreover, he liked to stop by one of the Fast Food franchises after a show to check out the amount and type of their Late Trade.

On weekend days, Tom played golf. He had tried to interest Elaine in the game, but she had never been athletic and her body motions were clumsy; after a few tries, she had given up. It was evident to her that she could never keep up with Tom, and would only spoil his fun. Several times Tom had suggested that she take lessons; in this way she would meet other women and could play with them. But Elaine was on the shy side, and did not make new friends easily. As the years went by, the very thought of a conversation with strangers was frightening to her. She spent her weekend days the same way she spent her weekdays—occasionally doing a little typing for Tom, mostly watching TV. She didn't mind. She knew Tom was happy; moreover, as he explained, his golf game was a way of getting to know the local people who could influence the Superdog hearings, and this, of course, would assist him in his career. Elaine recognized the importance of Tom's career, and though she could not help him actively, outside of the opinion poll and the typing jobs, she would never have stood in his way. If she ever felt a little lonely, the deep affection she had for him sustained her.

Before Tom left for work in the mornings he always tried out the motel's TV to be certain it worked. Once they had stayed in a motel where the TV was broken; another time, in a motel which did not have a TV. Tom—ever thoughtful—had bought a Sony portable, and they carried this with them to be on the safe side.

Tom had his breakfast alone, while Elaine was still in bed, always making sure to leave enough coffee for Elaine. After he kissed her goodbye, she would reach over and flick on the set and leave it on while she brushed her teeth and her hair and had her coffee and Danish. She didn't bother to dress until just before Tom came home. She watched TV through the morning and into the late afternoons with the blinds drawn. The maid always opened the blinds when she came in to do the room, but as soon as she left, Elaine closed them again. Around four o'clock, she was usually sleepy and lay down for a nap. Tom tried to be home by five-thirty; in the evening he often had planning or council meetings or meetings with the new owner-to-be. Elaine would watch TV until he returned.

During the first years of this life, she enjoyed almost all of the national network programs. She was particularly fond of The Guiding Light and reruns of old movies, particularly ones that took place in olden times. In the evenings, at six-thirty, she watched the Roundup of national and international news events with Tom.

Then, one day, in a suburb somewhere on the outskirts of San Jose, Elaine made a discovery which brought about a change in her life. This discovery was the commercials—

not just any commercial, but the commercials that featured local folks advertising their own businesses or products. In this way she felt she came to know the people of
the community and from this time on these personalized
commercials became more important to her than the shows.
The commercials varied from place to place, but, after a
while, she recognized a sort of pattern.

There was usually a Pharmacist. The Pharmacist wore
a white lab coat and had a kindly family physician air.
Often he stood in back of his counter, with its vials and
potions and old apothecary jars. He might be talking on
the telephone.

"I'll have your arthritis prescription ready for you in
fifteen minutes, Mrs. Caldwell. In the meantime, keep
yourself cozy and warm."

Then he would step out in front of the counter and introduce himself. He might give health and safety tips, reminding mothers to be sure their children had a good hot
breakfast before they went off to school, or warning parents
to cover electric floor sockets with tape if they had toddlers.
He might show you his Specials for the week. Aspirin or
vitamins or pills to relieve tension, or hemorrhoids, or that
stuffy feeling that came with colds. Any prolonged symptom, however, should always be reported to your doctor, he
would say.

In one of the towns, the Pharmacist introduced his viewing audience to his daughter, Linda. Linda was timid about
being introduced, you could tell. She fidgeted and giggled.
But the Pharmacist was proud of her. Linda was going to
help out in the Pharmacy this summer, then she was going
to college on a scholarship. She was going to study Pharmacology.

"It wouldn't surprise me if Linda wasn't planning to
take over my job," the Pharmacist said, with a sly wink at
Linda. "She may have a little trouble, though, getting rid

of her old man. The trouble is, I like my profession," the Pharmacist said. He said this with such sincerity that Elaine knew he wasn't putting you on.

Another Pharmacist introduced his wife, Bernice. Bernice was not at all timid about being introduced. She wore a stylish pants suit and high heels and had long dangling earrings; her blonde hair was meticulously coiffed.

Bernice, said the Pharmacist, was a cosmetic specialist, and if you came into the Pharmacy she would be happy to tell you what kind of cosmetics went with your skin and coloring and show you how to apply them. She thinks of it as an art, the Pharmacist said.

Bernice smiled, graciously.

"How do you like my foxy wife?" the Pharmacist said.

There was the Used Car Dealer, E-Z Morton or Okay All the Way Briggs or Why Pay More Perkins. The Used Car Dealer would stand in front of his Special-for-the-Week, explaining its advantages, and showing you all the extras, warning you to hurry on down while he still had some left.

"Bring the whole family, and don't forget your checkbook and your pink slip, this extra-special holiday bargain won't last long."

"Act now, before it's too late. Don't put off for tomorrow the one chance of a lifetime!"

The Used Car Dealers always spoke in a rapid, staccato voice and shouted to be sure you heard. They gave you the feeling it was an emergency situation, and Elaine would feel ashamed that she did not drive and could not respond to their well-intentioned appeal.

Frank Friendly, who owned the House of Quality—three furniture warehouses in the Salinas area—was another favorite, too. He had everything you needed to furnish your house.

"You name it, we've got it," he would say. "Contemporary, Oriental, Scandinavian, Traditional, in stock, immediate delivery at warehouse prices. If you don't know what you want, we're here to help you."

Frank Friendly was open seven days a week, and evenings up to ten, and offered low terms on approved credit. But what she enjoyed most about Frank was his relaxed and intimate manner. He was usually sitting down on one of his dinette chairs or a Rel-X-Or Lounge; sometimes he even lay down on a sofa bed to show you how comfortable it was. He had trouble, he said, keeping his eyes open. "Don't be surprised," he said, "if I just snooze off."

But most of the time Frank did not talk about furniture at all. He talked about his philosophy of life. He had an excellent philosophy of life, Elaine thought. He wasn't in business just to make money, he told his viewing audience. He was in business because he felt that the home was the backbone of this great country, the U. S. of A. The home was where the heart is, he said. The great poets and writers of all periods of history had written about the home. Sometimes he would recite a passage of a poem, to prove his point.

"It takes a heap of livin' to make a house a home"
"East, West, home is best"
"Be it ever so humble, there's no place like home"

Frank was a poet, too, himself. "Listen, I wrote this just the other day. I want to share it with you out there. My feelings run deep on this particular subject."

A home isn't just furniture. A home is a bouquet of flowers from the garden, the succulent odor of a casserole in the oven; a home is a nest. A home is where you gather with your nearest and dearest. Your Home is what you make of it.

"Now that's what's called blank verse. I never could rhyme,

so whoever invented blank verse must have had me in mind."

Frank showed snapshots of his own family. He showed them around the table at Thanksgiving and Christmas time. He showed his two boys and himself shooting baskets into a net in their backyard, while his wife looked on happily. He showed them his teenage daughter's newly decorated bedroom. "I let her pick things out herself. She's pretty proud of it. You know how girls are at her age. They're little women. They like to put their personal touch on something, and their own bedroom is a good place to start. It's good psychology, too," said Frank, with a wink. "Keeps 'em busy and out of trouble."

Frank always kept a pot of coffee going, and invited his audience to come in and have a cup of coffee with him and browse around, or just have a chat, no pressure to buy, he'd be happy just to meet you. "People count more to me than business," he said.

Elaine would have liked to have accepted Frank's invitation, but she did not think it was fair to take up his time, when she did not have a home of her own. Just the same, if she had a home, she would certainly patronize Frank, she decided.

Once, she asked Tom why the Superdog franchise owners never appeared on Superdog ads. Tom explained this to her in his intelligent way. He told her it was against the company's policy; that being a good Superdog owner did not make you a television personality. Part of Superdog's success was its professional and carefully adhered-to trademark. Moreover, anyone could drop in on the local cafe, where they knew the owner. It was that very fact that made Superdogs different. There were Superdogs all over the nation, as well as in Europe and Japan. If local owners started to put their individual stamp on the Superdog Image, where would it end? An owner might start using his own napkins and paper plates, instead of buying them from Superdog; he might decide to alter the menu. Little things like that could lead to bigger ones. Some small town egoist might even change Superdog's sign—put his own name on it, for example, "Red's Superdog"—something like that. The thing about Superdog was that people knew exactly what to expect and this gave them a sense of security; any variation on the Superdog theme could destroy this.

"The whole structure could come unglued," Tom said.

Elaine could see Tom's point. She felt dumb even asking the question. She even felt a little guilty, preferring, as she now did, these personalized commercials over the more professional national network commercials made in L.A.

"Red's Superdog," she said with a laugh.

Now it was late August and they were in a hot and muggy town in the San Joaquin Valley. It was nine on a Tuesday morning. Tom had just left and she already had the air conditioner on high. She was watching an ad for a TV Repair Service Center. Four men were standing in front of a Service van, parked in a lot in front of the Center. Three of the men wore dark shirts, with Andy's TV printed on the pocket. The other man—Andy—was dressed up to go fishing. He had on a fisherman's hat, waterproof jacket and waders, and was holding his fishing gear. He was speaking in a cheerful, chirpy voice. "You know us. We've provided fast, dependable, cheerful service for all you folks in the valley, now, for twenty-five years. All makes and types of sets. Most repairs made right in your home. But I want to tell you something. Today is a special day. It's my birthday. From now on I'm sweet sixteen, all the way. You know what I'm going to do? The trout are jumping up at Bonanza Dam, and the missus and I are going to check out our new spinning reels. I'm gonna take a whole week off. How about that? You know you don't have nothing to worry about, because you know my crew. Just in case any new folks in town aren't acquainted with them yet, I'll introduce them to you. Come on over, boys, and meet the folks. This here is Happy." Happy was tall and loose jointed, with a long and solemn face.

"Let's see you smile, Happy. Give the folks a smile," Andy said.

Happy smiled. From his smile you could tell he wasn't solemn at all; his solemn look was part of a joke. Happy was a Joker.

"This here is Vern," said Andy.

Vern was young, in his late twenties, maybe, with short curly hair, and an earnest expression.

"The only problem I have with Vern, here, is he's a Workaholic. I can't get him to take a day off. He'd work all night if I let him. Right, Vern?"

Vern nodded, a bit curtly. He appeared uncomfortable at Andy's personal remark.

"Now for my old standby, Ken. Ken's been with me since Andy's Service Center opened its door. I call him Old Faithful. To be honest I don't think I could run my business without Ken. It's hard to say what Ken has, but I call it Customer Appeal. I know a lot of you folks out there in the Viewing Audience are acquainted with Ken, and you understand what I mean."

Ken was fortyish. He was on the short side, with hairy muscular arms. He wore horn-rimmed glasses. His eyes, under the glasses, were large and dark and shrewd. He didn't smile, he just looked straight at the viewing audience with his big dark shrewd eyes. Elaine could understand why Andy called him Old Faithful. He had a solid, reliable appearance that gave you confidence. You could count on Ken, she thought. He was a man, she decided, who knew exactly how he felt about things, who brooked no nonsense. He had a no-nonsense outlook on life. Looking into Ken's knowing eyes, Elaine gave a little shiver. Ken, she said to herself, you couldn't put anything over on Ken.

"Ken and I have a little bet going," Andy was saying. "Ken's bet me twenty bucks I won't catch my limit. How about that? When I get back next week I'm going to show you folks photographs of my catch, and you can watch Ken pay up. This is the one time in Ken's life he's made a bad boo-boo."

It was hard to imagine Ken ever making a boo-boo, Elaine thought. Ken must have had good reasons for making a bet like that. Maybe he knew more about fishing conditions than Andy, or maybe he didn't have confidence in Andy as a fisherman. Whichever way, you could tell that Ken stood squarely in back of his conviction and wasn't worried about losing his money. A man like Ken would never make an impulsive bet. He would have given it careful consideration.

"So you don't have to worry about a thing, folks, with Ken holding down the fort. You know our number. You know our name. Andy's TV Repair Service. Just dial 341-6011 or 341-6012 and if you have any problems, one of our boys will be at your place before you can say Jack Robinson."

The picture faded out and a printed ad came on. Andy's TV and Repair Service, it said. Underneath was the address and the two telephone numbers.

Elaine said over the first number in her head, then she reached for a pencil and a postcard of the motel on the bedside table, and wrote the number down on the back of the postcard. All the time she was writing she could see Ken's no-nonsense eyes.

A man like Ken, she thought. A man like Ken didn't just throw his money away. On the other hand, Andy had appeared confident about the bet. He had publicly announced that Ken would have to pay up. Andy was the Boss. He *owned* Andy's TV Service. And can't be dumb, thought Elaine. Still, wasn't it possible that Andy might have inherited the business and that Ken really ran it? Andy had said himself, that he couldn't manage without him.

She glanced at the postcard she was holding in her hand. There was the number in her own handwriting. If it had not been her handwriting, she would never have imagined she had written it down herself. If I wrote it down, I must have had a good reason, she thought. You wouldn't write a number down, unless you intend to use it. She could think of no other possible reason for doing so.

She picked up the phone and dialed the number. When she heard the rings, she got a funny feeling. For a moment, she was tempted to hang up.

A busy man like Ken, she said to herself. Maybe I shouldn't bother him. I don't have any problems. Not any important problems anyhow. He'll probably think I'm nuts, bothering him like this, while he's holding down the fort. On the other hand, Andy said not to worry about a thing, with Ken here. Well, she wouldn't worry, then. She felt a relief, knowing she had nothing to worry about, with Ken in charge. It was extremely important to see Ken. That was what mattered at the moment.

"Andy's Repair Center," said a voice. Elaine was pretty sure this was Vern.

"I'd like to speak to Ken, please," she said. Hearing her own voice speaking these words gave her a peculiar sensation. It was as if somebody else had spoken them.

"Ken's out on a call. You want somebody else or you want Ken," said Vern.

"Ken, please," said Elaine.

"Okay, lady. If you leave your number, I'll have Ken call you back."

Elaine gave Vern the motel's number. "Will he call shortly?" she said, in her peculiar, somebody else's voice.

"That's hard to say when Ken's out on a call. I'll radio the truck and he'll get back to you. What's your name, lady?"

"Elaine," she said, and hung up.

She sat down on the bed. She was shaky, light-headed. I have to pull myself together, she thought. There's a lot to do before Ken gets here. I have to fix up the place for Ken.

The maid had not been in, so she got up and made the bed herself, pulling on the heavy spread and tucking it into the pillows. Then she dressed. She put on a pair of black slacks and the sheer flowered blouse Tom had given her for their wedding anniversary. She sat down at the motel's dressing table and brushed her long hair; then she combed it. She put on lipstick. I look pale, she thought. She dabbed lipstick on her cheekbones, and rubbed it in with her fingers, like rouge. The TV was still going. An organ was playing church music. She turned it off. Usually she kept the TV on, even when she was in the bathroom or kitchen, but now she had other things to think about and could not allow herself any distraction. Ken was a man who would want things to look orderly. She was positive this was the way he was. I have to clean up the kitchen, she thought. Ken wouldn't approve of dirty dishes in the sink. She hurried into the kitchenette and rinsed off Tom's breakfast dishes, which he usually did while he was fixing their dinner. Then she poured out the coffee he had left her, and made a whole new pot.

Ken probably likes to see a pot of coffee going. It would only be polite to offer him coffee, she told herself.

She had just finished plugging in the coffee maker when the phone rang. She ran into the bedroom and picked up the phone. She felt sure that Ken did not like to be kept waiting.

"Ken speaking," a voice said. It was a deep, masculine,

curt voice, precisely the sort of voice she had imagined Ken would have.

"This Elaine?" said Ken.

"Yes," she said. Her voice came out a whisper. She cleared her throat. "Yes," she said again.

"What's your problem, Elaine?"

"My problem?" she said. It occurred to her that she had expected Ken to tell her what the problem was. She had to think this through. "Well, it's my television set," she said, after a pause. She felt better after saying this. It seemed, under the circumstances, exactly the right thing to say.

"Where do you live, Elaine?" said Ken.

This presented another difficulty. She could not, just at this precise moment, recall the name of this particular motel. The El Rancho? The Thunderbird? Oh, my God, she thought in panic. Then she remembered the postcard and picked it up. "Riverside Manor," it said. "I'm at Riverside Manor, out on 91," she told him.

"If something's the matter with the set, you should report it to the manager," said Ken.

This had not occurred to her, either. Then she remembered the Sony. "It's my own TV," she said. "A Sony portable."

"I'm out on B Street, now, Elaine. I have another call out your way. I can stop by first. Is that what you want me to do?"

"Yes," she said. "Yes, please."

"What's your number out there, Elaine?"

She gave him the phone number.

"The number of your *room*, Elaine."

"My room?" She glanced at the phone's dial. It had the number printed on it. "Fourteen," she said. "Number fourteen."

"See you in ten minutes or so, Elaine," said Ken.

She put the phone down and sat there for a moment.

Then she got up and straightened the bed where she had sat and glanced in the mirror at her face. She added more lipstick to her mouth and cheeks. There was a knock on the door. She jumped.

"Maid," said a girl's voice.

"Could you come back later, please?" Elaine called out.

She waited until the maid's footsteps went away; then she opened the door, and put out the Do Not Disturb sign.

"Ken wouldn't want to be disturbed by the maid," she thought.

Then she sat down on the chair, so she wouldn't mess the bed, and turned on the TV to a different channel and watched the rerun of an old movie that had ladies in peaked caps, with long veils hanging from the back of the caps, sitting in a castle, embroidering, while knights in armor rode by on horseback outside the castle walls. The knights seemed to be gathering for a tournament. One of the ladies leaned out of a little window with many panes of glass and waved a long scarf at a passing knight; the knight saluted her; then the lady leaned her back against a tapestry on the wall and wept softly. It was obvious she was concerned about this special knight. After that, she returned to her embroidery. Elaine thought the movie looked familiar; it was possible she had seen it before.

In ten minutes or so, there was another knock. It's Ken, she said to herself. She got up and opened the door. In back of her she could hear cries and the pounding of horses' feet and the clash of swords as the tournament started.

"Elaine?" said Ken.

He was shorter than he had looked on TV, but it was Ken for sure. He had the same hairy muscular arms and the same big shrewd brown eyes, and he was wearing the same cap. The cap had ventilating holes at the top and his dark hair showed through. She hadn't noticed that on the screen. He was wearing the Repair Service's shirt, with

Andy's TV Center emblazoned in red letters on the pocket.

"Yes," she said, nodding.

"We don't get too many motel calls," he said, as he came into the room. He stood close to her. She could feel his breath. It was warm and had a spicy odor. He's been chewing gum, she thought. Dentyne? Liquorice, she decided.

"Okay, Elaine, what can I do for you?" said Ken.

She leaned against the wall. She could feel her heart beating in her throat. She laughed.

"Something funny?" said Ken.

"Seeing you this morning, on TV, and seeing you now," she told him.

He came closer. He was standing eye to eye with her. "What kind of a rating would you give me, Elaine?" he said.

"Rating?"

"You know. As a TV Personality?"

"I would say you were excellent," she said. "Andy and Happy and Vern were all right, but you were really excellent."

"You think I should go professional?"

"I wouldn't rule out the possibility. Can't you take tests or something?"

"Listen, Elaine, I have news for you. I wouldn't hang out with those Hollywood creeps if they offered me a million bucks."

"Not for a million?" she said.

"Nope. Not me. I'm satisfied with things the way they are."

"I thought you were. I could tell," she said.

"So what's your problem, Elaine?"

"My problem?"

"You must have had something in mind when you called me."

"Oh, yes, I did."

"You mentioned the Sony. Is it the Sony, Elaine?"

"I forgot to get the Sony out. I mean, I didn't have time. You came so fast. Just like Andy said you would. I never dreamed it would be that fast, though." She went over to the closet. Her legs felt wobbly. She opened the closet and pulled the Sony out and put it on the dressing table.

Ken looked at the Sony, then he looked at Elaine. He pursed his lips and made a whistling sound. Then he went to the dressing table and squatted down and plugged in the Sony and turned it on and waited for the picture to come on. The whistle became a jaunty tune. He continued whistling as he played with the dials. Elaine stood in back of him. She noticed Ken's neck. He had a thick, sturdy neck. There was a mole on his neck in the space between his collar and his hair line. His hair line was evenly trimmed. He's just had a haircut, she thought. She didn't think he had that haircut on the screen. "Do you think you'll win your bet?" she asked him.

"Already won it," said Ken without looking up. He turned the set around, took out a screwdriver and tightened a bolt.

"You mean—? Since when? Is Andy back already!"

Ken pushed the Sony back in place, still playing with the dial. "They did that spot two weeks ago, Elaine. Andy's been back since Sunday."

"You mean, when I saw you, Andy was back?"

"Yep."

"You're kidding."

"Do I look like the kind of guy who'd kid about something like that?"

She stared at him, without answering.

"Do I, Elaine?"

"No," she said softly.

"I'm a winner," he said.

"Did—Andy pay up?"

"Damn right he did." He turned off the Sony and stood up.

She was struck again by how short he was. I knew he

was shorter than Happy or Vern or Andy, but he didn't seem that short on the screen, she said to herself. She was trying not to think about the bet.

"You won't be seeing Andy pay up on the tube, though," said Ken. "He'll make like he won and *I* paid up. That's how he is. He doesn't want to destroy his image."

"What about you, Ken? What about your image?"

"I don't worry about my image, Elaine. I know I won. My wife knows I won. My kids know I won. That's what's important. I don't care what the viewing public thinks."

"The viewing public," she said.

Ken gave the Sony a quick glance. He put the screwdriver in his back pocket. He walked toward her. He had an assured way of walking. "I'm not a loser," he was saying.

She backed slightly away. "You look different than on television," she said.

"Different how?"

"I don't know. Just different. It's hard to put your finger on. Well, your hair, maybe. You've got a new haircut. That makes people look different." She noticed another mole, on his right cheek, but she decided not to mention this.

"You're the observing type, then?" said Ken. "Okay, Elaine. Now what's a pretty woman like you doing all alone in this motel?"

"I'm not actually alone," she said. "I'm traveling with my husband. My husband works for Superdog. He travels from place to place and I accompany him. I'm alone in the daytime and some evenings, but I'm not actually alone."

"Keeping tabs on hubby, eh?"

"Tabs?"

"You'd probably worry, having him on the road, without you. Maybe he'd get lonely, too, and do something about it. Ordinarily, a woman's place is in the home. Isn't that why you don't stay home, Elaine?"

"I don't have a home," she said. "Not at the moment. Someday, we'll have a home, but my husband's career pre-

vents us from settling down in a home for the time being.
He's a Junior Executive."

He took a package of Camels out of his shirt pocket and
offered her one. She refused. He lit one for himself. "You
don't have kids?" he said.

"For the time being, my husband's career prevents us
from starting a family."

"That's too bad, Elaine." His eyes traveled down her
body. "You've got the right build for having kids," he said.
"How old are you?"

"Twenty-nine," she said.

"The best child-bearing years are between twenty and
twenty-four. At your age, the risks get higher. Have you
ever considered staying in one place and raising a family?
Instead of worrying about hubby on the road?"

"I thought I did, once. I'm not sure, now. You get used to
not having them."

"That's not normal, Elaine." He squashed out the cigarette in an ashtray, and came closer again.

"Would you care for a cup of coffee, Ken?" she said.

"You didn't call me out here just to have coffee," he said.

"It's crazy. I called you about the Sony, and now I forgot
to even ask you about it."

"Nothing wrong with the Sony, Elaine. I tightened a
screw for you."

"I knew it was something," she said. "I knew you'd find
out what it was. The coffee's fresh," she said. "I just made
it."

"My wife makes me a thermos of coffee for the truck. I
can have coffee whenever I want it."

"I bet you have a good wife," she said.

"You're damn tooting I have a good wife. What other
kind would I have? But you're not bad yourself, Elaine.
Your hubby ever tell you that?"

"I guess he does. Yes, he does, sometimes."

"It doesn't hurt to hear it from other sources, though?

Right? It's my guess that you and Hubby have a few little sexual hangups. Wouldn't you say that's the real reason you called me, Elaine?"

"My husband and I have an excellent sexual adjustment," she said.

"Oh, c'mon, Elaine, I'm a busy man!" He stepped up to her, and put his hands around her waist. He held her like that for a moment. His hands were strong.

"You're trembling," he said. "You're the nervous type. It's because you don't lead a normal life." He reached around her waist and unzipped the back of her slacks. "Let's have a little cooperation, here, Elaine," he said.

She stood without moving, as the slacks fell down over her hips to her ankles.

"You're going to play coy?" he said. "Okay, if you want to play coy. Step out of your slacks, Elaine."

She obeyed him.

"Good girl. Now, over here." He led her to the bed, gave her a little push, and she toppled over on to it, like a wooden doll. "Now, the panties," he said. He was pulling at her panties. "You're not exactly the helpful type," he said. He rolled her panties down and pulled them over her shoes and tossed them on the floor. Then he stood at the end of the bed and looked down at her. "I'm going to give you a tip, Elaine. The next time you make a call to a busy professional man, you ought to dress right for the occasion. Don't you have any of those frilly robes? The transparent kind? You don't even know the right etiquette."

She began to cry. Big tears fell out of each eye and rolled down her face.

"What the hell, this ain't no funeral, Elaine. Let's have a little wiggle. Show me you're for real."

"That's just it," she whispered.

"What's 'it'?"

"Real," she said. "You looked realer on TV."

"I'm real, Elaine. You want to see how real I am?" He

stood back from the bed a step or two. He unbuttoned his
fly. "I'm real all right. Ever see anything more real than
this?"

She opened her eyes wide; then shut them.

"Come on, admire it. It isn't every day you get a chance
like this, is it? Open your eyes for Christ's sakes. You called
me, Elaine. I didn't call you." With one hand he was pushing her thighs apart. She held them tight, but he was too
strong for her; with a sudden, swift movement he opened
them, as if he were opening a nutcracker. Then she felt his
weight upon her, his liquorice breath. She shrieked. The
sound of her shriek startled them both. He crouched back
on his knees. "So that's your little game, is it, Elaine?" he
said. The shrewdness in his eyes had turned to rage.

As he crouched there, she rolled herself up in a ball and
slid from under him and jumped off the bed. The shriek
still echoed in her ears.

In a moment he was up, too, buttoning his fly. "It won't
get you nowhere, a trick like that," he said. "I'm well known
in this town, and you're just a transient. A dirty little
tramp. Your word against my word wouldn't be worth a
sack of shit," he said. "You know what I'm going to do?"

She stared at him, blinking her eyes; she shook her head,
no.

"I'll tell you what I'm going to do. I'm going to charge
you for this call. Ten bucks, service. You didn't expect that,
did you? Ten bucks, please, Elaine."

She moved slowly across the room to the closet, opened
the door, and took out her purse. Then she remembered
she was not dressed. She reached for her chenille robe and
put it on. She opened her purse and took out two fives and
put them down on the table in front of him.

"—Paid in cash," he said, writing. He signed the slip.
"Now, you sign here," he said, handing her the pen, and
pointing to a dotted line.

She signed.

He tore off the duplicate and handed it to her. "For hubby," he said. "In case hubby wants to know where his money goes." He looked at his watch. "I ought to charge you more, but I'm letting you off easy." He looked at her. "You know why I'm letting you off easy, Elaine?"

She shook her head, no.

"Because I feel sorry for you, you're so fucked up," Ken said.

After Ken left, Elaine poured herself some coffee and took it into the other room and sat down on the bed and drank it while she watched TV. She watched an old movie. A group of men in Western costumes were sitting around a poker table. One was obviously the villain. He was laughing and raking in the pot. Then the young sheriff entered. He stood in the doorway, looking over the game. The villain knew he was there, but did not glance up.

"Anyone's welcome to join the game if they're willing to play for high stakes," the villain said.

"I'm willing to play for high stakes," said the sheriff.

Elaine felt chilly. She got up and turned off the air conditioner. When she returned to the set, the commercial break was on. Andy and Happy and Vern and Ken were standing in front of the service van. Ken's mole didn't show on the screen, and, standing next to Vern, he looked taller, again. She thought about the mole and about how he really wasn't that tall. Thinking about this made her angry.

"Today is a special day," Andy was saying, "it's my birthday."

"It's not your birthday," said Elaine, out loud.

Then Andy said he was going fishing.

"You've gone fishing and you're back already. You're all a pack of liars," she said.

She reached over and flicked off the set. She sat staring at the shiny black screen. She could see her face mirrored in it. Tom was right about hiring actors, she thought.

Imagine calling up anyone from a Superdog commercial! It would never occur to you to do a crazy thing like that. Superdog's commercials had professionals. You knew all the time they weren't real. It was hicks like Andy and Vern and Happy and Ken with their personal and highly unprofessional behavior that got you into trouble, she said to herself.

Just before Tom came back, she took a shower and dressed. She put on a pair of slacks and a different blouse.

Tom kissed her; then he changed his clothes and went into the kitchen to start dinner. She followed him in. He was standing at the stove, frying a steak, and drinking a beer out of a can. He was humming a tune under his breath. He smiled at her. She could tell he had had a good day.

She hated spoiling Tom's day, but she felt it was only proper to tell him about Ken.

"Jesus, Elaine," said Tom, after she told him. He put down his beer can. His face was white. "That guy tried to rape you?"

"I don't know. I don't think so." She thought about it. "Maybe, well, he thought it was what I wanted," she said.

"Was it what you wanted?" said Ken.

She shook her head, no.

"What did you want, Elaine?"

"I don't know," she said. Then she said, "It wasn't that, though."

"You're sure?" said Tom. He looked sad and frightened. She nodded gravely.

"Would you care for a drink?" said Tom.

She shook her head, no.

Tom poured out his beer and fixed himself a gin drink. He turned off the steak. "A real dumb thing," he said. He was speaking in a funny, faraway manner. "I always thought you were safe and snug—here at the motel," he said. "I never dreamed you'd call some spooky service man. I could have come back and found you—" His voice trembled. He stared at her, then he stared into the glass. He took a gulp of the gin. "Jesus," he said.

Elaine went back into the other room and sat down on the bed. After a while, Tom joined her. He put the gin glass down on the silent TV and took her hand. His hand felt cold. He kept shaking his head in wonder and sorrow. She could tell he was trying to organize his ideas. They sat there for a time, then Tom cleared his throat. He began to speak in a slow and cautious and sober fashion. "A thing like this could screw up our sex life," he said. "You could have nightmares about it. Both of us could. We've got to forget it. That's the only sensible approach to this kind of thing." He paused, deliberating. "The way to forget it," he said, "is to pretend it was just a dream." His hand tightened on hers; she could feel the warmth returning to it. "You know how crazy dreams are, Elaine?"

She nodded.

"Just tell yourself you had this crazy dream." He ruffled her hair and kissed her on the forehead. "Okay?"

She said, okay.

Tom went back into the kitchen. She could hear the steak frying. "Tom's right," she thought. He had Know How and Ability. His advice was always excellent. She began to practice his advice.

"It's just a dream," she told herself. "A crazy dream. I never called Ken." She repeated this three times, in a careful manner, concentrating on the words.

Then she reached over and flicked on the TV. It was the middle of an Outer Space show, part of a series. A pretty Earth girl with long blonde hair, her hands tied behind her back, was standing between two Extra-Terrestrial Guards, in front of a throne. On the throne was Zor. Music of an extra-terrestrial type was playing. Zor's little green eyes examined his victim as he pondered her fate.

But I did call Ken, she was thinking. It wasn't a dream. I called him.

It was the first time in their married life that she had not found Tom's advice useful.

In the kitchen she could hear Tom humming as he fried the steak. Soon he would call her to dinner, and, after dinner, they would watch the News. It was even possible he would want to have sex, just to assure himself that their sex life wasn't screwed up. Everything seemed just the same as always, except she had called Ken, so it could never be the same, the whole structure, she thought, had come unglued.

(The Ohio Review)

About the Authors

ANN BEATTIE is the author of two collections of stories, *Distortions* and *Secrets and Surprises,* and two novels, *Chilly Scenes of Winter* and *Falling in Place.* A new book of stories will appear this year.

FRANK BIDART has published two books of poems, *Golden State* and *The Book of the Body.* He teaches at Wellesley College.

RICHARD BLESSING has written two volumes of poems, *Winter Constellations* and *A Closed Book;* critical studies on Stevens and Roethke; and a young adults' novel due soon from Little, Brown. He won a Guggenheim Fellowship in 1972 and an NEA Fellowship for 1982.

EMILE CAPOUYA teaches English at Baruch College of the City University of New York and is editorial director of Schocken Books.

RAYMOND CARVER'S latest collection of stories, *What We Talk About When We Talk About Love,* appeared last year. His other books include three collections of poetry—*Near Klamath, Winter Insomnia,* and *At Night the Salmon Move*—and a collection of stories, *Will You Please Be Quiet Please,* which was nominated for a National Book Award. He teaches at Syracuse University.

TERRENCE DES PRES is the author of *The Survivor: An Anatomy of Life in the Death Camps;* he writes essays and reviews and teaches at Colgate University in Hamilton, New York.

JIM GAUER has published in *Poetry, The Iowa Review,* and *The Kenyon Review.* He works as a computer consultant in Washington, D.C.

LINDA GREGG'S latest collection of poems is *Too Bright to See.*

STEPHANIE C. GUNN received an M.F.A. from Columbia University in 1979, and a grant from CAPS 1979–80. She is at present living in Toronto, working on a novel, *The Life Itself Is Too Strong.*

ROBERT HASS is the author of *Field Guide* and *Praise.* He lives in Berkeley, California.

AMY HERRICK is a graduate of the Iowa Writers' Workshop. She now lives in Brooklyn, New York. "Outerspace" is her first published story.

DENIS JOHNSON is the author of two chapbooks, *The Man Among the Seals* and *Inner Weather.* His book *The Incognito Lounge* will appear in the spring of 1982.

BILL KNOTT's recent books include *Rome in Rome* and *Selected and Collected Poems*. He teaches at Emerson College in Boston.

RICHARD LEIGH is primarily a short-story writer and a novelist. He was born in New Jersey in 1943; he was educated at Tufts, the University of Chicago, and the State University of New York, where he received his degree in literature. Since then he has lectured at various universities in the United States, Canada, and Britain.

WILLIAM LOGAN was born in Boston in 1950 and was educated at Yale University and the University of Iowa. He received the Amy Lowell Award and a grant from the Ingram Merrill Foundation. His most recent book is *Sad-Faced Men*. He now lives in England.

THOMAS LUX's latest (full-length) collection is called *Sunday*. Two recent chapbooks are *Like a Wide Anvil from the Moon the Light* and *Massachusetts*. He has been a member of the writing faculty at Sarah Lawrence College for several years and has also taught (most recently) at Columbia University, University of Houston, and Boston University.

HOWARD NEMEROV teaches at Washington University. He is the author of some twenty books of poetry, fiction, essays, and memoir.

KATHA POLLITT's first book of poems, *Antarctic Traveler,* appeared this winter. She lives in New York.

MARK RUDMAN was born and lives in New York City, but spent most of his boyhood and youth in the Midwest and the West. His poems, essays, and translations have appeared in a wide variety of magazines and anthologies. His recent books are *In the Neighboring Cell* and the translation (with Bohdan Boychuk) of Boris Pasternak's poems, *The Highest Sickness* and *My Sister—Life*.

ALAN SHAPIRO's last book, *After the Digging,* was published this fall. He is looking for a publisher for his second book, *Courtesy*. He teaches at Northwestern University.

PETER TAYLOR is the author of numerous books of stories, most recently *In the Miro District*. He lives in Charlottesville, Virginia, and Key West, Florida.

JEAN THOMPSON is the author of a collection of short fiction, *The Gasoline Wars*. She has published in numerous magazines, including *Mademoiselle, Ploughshares, Fiction International, Southwest Review,* and *Ascent*. She is now teaching creative writing at the University of Illinois.

LINDA VAVRA lives and works in Chicago. She is a recent graduate of Oberlin College.

C. K. WILLIAMS' books of poetry are *Lies, I am the Bitter Name,* and *With Ignorance.* He is also the co-author of a translation of Sophocles' *Women of Trachis.*

TOBIAS WOLFF is a native of Washington State. His first collection of short stories, *In the Garden of the North American Martyrs,* was published in the fall of 1981. He teaches at Syracuse University.

CHARLES WRIGHT, who teaches at the University of California at Irvine, is the author of five books of poems, *The Grave of the Right Hand, Hard Freight, Bloodlines, China Trace,* and *The Southern Cross.*

PATRICIA ZELVER is the author of two novels, *The Honey Bunch* and *The Happy Family,* and, most recently, *A Man of Middle Age & Twelve Stories.* She has been included in the *Esquire* anthology, *All Our Secrets Are the Same, The Pushcart Prize,* and has won O. Henry awards. She is now working on a novel.